SACRAMENTO PUBLIC LIBRARY
828 "I" Street
Sacramento, CA 95814
12/12

D0046132

THE LION SLEEPS TONIGHT

Also by Rian Malan

My Traitor's Heart

THE LION SLEEPS TONIGHT

and Other Stories of Africa

RIAN MALAN

Grove Press
New York

Copyright © 2012 by Rian Malan

All rights reserved. No part of this book may be reproduced in any form or by any electronic or mechanical means, including information storage and retrieval systems, without permission in writing from the publisher, except by a reviewer, who may quote brief passages in a review. Scanning, uploading, and electronic distribution of this book or the facilitation of such without the permission of the publisher is prohibited. Please purchase only authorized electronic editions, and do not participate in or encourage electronic piracy of copyrighted materials. Your support of the author's rights is appreciated. Any member of educational institutions wishing to photocopy part or all of the work for classroom use, or anthology, should send inquiries to Grove/Atlantic, Inc., 841 Broadway, New York, NY 10003 or permissions@groveatlantic.com.

Some of the pieces in this collection first appeared, some in a different form, in *The Spectator, Esquire, Rolling Stone, Maverick, Daily Telegraph, Sunday Telegraph, The Observer, The Independent on Sunday, Empire, The Wall Street Journal, Frontiers of Freedom*, and in liner notes published by Fresh Records.

Published simultaneously in Canada
Printed in the United States of America

FIRST EDITION

ISBN-13: 978-0-8021-1990-2

Grove Press
an imprint of Grove/Atlantic, Inc.
841 Broadway
New York, NY 10003

Distributed by Publishers Group West

www.groveatlantic.com

12 13 14   10 9 8 7 6 5 4 3 2 1

ACKNOWLEDGMENTS

I'd like to doff the hat to all the brave and patient editors who assisted at the birth of these pieces, especially Bill Tonelli at *Rolling Stone*, Rosie Boycott at *Esquire* UK, Alan Jenkins at the *Observer*, Stuart Reid at the *Spectator*, Branko Brkic at *Maverick*, and Graham Boynton at the *Sunday Telegraph*.

Sincere thanks also to Kevin Bloom for an astute reading, and to Ann Seldon Roberts for the WABI.

And, finally, thanks to Morgan for heroic feats of patience and forgiveness, and to Peter Blackstock and Michael Hornburg in New York for their labors on this edition.

CONTENTS

FOREWORD

Once upon a time in America, I worked for a semiunderground newspaper that had offices on a seedy stretch of Hollywood Boulevard and at least one great writer on its masthead. Michael Ventura was a New Yorker who'd somehow reinvented himself as a straight shootin', hard drinkin' cowboy from the lonesome plains of Texas. I guess that was the Larry McMurtry part of his complex persona. He also had a Kerouac aspect and broad streaks of Mailer and Hemingway, but on the page, the spirit he most often channeled was Thomas Wolfe, whose incantatory rhythms he could mimic with uncanny accuracy. Ventura started out as a reporter but decided that "nobody can write fast enough to tell a true story" and moved on to movie reviews. If we were lucky, he'd pitch up on deadline day with black rings around his eyes and two days' stubble on his chin, bearing a searing five-thousand-word essay on whatever Hollywood blockbuster had irritated him that week.

The best of those reviews concerned a movie about Jack Kerouac, the bebop hophead whose amphetamine-fueled prose more or less defined the Beat Generation. Hollywood had (of course) turned Kerouac into a likable middle-class guy with straight teeth, a cleft chin, and a lifestyle that deviated from the American norm only to an extent likely to titillate the good folk in Peoria. Ventura was hugely offended. His review began, "This is a chickenshit movie," and by the time it was done, several Hollywood reputations had been reduced to dog meat.

I dread the thought of Ventura getting his hands on this book. He'd say, "This is a chickenshit collection," and he'd be right. But I'd like to proffer some excuses, if I may. Let's begin with Ventura's aphorism about the alleged impossibility of writing a true story. This is of little consequence to news reporters who glance at the police blotter and produce a dry recitation of the basic facts, but hacks of my generation had other dreams, inspired for the most part by the incendiary revelations of American New Journalism. I suppose the ideal was a piece of nonfiction so carefully observed and exhaustively reported that reading it was almost as good as being there.

This was a fiendishly difficult thing to pull off, even in America, where people spoke the same language, shared most values, and understood with a reasonable degree of certainty the boundaries of the matrix they inhabited. The laws of cause and effect were known. The narrative might twist and turn but the forces that drove it were quantified. Even so, your chances were slender. You could set the words down and polish them until your fingers bled, but Ventura was generally right: the ideal was beyond attainment. *Nobody can write fast enough to tell a true story.*

In America, this was an artsy verdict on the limitations of the form. In South Africa, it's like a law of nature: there's no such thing as a true story here. The facts may be correct, but the truth they embody is always a lie to someone else. Every inch of our soil is contested, every word in our histories likewise; our languages are mutually incomprehensible, our philosophies irreconcilable. My truths strike some South African writers as counterrevolutionary ravings. Theirs strike me as distortions calculated to appeal to gormless liberals in the outside world. Many South Africans can't read any of us, so their truth is something else entirely. Atop all this, we live in a country where mutually annihilating truths coexist entirely amicably. We are a light unto nations. We are an abject failure. We are progressing even as we hurtle backward.

The blessing of living here is that every day presents you with material whose richness beggars the imagination of those who live in saner places. The curse is that you can never get it quite right, and if you come close, the results are often unpublishable.

I would say, looking back, that the only worthwhile writing I've done over the past two decades appeared in letters to friends in whose company I could ignore the crushing taboos that govern discussions of race among civilized people. In public . . . I don't know. I think it was T. S. Eliot who said the purpose of all exploring is to return to the place from whence you came and see it as if for the first time. I spent eight years on the far side of the planet and when I came home, in the late 1980s, I saw that I was in Africa, and that changed everything. Those I'd left behind remained obsessed with apartheid. I became obsessed with what replaced it. They thought apartheid was the source of all South Africa's pain. I thought we were doomed unless we figured out what had gone wrong elsewhere in Africa, and how to avoid a similar fate. I was an atheist in the great revival tent of the new South Africa. The faith on offer was too simple and sentimental, the answers it offered too easy.

Those who stayed saw it differently, but to me the most telling creation of apartheid was not the system of laws designed to keep blacks in their place, or the passes that restricted their movement, or the secret police, or the mines and factories that generated the taxes that paid for repressive measures. Apartheid's great triumph was the world I grew up in—the whites-only suburbs of northern Johannesburg, where whites took their cues from the great white mother culture, reading the same books, enjoying a similar lifestyle, espousing similar values, and somehow imagining that all this was normal and would continue indefinitely. The denizens of this world were not racist, at least not overtly so. We listened to Bob Dylan and voted the white liberal ticket. We read Norman Mailer and Carlos Castaneda. After high school, we attended the University of the Witwatersrand, where white professors faithfully propagated doctrines laid down on the far side of the planet by the high priests of white civilization.

By the time Nelson Mandela came out of prison in 1990, those doctrines were generally of the variety called "progressive," which rejoiced in the downfall of white supremacy. Practitioners of this doctrine saw themselves as part of, sometimes even heroes of, the uprising of the natives. They thought the wrath of the masses would fall on the bad whites responsible for apartheid, while "good" whites merged into a smiley-face culture of soft socialism and interracial harmony. I said, bullshit, gentlemen, Africa calls for another outcome entirely. The wind of change will eventually sweep everything away—your job, your illusions, your university as presently constituted, the wires that bring light at the flick of a switch, the pipes that discreetly remove your turds, the freeways on which you drive, the high-tech chemical farms that put food on your table, the investments intended to sustain your comfortable old age, and the clean, efficient hospitals in which you plan to expire. All these things are creations of the white empire, and when it fades they will, too.

That was more than two decades ago. Every day since has brought thunderous confirmation of the rectitude of my prognostications. Every day also brought irrefutable proof of the fact that I was mistaken. I cursed Mandela when he refused to shake F. W. de Klerk's hand during some televised debate during the early 1990s peace talks era. A few months later I was fighting back tears at his inauguration. I claimed vindication when our currency began its great collapse, and ate my words when it bounced back again. Every white murdered on a lonely farm seemed to herald the onset of generalized ethnic cleansing. Every visit to Soweto left me believing in the brotherhood of man again.

There was a time when I thought these howling ambiguities could only be resolved by a great cleansing apocalypse, but apocalypse never came. Instead, we had the miraculously peaceful transition of 1994, followed by the delirious triumph of the 1995 rugby World Cup, where hefty Boers wept and said, "That is *my* president," as Mandela raised a golden trophy into the blue heavens celebrated in our national anthem. The resulting goodwill was obliterated by the one-sided maunderings of Archbishop Tutu's Truth and Reconciliation Commission, but it made a comeback when the economy rebounded under President Mbeki. Five years later, the collapse of neighboring Zimbabwe put catastrophe back on the agenda, and by the time the lights went out in 2008, the end seemed nigh. Computers stopped working. Factories and mines fell silent. Traffic gridlocked on city streets. The national power company had been mismanaged back into the Dark Ages by incompetent bureaucrats who owed their appointments to "cadre deployment"—the reservation of important jobs for loyalists of the ruling African National Congress.

The great blackout of 2008 was not an isolated event. It was a metaphor for a country in which everything seemed to be disintegrating: the civil service, the sewerage system, the highways, the hospitals, the schools, and, above all, the moral integrity of the Rainbow Nation, shredded by ceaseless corruption scandals. But even as the rot deepened, we saw the rise of the only force that could check it—black people willing to stand up and say, *This cannot be tolerated.*

This was a development I had not anticipated, because the chains of black solidarity are far heavier than the taboos that keep timid white liberals quiet. Forged by centuries of oppression, those chains bound black South Africans in absolute loyalty to the party that liberated them. For years, no thoughtful African dared speak out in public against Nelson Mandela's mighty African National Congress; to do so was to be instantly branded a traitor. But something changed once it became clear that Mandela's party was turning into a self-enrichment machine for the ruling elite. The black poor rose up in a thousand shantytowns, demanding the removal of corrupt municipal councillors. Black intellectuals started speaking out in terms that made my plaints seem ladylike. Black journalists began to expose corruption and malfeasance, often in alliance with black commentators who did not flinch from calling the disease by its name: South Africa, says trade unionist Zwelinzima Vavi, is ruled by a "predatory class" of political opportunists who feed "like hyenas" off the carcasses of the poor. If you'd told me in 1990 that I would one day find myself in agreement with Comrade Vavi, a stalwart of our Communist Party, I would have laughed. But here I am, eating my hat. Again!

Which brings us back to Michael Ventura. I imagine him shaking his head in disbelief as he reads this. "Chickenshit," he says. "Malan can't make up his mind. He's been sitting on the fence so long the wire is cutting into his cowardly ass." I agree entirely, but if there is an overarching truth here, it eludes me. The only true line I've ever written about South Africa is this one: "We yaw between terror and ecstasy. Sometimes we complete the round-trip in fifteen minutes." Anyone who has lived here understands these oscillations, but I'm a journalist, which means that I leave behind a trail of judgments that often turn out to be mortally embarrassing in retrospect. There is no excuse for such failings, but if I may, some evidence in mitigation.

In the past two decades, South Africa has been stricken almost weekly by scandals that would have toppled governments in the West but seem almost meaningless here. Did Nelson Mandela really ask the Zambian government to jail a troublesome witness against his wife Winnie, on trial for kidnapping and murdering a child? Did President Mbeki really negotiate our $8 billion arms deal on a "government to government" basis and pocket the resulting commissions? Did he really tell state investigators to bring him the head of his archrival Jacob Zuma, even if that entailed fabricating evidence and setting honey traps? When these stories break, you think they're going to tear the country apart and alter everything, forever. But they don't. They linger for a week or two and then fade into oblivion, blown off the front pages by the next dumbfounding scandal. The ordinary laws of cause and effect don't seem to apply here. The boundaries of the matrix we inhabit remain unknown.

But anyway, there's something to be said for practicing journalism on the edge of an abyss, trying to follow your targets into the murk that surrounds. In the pieces that follow, I often miss, but there are a few passages that come close to disproving Michael Ventura's dictum. For the rest, I tried my best, and provoked reactions as richly varied as the reality we inhabit. A few people said nice things—"a born storyteller," according to the judges on some American awards jury—but the reactions that lodge in my memory are mostly the angry ones. Some said racist, but that's so commonplace it's barely worth mentioning; any

South African journalist who hasn't been called a racist or a self-hating house Negro is a fawning ingrate whose lips are chapped from sucking the unmentionable appendages of those in power. The more interesting accusations were incest, homosexual tendencies, heterosexual debauchery, incompetence, deceit, murder, sissiness, "carbuncular" practices, a secret alliance with the diabolical President Mbeki, spying for the Zulu nationalists, drinking too much, taking drugs, and smelling bad.

What can I say? My name is Rian Malan and I called it as I saw it.

PART ONE
POLITICS

THE LAST AFRIKANER

*T*he early 1990s was a time of ago-
*nizing crisis for Afrikaners. After 350 years in Africa, we'd come to the end of
the line. Nelson Mandela was free, the country was burning, and President
F. W. de Klerk was negotiating the terms of our surrender. Some Boers were
willing to follow him into an uncertain African future. Others said,* Over
our dead bodies. *It was in this climate of massive psychic dislocation that I
stumbled upon the parable of Tannie Katrien, a little old lady whose experience
defied at least some of our myths about darkest Africa.*

Once upon a time there was a British colonial family named Hartley who had a magical farm in Africa. It lay on the slopes of Mount
Meru, a cool green island in a sea of sun-blasted yellow savannah.
Twice a year, monsoon winds deposited heavy rains on Meru's lee-
ward slopes, which were clad in dense rain forest, full of rhino and
buffalo and elephant. Several swift, clear streams came tumbling out
of the jungle and meandered across a level plain where the soil was
so rich and deep that anything you planted bore fruit in astonishing
profusion—peaches, apricots, beans, maize, and the sun so close you
got two harvests every year.

The Hartleys bought this farm in 1953. Their homestead lay on
the shoulder of the volcano, so high that it was often above the clouds.

3

Sometimes they would wrap themselves in blankets at night and sit on the veranda with the clouds at their feet, watching the moon rise over the glittering summit of Mount Kilimanjaro, forty miles away. In the morning, it would be burning hot again, and you could sit on the same stoop with a pair of binoculars, tracking the movement of elephant herds across the parched plains far below. "I loved that house," Kim Hartley told me. "The veranda was ninety-nine feet across. It had big white Cape Dutch gables, and the previous owner had left a portrait of Hitler in the cellar." I didn't have to ask who'd built it. It had to have been a Boer.

In 1902, in the aftermath of the Anglo-Boer war, disaffected Afrikaners sent a scouting party up the spine of Africa in search of a place where a Boer could live free of British domination and rid his mouth of the bitter taste of defeat. They found Mount Meru. Two years later, the first ox wagons came trundling across the savannah, carrying Afrikaners who settled in a giant semicircle around the northern base of the volcano. At first they lived by the gun, but in time they cleared the land and began to till it with ox plows. In the beginning, they dreamed of linking up with Afrikaners who'd settled in Kenya and resurrecting the lost Boer republics, but there were too few of them, so it came to nothing, and what they had was fine, anyway: perhaps the best farmland in the world.

By the time the Hartleys arrived, the Boers had created a paradise under the volcano. The lower slopes of Meru were dotted with whitewashed farmhouses, shaded by blue gums and jacaranda trees. Around them lay a mile-wide belt of orchards and wheat fields, segmented by whitewashed wooden fences and crisscrossed by irrigation furrows. Below the cultivated lands, literally at the bottom of the garden, lay the dusty savannah, teeming with antelope and big game, and on the far horizon was Mount Kilimanjaro.

A few days later, I met Kim's mother, a grand old white Kenyan, charming, well preserved, and full of astonishing tales about good chaps who'd been gored by buffalo or died in light plane crashes. Mrs. Hartley was fascinated by the Boers, whom she clearly regarded as a subspecies of noble savage, almost as exotic as the Masai. Their leader was General Wynand Malan, a dapper old fellow with a white goatee, remembered for his suicidal commando exploits behind English lines in the war of 1899–1902. General Malan was rich and fairly civilized. So was Sarel du Toit, the haughty man who built the Hartleys' hill-top mansion and dreamed of becoming governor of Tanganyika. Mrs. Hartley was more interested in the wild Boers, the biltong hunters and farmhands on the community's fringe.

They were tall and strong and very good-looking, she said, but when they smiled, their teeth were black, stained by fluoride in the river. Some had never seen electric light, or talked on a telephone. The men wore funny hats and home-crafted shoes called *veldskoens*, and women seldom ventured outside without a *kappie* or bonnet. They were full of obscure bush lore regarding edible plants and *geneesblare*, healing leaves. They quarried their own whitewash and made their own soap from elephant or hippo fat. They'd disappear into the bush in battered old trucks and return weeks later with loads of biltong and ivory. On market day, they'd pass by in ancient Fords piled high with wheat, oranges, beans, and geese, heading toward Arusha.

Arusha was the nearest town, population 5,000 or so. To get there, you had to cross a plain covered with fever trees, and then follow a rough track through the elephant-infested rain forest. Beyond the rain forest was a region of coffee plantations, and then you came to Arusha, a cluster of white houses with red-tiled roofs, bisected by a rushing stream in which colonial gentlemen cast flies for trout. After market, the richer white farmers would gather at the country club, where the men told hunting stories and drank too much and sometimes played *bok-bok*, an extremely violent form of indoor leap-frog introduced by the Afrikaners.

Meanwhile, the ladies sat in the ladies' lounge, rolling their eyes, sipping gin and tonic, and talking about children and servants. "The Boers had a habit," said Mrs. Hartley, "of twinning their sons with a black boy. They went everywhere together, a little Boer boy with hair this short and his little black companion. But when they grew up, the white boy was expected to be the master, and take a strong line with the blacks." Too strong a line, in Mrs. Hartley's estimation. "They thought I was stupid," she said, "because I didn't know the golden rule: if they did something wrong, you had to beat them. They were very hard on the natives."

And yet, and yet. African laborers seldom stayed long with English gentleman farmers, but they often stayed with Afrikaners all their lives. "It was curious," she said. "They seemed to understand each other better than we did."

Maybe so, but when the wind of change began to blow in the fifties, the Afrikaners of Mount Meru grew unsettled. They thought of Africa as a place where only the strong survived, where a white man had to stand his ground with gun in hand or else be overwhelmed. Many were convinced they'd be massacred. As soon as independence day was set, they started packing up and heading south in convoys of heavy trucks, laden with furniture and bedding and prize cattle. Some sold their farms but the market was collapsing so many just locked their doors and walked away.

A few dozen diehards stayed on after *uhuru,* but life grew tougher and tougher, and utterly impossible after 1967, when Tanzania committed itself to socialism. The Red Chinese were invited in. Factories and banks were nationalized. Most remaining white farmers—the Hartleys included—were given twenty-four hours to quit the country. One of the last Boers to leave was a bearded ancient named De Wet, who had come to Meru as a young boy and could not bear to go. But what could you do? There was no appeal. So he loaded his truck and set out for South Africa, only to die of a broken heart two days down the road. And that was the end of the Mount Meru Boers. "They all left?" I asked. "Yes," said Mrs. Hartley. "They all died, or went back home."

It might have ended there, but her son Kim was stricken by longing for the landscape where he'd spent his first years, so he took me on a pilgrimage to Mount Meru. Our first day was dismaying. The Hartleys' old house was a ruin. The surrounding farmland was turning in part into dustbowl. The Boers' irrigation pumps lay rusting in the dirt. Their fruit orchards had been uprooted and burned. Here and there, an old Boer farmhouse was still standing, inhabited by people who sometimes had vague memories of the people they called kaBuru. "This belonged to Bwana Billem (boss Willem)," they would say. "He was a kaBuru. We chased him away."

The kaBuru were not always fondly remembered. "They were a strong, harsh people," one man told me. "Like this!" He balled his fist and raised his forearm as if to strike me. A graybeard chipped in with an amused demurral. "I worked for a kaBuru once," he said. "In six months, I saved enough to buy a white shirt and a bicycle." The first man laughed, clapped me on the shoulder, and said, "You are welcome. Do you want to see the kaBuru graves?"

So we piled into the Land Cruiser, our guide and ten others, and headed off through the bush on a goat track. Storm clouds were gathering over the volcano. We came to a narrow bridge that crossed a deep canyon, in the depths of which there was a swift river with deep, dark pools. A little farther on was kwaJannie, where Jannie Pretorius had once stayed. His house was still standing in the middle distance, unpainted for three decades and now blending into the dusty gray desolation.

As we stopped, a crowd of young men appeared as if from nowhere, wearing ragged jeans and T-shirts and demanding to know what was happening. I said, I am a kaBuru, I've come to see the graves of my people. This did not go down well. There were scowls and unfriendly mutterings in a language I could not understand. Our guide said, "Socialism is finished here. Whites and coolies are coming back. Some are reclaiming properties that were nationalized by the Revolutionary Party. These people think you have come to take their land away."

I said, no way, I'm just a tourist, but they weren't impressed, so I produced some snaps of a small farm in South Africa in which I owned a one-sixth share. I said, "I'm not interested in your land, I've got my own, in Afrika Kusini." The snapshots passed from hand to hand. They were studied very closely. Aha. Nice. Cattle? You have cattle? Soon everyone was smiling. Their spokesman said, "Up there is what you want to see."

So we walked up the hillside, sloughing through deep drifts of powdery red dust until we reached a tall thorn tree under which lay sixteen old graves. They were buckling and cracking, sliding slowly into a *donga*. Only one bore a legible headstone: General Wynand Charl Malan, 1872–1953. Three teenaged waMeru girls were standing beside me. I asked, "Do you know anything about these people?" They were overcome by shyness. Two little ones hid away behind the biggest, who giggled and said, "We were not born yet. All we can say is, they were kaBuru."

And that was more or less that. Kim and I returned to Arusha and checked into a motel called the Tanzanite. The phones were out of order. The power had failed. Toilets wouldn't flush and there was no toilet paper, but the beer was ice cold and the company was interesting —a party of Indian diamond smugglers from Jo'burg, on their way home from an extremely dangerous but lucrative trip to Zaire, and some Zanzibaris who were intrigued to meet a white South African. They assumed I'd come in search of a deal—diamonds, land, a tourist concession, maybe some Swahili pussy. "Our girls are taught to play sex from when they're this small," one told me. "You should try." They were perplexed when I said we were actually looking for relics of the Boers. The Boers? KaBuru? Blank stares. No one reacted save William the bartender, who said he knew someone who'd heard a story and, when he told it, it struck me as wildly implausible. I said, "I don't believe it." William said, "Come tomorrow, I'll show you."

In the morning, we headed out of town on a road clogged with ancient, listing minibus taxis, all weaving back and forth as if drunk, dodging cavernous potholes. The verges were lined with *spaza* shops, rickety little wooden shacks with brand-new Coca-Cola signs, vivid splashes of capitalist color against a prevailing backdrop of socialist gray. "I hate Socialism," said William. "Nothing happened in this country for twenty years. Kenya got rich, and we couldn't even eat."

After a while, we peeled off on a dirt road, crossed a vast state-owned coffee plantation, and passed under a derelict archway that said, "Arusha National Park." Beyond that, we were in rain forest. The canopy closed over our heads. The light was green. There were still a few elephant, apparently, but they hid away on the volcano, and all the rhino had been shot by the park's own rangers. That's what William said, at any rate. He waved to a strapping young ranger with dreadlocks and a rifle over his shoulder. "That man," he said, "reported his boss for poaching rhinos. What happened was, they put *him* in jail."

Thirty minutes later, we emerged onto a broad plain covered with fever trees. The clouds parted, and there was Mount Kilimanjaro, looking just like it does on a postcard, save that there were no elephants or lions intervening. This was not the Africa of coffee-table books. This was the real thing, a densely populated zone of mud huts, banana plantations, and mealie patches. The grass was grazed flat as a billiard table. The limbs of many trees had been amputated by woodcutters. William pointed to a distant clump of blue gums, so we left the road and headed in that direction. We forded a shallow river, climbed a short rise, and came upon a landscape dotted with mud huts and patches of cultivation. One of the houses was set apart from the others. It was made of gray mud and thatched with grass from the nearby fields. It had no windows, just planks to keep out prowling night creatures.

Outside the sun was like a hammer. I walked up to the door, upon which someone had scrawled *karibuni*—Swahili for *welcome*. I knocked but no one answered, so I went around the back, into a dusty yard full of goats, rubbish, and emaciated dogs and chickens. In the center of it stood a smoke-blackened hut roofed with banana leaves—a Swahili kitchen. I peered inside. There was a figure within, a withered old crone, hunched over the fire. She had sharp blue eyes and a long sharp nose, the face of a bird of prey. There was an old *doek* on her head, and down below a *kanga*, and dusty feet in plastic sandals. I greeted her in Afrikaans. She came to the door, squinting at me in amazement. Her name was Katerina Odendaal. She had not heard Afrikaans in three decades. She was the last Afrikaner.

The first recorded use of the term "Afrikaner" took place in the village of Stellenbosch on a wild night in March 1707. The magistrate, a German nobleman named Starrenburg, was roused from his slumbers to deal with some drunk youngsters who were causing an uproar in the town square. When the magistrate ordered them to desist, a teenager named Hendrik Biebouw told him to get lost. "I am an Afrikaner!" he cried—I am an African. "I will not be silent!"

The Dutch colony at the tip of Africa was barely six decades old at that point, but the authorities were already failing in their efforts to stop their minions going native. Biebouw, for instance, came from a family whose European identity was rapidly fading. His illiterate father cohabited for years with a slave named Diana of Madagascar. At least one of his siblings was a half-caste, as were many of his friends. Young Hendrik was flogged for his insolence, a punishment that surely deepened his alienation from polite white society. In the aftermath, he sailed away on a passing ship, but many of his Afrikaner peers trekked off into the interior, becoming semioutlaws who wandered the sub-continent like nomads, driving their cattle before them, living in huts made of reeds, and hunting with bows and arrows when their ammunition ran out.

In apartheid's schools, Afrikaans boys were taught to think of those early *trekboers* as pioneers of white civilization, carrying the torch of Christianity into places of darkness. This was true for some, I suppose, but for others it was just the start of a hunting safari that continued for centuries, interspersed with occasional battles against African tribes and nights of ecstatic intoxication on home-brewed liquors. The early wanderings of the Odendaal clan are lost to memory, but the patriarch Piet Odendaal, comes into focus in the 1890s as a transport rider and biltong hunter on the wild peripheries of the doomed Transvaal Republic.

When the Anglo-Boer War broke out in 1899, Piet joined President Paul Kruger's ragtag militia and saw action in several set-piece battles during the war's conventional phase. After that, he joined General Wynand Malan's guerrilla commando, which wreaked havoc on British supply lines in the northern and eastern Cape. Malan's commando fought until all was lost, and then fought on, refusing to give up until the very last day, when they were cut up in what was probably the war's very last skirmish.

Peace did not sit well with bitter-enders like Odendaal and his general, especially not the bit about crooking the knee to the British queen. They would not hands-up. They would not concede. And so, in the aftermath, they trekked away in search of a place where a Boer could live as he pleased. General Malan loaded his wagons on a ship and set sail for East Africa. Piet Odendaal followed later, heading north in a convoy of four big ox wagons, navigating by the sun and stars. He took a wrong turning in the trackless bush beyond the Zambezi River and wound up in the Congo, where he wandered aimlessly for many years, but that was no cause for concern; the life of a trekker was quite sweet in its way; game was plentiful, each day was an adventure, and the land went on forever. A new generation of Odendaals was born on the back of the wagons, among the chickens and gunpowder sacks. They could barely read. Their clothes were made of animal skins. It was 1914 before their father caught up with his old general, who had settled under Mount Meru.

Piet Odendaal got himself a farm not far from the general's, where he planted corn and pumpkins and tried to settle down. But all those years of trekking and freedom had spoiled him for civil society. After a year or two, he reloaded the wagons and spent the rest of his life endlessly circling the volcanoes with his goats and cattle, following the rain and the game.

Katerina was born in 1929, the youngest of five. Her mother died when she was twelve days old, and she was brought up by her grandmother, who called her Katrien. She spent a few years at the Dutch Reformed boarding school in Ngare Nanyuki, and then rejoined her wandering family. "We went here, we went there," she says. "Sometimes we plowed and planted wheat for other farmers, but we never stopped long in one place. We had our own sheep and goats and cattle. If there was no meat, we shot game."

She pulled out some old photographs, yellow with age, the edges chewed ragged by termites. A grinning oaf stands on a featureless plain with a dead buck at his feet, at least eight inches of bare skin between his trouser cuffs and his handmade shoes. Dashing young men pose with ivory tusks. A young girl sits on the head of a dead bull elephant, surrounded by khaki-clad hunters. It's Katrien in her teens. She points to some tiny, half-naked figures on the fringe of the tableau. "These little people we called the Dorobo," she says. "They hunted with

11

poison arrows. They got used to the Boers. When they heard our engines, they'd come out of hiding and guide us to where the big bull elephants were. They kept the meat, we kept the ivory."

"This was a wonderful place then," she says. "It was the Garden of Eden. There was game everywhere. There was room for everyone." So the Odendaals kept wandering until 1950 or thereabouts, when the Tanganyika frontier finally closed. The population was growing and you could no longer shoot game as you pleased. Farmers were no longer willing to share their grazing. The Odendaals had to sell their livestock and look for jobs in town. Katrien was about twenty. Both her grandparents were dead by now, and her eldest brother, Jan, was looking after her. He landed a job in a sawmill at Makuru, south of Kilimanjaro, and took her there to stay with him.

The sawmill had electric power, a great novelty for her, and a luxury she would never see again. It also had an office with typewriters, manned, inter alia, by a handsome young African named Shabani Lulu. He came from the Mbulu tribe, a tall seminomadic people, renowned for their high cheekbones and aquiline noses. Everyone liked Lulu, especially Katrien. He was handsome. He made her laugh. She had feelings for him that were absolutely forbidden for an Afrikaner girl. She came from a culture in which, as she put it, "We were taught to keep ourselves separate. If you were a white girl, you weren't even allowed to talk to a kaffir. That's how we were raised, and what did I know? I was just a child." But now she was a woman, and falling in love with an African.

It was a difficult thing for the old lady to talk about, even forty-three years later. She was breaking a taboo so deeply ingrained that somewhere in her heart she still seemed to see herself as a sinner. But she couldn't help herself. She was in love. She and Lulu had an affair. It had to be secret, because her brothers would have killed both of them. Her brother Coen was a thickset man who drank too much and got into bar fights. The other brother, Jan, was tall and gentle, but even he could not be trusted. Katrien enlisted the help of a kitchen boy, who made his house available for rendezvous. The lovers dug a hole in his kitchen floor. If the brothers showed up, Lulu would duck into it. Katrien would cover his hiding place with a plank and a table and pretend that nothing was happening.

And then she became pregnant, an absolute disaster. Lulu ran away, terrified of the wrath of her brothers. Katrien didn't know what to do. When the pregnancy began to show, she had to confess. The brothers went mad. "They wanted to shoot us," she says. "I'm telling you, *bwana*, a Boer's heart is just like a Masai. They don't worry about killing people." So she packed a few things in a bag and fled. She slept in the bush, stealing food from *kraals* to stay alive. She had the baby all on her own, under a thorn tree, and she didn't know what to do with it. "I didn't know how to cut the cord," she says. "I didn't know anything." An old African woman found her wandering around with the baby boy in her arms and took her home, where the cord was severed, along with all Katrien's ties to her own people. As far as Afrikaners were concerned, she was as good as dead.

In the aftermath, she returned to the sawmill where Jan was working, but he was deeply shamed by her and her half-caste baby, to whom she'd given the Afrikaans name Boetie. "They wanted to send Boetie away," she says, "but I fought. They weren't going to do anything to my boy." Then one day she got a letter and some cash from her lover. He was back in the district, but wouldn't come to the sawmill for fear the Afrikaners would kill him. So Katrien joined him in Arusha, where they lived together in bitter poverty and had four more children over the next fourteen years—Elizabeth, Christina, Flora, and Corneliu.

The children were brought up in the stern Afrikaans tradition, with brutally short hair and regular hidings. During the week they went to school with Arusha's Indians, and on Saturdays to church with the Sabbatos, the Seventh-Day Adventists. It was the time of *uhuru*, time of the Mau Mau uprising. Two or three isolated farms were attacked, their owners murdered. The Boers grew paranoid and took to posting armed guards at night. Katrien didn't care. "I said, 'Let it happen. The Boers rejected me. They hated me. If someone hates you, you can't have pity. They spat at me, and I spat back.'"

As independence drew nearer, the Boers started leaving. Katrien was barely affected. Even her sisters didn't say good-bye when they went home. In the end, there were only three Afrikaners left under Mount Meru—Katrien and her two brothers, both bachelors. Coen stayed because he drank too much and knew nobody in South Africa. Jan stayed because he'd promised their dying grandmother he'd take care of his little sister.

Once the other Boers had gone, Jan and Coen relaxed a bit. There were no more expectations to live up to, no pious chuch ladies to sneer when they visited their disgraced sister. They were taken by Katrien's children, who were half-caste, to be sure, but good-looking, the girls slender, light-skinned, and high-cheekboned, the boys well brought up and dutiful. When Lulu abandoned his family in the late sixties, Jan bought a *shamba* for Katrien, a tiny chunk of an old Boer farm on the far side of the rain forest, just enough land to subsist on. Soon after, Coen died of a heart attack, and Jan passed away exactly one week later. On his deathbed, he told Katrien, "Now you're alone. Now you will truly suffer."

This was true. It was 1971, and Tanzania had just started its long descent into socialist paralysis. Nationalized factories were dying of inefficiency. Cadres of the Revolutionary Party were stalking the countryside, setting up spy networks and trying to force sullen peasants to collectivize. Commodity prices were set so low that farmers hardly bothered to plant. Even if you had money, there was nothing in the shops to buy. No sugar. No fat. No soap. No cooking oil. No tick dip. No petrol. No toilet paper. No cigarettes. No clothes. Sick people dosed themselves with veterinary medicines. Anything that broke stayed that way, because there were no spare parts, no tools. When Katrien's hand-cranked Singer sewing machine gave out, it had to be thrown away, her son's beloved motorcycle likewise. By 1978, she was washing her clothes with bitter apples, like a Voortrekker in the 1830s.

These ordeals would have defeated others, but Katrien was in many ways a living fossil, armed with survival strategies from an earlier century. She knew how to cure disease with herbs from the veld, how to turn cow dung into a serviceable floor, how to butcher a hippo and turn its fat into soap. She could plow with oxen, snare birds, and spear catfish in the veld when the river flooded its banks. Her vocabulary was full of quaint archaisms, among them the word *kaffir,* or in Afri-kaans *kaffer,* from the Arabic *kafir,* meaning unbeliever. She had no idea that it had become a forbidden term. For her, it was just the name Af-rikaners had always used for Africans.

She'd sit there with a pitch-black grandchild on her lap, chatting animatedly about the kaffirs and their idiosyncrasies. Sometimes her judgments were favourable, as in, *"Die kaffer sien nie eers jou kleur raak nie"*—the kaffir is color-blind. Sometimes they were less so. *"Ek sê jou, bwana, dis 'n ander nasie die,"* she told me one afternoon—these people are strange. "They eat food you've never heard about—bananas and blood and curdled milk. It's a sin to drink blood, because you're drink-ing the animal's life. That's why I say, you can't live in the same house as them. I was brought up different. I'll die an Afrikaner." The baby gurgled. The old lady said, "This one's called Mannetjie," and planted a kiss on his plump black cheek.

Any contradictions here were invisible to her, and she seemed bewildered by my South African obsession with race. I kept asking, "What have you learned here?" And she kept saying, "What do you mean?" I said, Afrikaners have always believed Africa is a place where only the strong survive. You were the last Afrikaner, left alone and de-fenseless in a great sea of black people. Why are you still sitting here talking to me?

Tannie Katrien chuckled and told a story from the darkest depths of Tanzania's socialist debacle, a time when even aid workers had left and trade had collapsed entirely and whites were so rare that people would come from miles around to stare at her. "Usually they brought children, because some of the young ones had never seen a white be-fore. They'd stand right there," she said, pointing to a spot ten yards from her kitchen hut. "But they never did anything to me. They were just curious."

She said she had no problems with her African neighbors. They helped each other at harvest time and punished their grandchildren for raiding each other's fruit trees. If her cattle got taken in a Masai raid, all the local men took up their bows and arrows and shotguns and gave chase. Whenever a woman went into labor, they called the kaBuru auntie, because she had some knowledge of germs and sterilization. She was afraid of many things—of disease and drought and famine— but she wasn't at all afraid of her African neighbors, perhaps because she owned no more then they did, which is almost nothing. She was the only white I'd ever met of whom that was true, anywhere in Africa.

She was dimly aware that South Africa was heading toward its own *uhuru*, but didn't find the details very interesting. "Ag," she said, "it will be just like here. They won't do anything to the whites." But she was equally adamant that black rule would lead to economic collapse. Her reasoning in this regard was based entirely on food. "When the Boers were here there was plenty of food," she said. "Butter, cheese, *boerewors*, chickens, peaches, plums, and macaroni cheese. And now look! *Ek sê jou, bwana*," she concluded, "*die kaffers kan nie boer nie. Hulle breek alles.*" These kaffirs can't farm. They break everything.

We returned to this subject several times during the time I stayed with her. I kept saying, "It's not really that simple," and she always said, "It is!" In the end, she lost her temper. "*Is jy onnosel?*" she snapped. Are you stupid? The subject was clearly closed. I crawled off into my allotted corner and went to sleep, thoroughly chastened.

The old lady rises long before sunrise. I hear her sweeping the yard outside. I find her in the kitchen hut, where she's brewing tea over an open fire, the kettle perched on three stones. Two calves are tethered to a post in one corner, and huge bunches of cooking bananas dangle from the rafters overhead. She has about five pots and pans, and five plates, but only three spoons, which will in due course become a source of agonizing embarrassment. She's huddled over the fire like one of Macbeth's crones, staring at the flames. She always sits that way, with her painfully thin knees drawn up against her chest like a bushman. It's the habit of a woman who's spent her life in houses with virtually no furniture, no running water, no electrical appliances. In her world, even tea is a luxury, so she boils it for ten minutes, and then throws in sugar by the handful, to make a brew that is dark and strong and very sweet. We drink a cup apiece, and go outside to milk the cows.

The sun's just rising over Kilimanjaro and the landscape is heart-breakingly beautiful. There are three milk cows, tethered to banana trees. Her cows. Even her sons are not allowed to milk them. "They don't do it properly," she says. "The milk dribbles down their forearms and off their elbows, picking up dirt and germs." If it's to be done properly, she has to do it herself.

She trusses up the cow's back legs, hunkers down with a plastic pail, and immediately starts cursing. The udder is covered with blue-black ticks, bloated and big as grapes. I say, "Why don't you buy some tick dip?" And she launches into an impassioned tirade about the shortcomings of the Tanzanian government with reference to agricultural chemicals. "You can't get tick dip anywhere. The government keeps promising, but nothing happens. I ask the coolie at the shop in Usa River to get some, but he can't get it, either. So I walked halfway to Kilimanjaro and talked to some whites at a safari camp. They promised to bring some from Nairobi, but that was weeks ago. It's just like the early seventies, when my son Boetie lost thirty-four cows to East Coast fever."

When I first came, Katrien and I struggled to find common ground. I was a creature of the twentieth century, my head crammed full of irrelevant information. I'd ask her about stuff I'd read in books, about *Ujamaa* and *kijiji* and the policies of Tanzania's ruling Revolutionary Party, but she'd never heard of these things. She'd turn to her son and ask, "*Was dit hier so gewees, Boetie?*" Did that happen here? The conversations that followed were stilted and seemed to bore her, but she'd go on for hours about her central obsessions: rain or the lack of it, seeds, plant diseases, and the techniques of Iron Age agriculture. She and her sons had dug a furrow that led water into her banana patch. She was also growing tomatoes, onions, beans, and pawpaws. She had sixteen orange trees, a guava tree with beehives in its boughs, and, on a distant hillside, a cornfield, about fifty yards by twenty.

In a good year, Tannie Katrien and her sons earn about $100 between them, selling beans, oranges, and honey. Of this, $70 goes to keep just one grandson in high school. The rest of the family makes do on what remains. They own almost nothing except the clothes they stand up in and their livestock. "Christmas is just another day," she says. "You eat porridge, you work, you sleep." The old lady has given up plowing, because the strain of handling the oxen has become too much for her, but she still hoes and weeds under the burning sun, still carries water, still staggers for hours across the plains, burdened like a donkey under firewood. She says, "You have no choice. If you're not tough, you die. You just have to be satisfied with what you have."

By now the sun is high overhead and it's getting hot. We squat on the bare earth outside her kitchen. The conversation peters out. Every now and then, one of her neighbors emerges, squints at the sky, and scans the fields for signs of human activity. The old lady says its time to plow but nobody wants to go first. "If you plow first, your crops ripen before anyone else's," she says, "and then the baboons and thieves steal everything." So you wait.

Flies buzz around your head, crawl into your nostrils. The hours pass with agonizing slowness. A battered old truck appears, crawling along a distant track. The old lady's eyes follow it across the horizon. When it comes abreast of us she changes her position so she can watch it go again.

Over the years, I'd sat outside a thousand similar huts or shanties, struggling to communicate with Africans who spoke no language I could understand. Tannie Katrien was the first African peasant I'd ever met whose every word made sense to me, but it was her interminable silences that provided the most eloquent answer to the question I was posing: what's it like to be you? The answer is: bleak beyond description. The only colors in your world are the colors of nature—the grass, the trees, the various shades of soil beneath your feet. The only stimulation comes from a battery-operated radio. The small pleasures that Westerners take for granted—a cup of coffee, a newspaper, a trip to the shops—are unobtainable fantasies.

After several days, I began to feel claustrophobic, but there was no escape. Okay, that's a lie. I had a credit card. I could have checked into the nearest safari lodge and treated myself to a hot shower and a cold beer. But it seemed shameful to display such selfishness in the face of my host's utter deprivation, so I sat there in the dust while the sun wheeled overhead, counting the hours until the evening meal.

One afternoon, I walked to the nearest village with Corneliu, aka Bushy, Katrien's youngest son. At age twenty-eight, Bushy was trying to work as a carpenter, but he had no tools apart from some chisels and a hammer. We were going to buy a live goat for a *braai*, a Boer ritual that involves cooking meat on an open fire, but the traders doubled their price when they saw white skin, so we settled for three fly-specked haunches.

On the way back, we ran into an old drunkard who asked my name. When I said Malan, he threw his arms around me. It turned out that he'd once worked for a Bwana Malan, a descendant of the pioneer general. "Take me home to South Africa with you!" he cried. I wanted to invite him to our *braai*, but Bushy cautioned against it. "My mother has no time for drunkards," he said. "This one she will chase with stones."

After sunset, we sat around a fire at the banana plantation, listening to the sound of singing and clapping from across the river. When the goat meat was done, everyone just sat there staring at it, looking embarrassed. After a while, I realized there were five of us but just three spoons, so I helped myself and began to eat with my fingers. The old lady said, *"Sien jy, hy's 'n Boer en hy eet met sy vingers"*—Look, he's eating with his fingers, and he's a Boer. At that, everyone relaxed and joined in.

Katrien's eldest son, Boetie, had come to eat with us. He was a quiet, shy man of forty-three, wearing a baseball cap to hide his receding hairline. "If I go to South Africa," he asked, "will the Boers shoot me?" I said, "That seems very unlikely." He said, "No, they'll shoot me. I know the Boers. They'll say I'm a kaffir. Will a Boer eat at the same table as me?" And so on. Boetie's childhood wounds seemed to be reopening, so I told a few stories that might ease his pain. "President F. W. de Klerk's son is engaged to a mixed-race girl," I said, "and nobody makes a fuss. De Klerk's Washington ambassador, Dr. Piet Koornhof, had a child by a mixed-race woman, and he didn't hide it away as if it was a sin. In fact, he stood up in front of everyone and said, 'This is my child.' Then he moved in with his girlfriend, to live as husband and wife."

The old lady cackled. "No," she said. "That can't be. Don't lie!" I said, "What do you know? You've never even seen South Africa." She said, "Yes, but my grandfather told me everything." Like what, for instance?

Well, she said, "There in the Transvaal around Johannesburg, it's bitterly cold but there's no firewood. That's why the Boers have to walk around behind their cows, collecting dung. They use that dung to make cooking fires that fill their houses with smoke. That's why you can always tell a Transvaler by his bloodred eyes."

Astonishing. The image was at least 150 years out of date. I cleared my throat and started explaining about skyscrapers, freeways, and houses with flush toilets, lights, and central heating. The old lady gaped, as if listening to an alluring but vastly improbable fairy tale.

Another day, more tribulations. Tannie Katrien is wearing her Sunday best. We're sitting in the dust outside a shop in Usa River, waiting. We have done a lot of waiting in the past two days. We came to town to do some shopping, and to meet her lovely daughters—Tina the school-teacher, married to a safari driver, and Flora the housewife, married to a mechanic. We have waited for taxis. We have waited for bank clerks. We have waited for shop attendants. Right now, we are waiting for Flora, who has some tropical wasting disease. Flora is at the Catholic hospital, waiting for the doctor, who is somewhere else, waiting for the government to supply him with medicine. A lot of waiting is done in Tanzania.

It's high noon. Trucks trundle by, weaving through the potholes. The sun wheels overhead. The *tannie* is hungry and extremely short-tempered. Perhaps her kidneys are bothering her again. Perhaps she knows what passed between me and Boetie in the bank. I can't really say. All I know is she's angry.

We wait until half past two, when a pickup stops alongside us. It's going our way, but first we must wait for a full load to accrue. Ten people get on, then twenty, carrying bags of mealies and beans. At last we head off. The old lady sits on a tire right behind the cab, clinging for dear life to the roll bar. She does not trust "kaffir drivers" and she won't even talk to me.

The *bakkie* drops us at a crossroad in the middle of a flat and featureless plain. I hold out my hand to help the *tannie* down but she slaps it away. "Leave me alone!" she cries. "Do you think I'm dead already?" She gathers up her purchases and stalks off across the plain, all on her own, like a thin, angry secretary bird. The rest of us straggle along behind. The path winds around a *koppie* and crosses the river on a precarious suspension bridge. Then it climbs a rise and arrives at the clump of blue gum trees in the shade of which lies her home. By the time we get there, the old lady has already changed into her everyday clothes. She's crouched over the fire, muttering angrily.

Her sons and I sit down in the last of the sunlight and light up some Sportsmans. I say, "Your mother has a temper, hey." They laugh. Boetie says, "*Ja*, you should have seen her when our sisters were teenagers. She threw stones at their boyfriends. She got a whip and chased them away." Then he turns serious. He says, "You know, I wouldn't be alive if she wasn't so tough, if she didn't fight for me. They wanted to send me away, you know. They wanted to drown me. Because of, you know, my father."

There is something that should be mentioned here, something that sheds light on the old lady's fit of ill temper. When I first arrived, I asked her husband's name. She thought for a long time, then said, "Uh, Johannes. Johannes van Reenen. He was a Baster, a half-caste Afrikaner." And your firstborn's name? Johannes, too. But while we were in town, I wrote a check for Boetie to deposit into his bank account, which is how I discovered that his real name was John Shabani Lulu. His father was an African. It was no surprise for me. I'd guessed the truth anyway. Boetie couldn't understand why his mother had lied, why half an Afrikaner was better than a full-blooded African, after all those years and all that pain. But I knew. "*Ek sal doodgaan as 'n Afrikaner*," the old lady said. I'll die an Afrikaner. And she was trying, she was trying.

21

When the sun went down, she came out of the cooking hut with a crooked smile on her face and a peace offering in her hands. *"De,"* she said. "Look what I made for you!" It was *pannekoek*, pancakes in the traditional Afrikaner style, with cinnamon and sugar and lemon juice. On a dark night, under a volcano, in the heart of Africa.

—*Fair Lady*, August 1994

INVICTUS

This is a story about Nelson Mandela, but I think it should begin with a halfhearted spattering of applause for F. W. de Klerk, the machine politician who led the Afrikaner *volk* out of its primordial *laager* and into the happy land of muddle-through in which South Africans now dwell so uneasily. Alas, poor F.W. Burdened by the reeking albatross of apartheid and cursed with a stiff, earnest personality, he never stood a chance against Mandela in the global popularity stakes. His biography sold a few thousand copies; Mandela's sold millions. His foundation limps along in the shadows. Mandela's grows more lustrous daily, its coffers bloated by donations from international celebrities desperate to be photographed alongside the supernaturally charming Madiba. As for motion pictures, we've already been treated to any number of sentimental confections celebrating aspects of the Mandela legend, while De Klerk languishes in almost total celluloid obscurity.

This is a bit unfair, considering that De Klerk was arguably the chief architect of South Africa's miracle of 1994, but what can you do? De Klerk was up against an opponent he couldn't possibly defeat, and the enemy was not Mandela. It was a great, syrupy myth conjured up by sentimental American liberals, who insisted on seeing the South

African struggle as a rerun of their own civil rights movement. There were no Communists in this sweet tableau, no bloody revolutionary excesses. The African National Congress was inevitably depicted as an army of hymn-singing Uncle Toms, initially led by English-speaking clerics who just wanted a smidgeon of justice and dignity. Then the prison doors swung open and into the spotlight stepped Nelson Mandela, instantly dwarfing Martin Luther King and Bill Cosby in the American pantheon of seriously nice black guys.

Among the hacks who serviced this myth was John Carlin, who covered South Africa in the early 1990s for *The Independent*. Details of my disagreements with Carlin are lost to memory, so let's just say that I saw him as something of a useful idiot, prone to giving the ANC the benefit of the doubt in any situation and averse to reporting the chicanery in which it was then engaged, purporting to talk peace with De Klerk while simultaneously plotting his violent overthrow. Carlin no doubt saw me as an unreconstructed reactionary, and he had a point; I disliked his line, and the ease with which he passed lofty moral judgments on situations that struck me as howlingly ambiguous.

It's usually pleasing to see a fellow hack score a movie deal, but I was horrified to hear that Hollywood was planning to turn Carlin's book about the 1995 rugby World Cup into a major motion picture. I once lived in Hollywood, under the *D* in the famous hillside sign. I know that town and its sentimental proclivities. The best line ever uttered about Hollywood was penned by film critic Joe Morgenstern, in an essay pondering *Gandhi*'s multiple triumphs at the 1984 Oscars. Why, asked Morgenstern, had the greedy, arrogant, and ego-bloated members of the Academy voted en masse for Richard Attenborough's movie about an Indian ascetic? "Gandhi was everything Hollywood moguls long to be but aren't," Morgenstern explained. "Thin, tan and moral."

The prospect of such people combining with John Carlin to make a movie about Nelson Mandela filled me with dread. Nothing good could possibly come of it. South Africa would be depicted as a country divorced from its continent, populated by caricatural white villains and noble black victims. Facts would be raped, truth subordinated to the requirements of a sentimental story line, and De Klerk and his ilk once again made fun of. And I would be forced to once again take up arms in defense of the tattered remnants of Afrikaner honor.

So then, the truth: I set forth to see Clint Eastwood's movie of John Carlin's book in a warlike frame of mind, armed with a digital recorder on which I intended to capture every cliché, every error, every outbreak of simpering political rectitude. There are several of these in the resulting recording, but there is also the sound of my girlfriend sobbing alongside me, and my own voice breaking as I repeat corny lines just uttered by the actors on-screen. I am dreadfully, dreadfully ashamed of myself, but the truth must be told: in spite of everything, I was deeply moved by *Invictus*.

As we all know by now, *Invictus* is set in the immediate aftermath of Mandela's ascendance to the state presidency, a time of massive psychic dislocation in South Africa. The ANC was struggling to find its feet in government; rising crime seemed to portend a slide into anarchy while centrifugal forces tore at the fragile center, among them right-wing Afrikaners who bitterly resented their loss of power. Mandela knew that these potential rebels had to be pacified, and he had the wisdom to spot the most likely means. When his own comrades moved to strip the national rugby team of its Springbok emblem (they wanted the Boks to be known as the Proteas, which came dangerously close to pansies), the old man stepped into the fray and ordered them to let rugby be, at least for the time being. Then he transformed himself into the Springboks' number one fan, memorizing the names of the most famous players, visiting their practice sessions, and urging them to win the 1995 World Cup for a nation that existed only on paper.

For many blacks, Mandela's behavior bordered on race betrayal, but the old man was playing a canny game. Afrikaners hold rugby sacred, and we found his interest in the sport inexplicable but hugely endearing, especially when he showed up at the World Cup final wearing Springbok colors. Screeds have been written about Mandela's political courage and generosity of spirit, but it was more than that: he seemed to be showing that he loved us, in spite of everything, and it suddenly seemed churlish not to respond in kind. So the boys pulled themselves together and proceeded, against all odds, to beat New

Zealand, a triumph that reduced even the hardest Boers to uncontrollable weeping and cries of "That's *my* president."

If this sounds like a Hollywood ending, well, it was; I know, I was there. Music swelled, deadly enemies were at least temporarily reconciled, and no one left dry-eyed. *Invictus* lays it on a bit thick, but what you see on the screen is pretty accurate. In fact, it's great, thanks to an uncanny performance from Morgan Freeman, playing Mandela. Much credit also goes to director Clint Eastwood and his screenwriter, who had the good sense to ignore Carlin's ideological digressions and let the story tell itself. There are one or two outbreaks of Boer-bashing, but the *volk* seem to have taken them in stride. In fact, Afrikaans critics loved the movie. One had minor quibbles about rugby technicalities (a certain try was apparently scored in the right-hand corner, not the left), but the rest found the movie "inspirational," and their bosses seized the opportunity to editorialize about Mandela's precious legacy of interracial tolerance and understanding.

Myself, I can't give up quite so easily. *Invictus* tells the truth as regards rugby, but it is otherwise riddled with errors of omission, several of which are laid out in *The Last Trek*, F. W. de Klerk's 1998 autobiography. Around the time of the World Cup, for instance, Zulu leader Gatsha Buthelezi was rattling sabers over Mandela's refusal to honor a promise to submit their differences to international arbitration. De Klerk (then deputy president in a Government of National Unity) says he offered to mediate, but Mandela wasn't interested. "He told me he wanted to crush Buthelezi," writes De Klerk—by force if necessary. Around the same time, Mandela was also refusing to grant amnesty to apartheid's police and soldiers—another less than generous move, considering that De Klerk had already freed thousands of ANC armed strugglers on the understanding that the gesture would be reciprocated. Atop all this, De Klerk claims that Mandela spurned his advice, insulted him at cabinet meetings, and downgraded his official residence, a move De Klerk's wife saw as "a calculated attempt by Mandela himself to humiliate us."

Such anecdotes sit awkwardly alongside *Invictus's* depiction of Mandela as a man of almost infinite wisdom, honor, and courtesy. In the movie, he memorizes the names of his lowliest minions, and inquires about their wives. He pours the tea himself, sparing his white maid the indignity. At almost every turn, he intones, "Bygones are bygones" and urges his followers to rise above their desire for vengeance. "Reconciliation begins here," he says. "Forgiveness begins here, too."

This is Mandela as we know him, and yet, and yet. In one of its most touching scenes, *Invictus* shows the great reconciliator addressing apprehensive white staff on his first day in the presidency. "If you feel you can't work with me, you're welcome to leave," he says, "but I need your help, and I'd really like you to stay." Heartwarming stuff, unless you consider that the ANC had guaranteed the jobs of all civil servants for at least five years; Mandela couldn't fire whites, even if he wanted to. This so rankled elements of his administration that they eventually used voluntary retrenchment as a tool to purge the bureaucracy of Caucasians, a move that plunged most government departments into instant crisis.

But including such details would have spoiled the plot, and you can't have that in a Hollywood movie. Nor is it entirely fair to expect an ex-cowboy like Clint Eastwood to think too deeply about America's curious love affair with a leader from the far side of the planet. When I lived among them, I often felt that American liberals would rather put out their eyes than see Mandela in all his dimensions. They downplayed his comradely friendships with Fidel Castro, Yasser Arafat, and Muammar Gaddafi, ignored the hammer-and-sickle banners at his rallies, refused to believe that he'd been jailed for plotting to start a war in which millions might have died. They saw him as a moderate civil rights leader, and when he spoke of forgiveness they swooned, possibly because they yearned to hear similar words from their own long-suffering Negroes and had never been thus gratified.

But who am I to talk? Mandela seduced me, too, first on the day of that great rugby match, and then again last Sunday, in the air-conditioned darkness of a Johannesburg cinema. On both occasions, I knew he was manipulating us toward an outcome of his own devising, but I went along anyway, partly because he seemed to be heading toward a better place than the one we'd come from, but mostly because it just felt so good to be in his company. I was not alone. The 1995 World Cup final was a watershed moment for an entire generation of white South Africans. We talk about it in much the way Americans once talked about the Kennedy assassination: where were you, and what do you remember? It was an event of almost no significance in the larger scheme of things, but nothing was ever quite the same again. For whites, at any rate.

It's just as well that *Invictus* ends where it does, because it spares Carlin and Eastwood from confronting a question that arose in the aftermath: did blacks share this exalted view of Mandela's rugby policy? In fact, did Mandela himself see it as anything more than a ploy to confuse and disarm his enemies? Oddly, De Klerk doesn't even mention the World Cup in his autobiography, possibly because his deteriorating relationship with Mandela left him too exhausted to pay attention. There's probably another side to this story, but De Klerk says the great reconciliator was in the habit of launching vicious attacks on his integrity, culminating in September 1995 in a "shocking" outburst at a corporate banquet.

South Africa's Government of National Unity disintegrated a few weeks later, and after that it was back to business as usual. ANC sports commissars renewed their efforts to strip the Springboks of their beloved emblem and threatened dire retribution if coaches failed to select more black players. Race relations resumed their oscillation between terror and ecstasy, warming in the lazy summer months and turning glacial in the aftermath of speeches like the one delivered by Mandela at Mafikeng in 1997, in which he attacked democratic opposition as a counterrevolutionary plot, accused media critics of racism, and called for "battalions of revolutionaries" to carry the struggle forward.

Those words alone tend to annihilate Carlin and Eastwood's central premise, and worse was to come. In 1999, Mandela was succeeded by Thabo Mbeki, who set about reracializing South Africa with a vengeance. South Africa was not one country, he said, but two—a desperately poor one for most blacks, and a comfortable one for parasitic whites who continued to wield far too much economic power. Such radical sentiments were presumably intended to endear the aloof and cerebral Mbeki to the African masses, but they failed, and the president's approval ratings sank ever lower. One sometimes got the feeling that Mbeki was haunted by his predecessor's global popularity, and that he yearned for the same adulation. In 2007, he too donned Springbok colors and joined the boys on the field to celebrate another World Cup victory, but by then we were all too cynical to care. Rugby had become, once again, just a game.

But enough of facts and political argument. Movies, especially Hollywood movies, are dreams that celebrate the triumph of likable underdogs, of good over evil and love over hate. That's why we adore them, and why the return to reality is so sad, especially for South Africans. As I write, we're steeling ourselves for humilation in the upcoming soccer World Cup, a tourney in which our national squad appears doomed to instant elimination. But they said much the same of the Springboks in 1995, and lo, a miracle intervened. I know, because I've seen *Invictus*.

—*The Telegraph*, January 2010

SEASON OF THE LEOPARD

*G*iven the way the world works, for-
eign coverage of South Africa's 1990s crime epidemic focused on the plight of
whites, once lords and masters of all we surveyed, now reduced to cringing
behind steel bars and electric fences, awaiting the onslaught of armed ban-
dits. In truth, we had it relatively easy; it was black people who endured the
most pain.

Once upon a time, the saPedi term *go befelwa kudu kudu* was seldom
heard in the rural backwoods of Sekhukhuneland, largely because it
denoted a state of mind so inflamed that it seldom occurred outside
wartime. These days, it's on everyone's lips, a tough term for trying
times. Here is how you might define it.

Your name is John Montle Magolego and you were born in a mud
house in a remote village called Ga-Malaka, son of a railway worker
and an old-fashioned mother who didn't quite see the point of educat-
ing her sons the white man's way. You spend your childhood herding
cattle, and you're fourteen before you see the inside of a schoolroom.
The odds against you are insuperable, but you're "a man of ambition,"
so you claw your way forward in life. At eighteen, you take a lowly job
at the post office, but you keep your nose to the grindstone, attend
night classes, polish your English, and save every penny you can.

In 1978 you open a small take-away restaurant beside a potholed road in a tribal area called Sekhukhuneland, after the great Pedi king who ruled hereabouts in the nineteenth century. The restaurant does well, and in due course you add a bottle store, a supermarket, and a small hotel, built with your own hands. By 1996 you're a man of substance, portly and solid, somehow Victorian in your stern morality and florid oration.

As such, you're in perpetual mourning for the lost world of your boyhood, when Sekhukhuneland was ruled by hereditary chiefs and white magistrates who deployed unarmed "police boys" in pith helmets to keep the peace. In those days, Sekhukhuneland was lovely and quiet. Now it strikes you as an awful mess. Tribal authority has been weakened by the freedom struggle. The police are slack and demoralized. Little boys are running wild, terrorizing their high school teachers, drinking and raping all night. You can barely sleep at night for worrying about your wife and six children, and hardly a week goes by without a burglary at one of your businesses.

This being a semirural community where everyone knows everyone else, people come to you with tip-offs. You take the information to the police, but they seldom act decisively, and you can't quite understand why. Sometimes you think it's all this human rights business brought in by Nelson Mandela. Sometimes you think it's corruption. On bad days, you blame democracy itself, which strikes you as a system where everyone thinks they can do whatever they want. You know it's unfashionable to talk this way, but you can't help it. You say, "I don't care what I look like. I've got to face facts and tell the truth."

And the facts are so grim they're almost funny. Every day there's a story in the newspaper. Convicts walking out of prison because they feel like a holiday. A spate of thefts in the House of Parliament. The National Intelligence Agency's computers stolen from under its nose. According to news reports, fewer than 10 percent of accused rapists go to jail. Only one in fifty-three hijackers is arrested and tried. As for the petty thieves who keep breaking into your shops, the odds of detection are infinitesimal, so they keep coming back, growing more violent and daring with each break-in. In the winter of 1996, eight shopkeepers are murdered in as many weeks in just your little corner of Sekhukhune-land. Incensed, you call on the local chamber of commerce to take a stand. "Let us put our feet on the floor," you cry. "No other business-man should be killed in this manner!"

Everyone agrees, so you found an organization called Mapogo a Mathamaga. The name means "Colors of the Leopard" in your native saPedi, and your logo is supposed to portray two snarling leopards. But the game in these parts was shot out a century ago and the local artist has never seen such a creature, so he draws two tiger heads instead. Nevertheless, the message is clear: the shopkeepers of Sekhukhune-land are getting angry.

Your first act as president of Mapogo is to organize a march on the provincial capital, where you present a petition demanding effective policing. Nothing happens. Weeks turn into months, and the politi-cians don't even reply. Meanwhile, crime is worsening. Cattle rustlers are active in the mountains. A young thug jailed for murder escapes from prison and returns to torment his victim's widow, helping himself to food from her shop, demanding protection money, jeering that he'll be coming for sex now that her husband's out of the way. The police are told, but they do nothing, as usual, and that's when you reach the state of terminal frustration known in the saPedi tongue as *go befelwa kudu kudu*, meaning madder than hell. A man in this state is very dan-gerous. Uncontrollable detonations of rage are likely.

On Friday, November 22, 1996, John Magolego summons the faithful and announces that the hour has come. Scores of suspected criminals are rounded up and dragged into Mapogo's headquarters. Those judged guilty are stripped naked, thrashed to a bloody pulp, and dropped off at nearby police stations. The thrashing continues all night and much of the following day. By Sunday, at least eight alleged villains are in hospital, along with two policemen allegedly caught drunk on duty. One of the hospitalized men dies of his injuries, and a second body turns up in the veld, beaten to death under unknown circumstances.

Vigilante attacks are common in South Africa, but there's some-thing odd about this one: the perpetrators declare themselves openly and vow to continue their campaign until crime is eliminated. "Enough is enough," thunders Magolego. "An eye for an eye!" In the next several months, his followers flog their way across Sekhukhuneland and out into surrounding provinces. Hundreds of thieves are beaten, bludgeoned, dragged behind pickups, or hurled into crocodile-infested rivers.

The death toll rises to five. Magolego finds himself in the spotlight, where he flourishes hugely, appearing in public in a comic opera general's uniform and making the most outrageous statements: "Human rights for criminals is a whip on the buttocks." Or, "If your ears won't listen, your skin will feel." Liberals issue appalled denunciations, but this only endears him to the crime-maddened masses. By 1999, Mapogo claims to have ninety branches and 35,000 members, ranging from African peasants and Catholic missionaries to white farmers and corporations with fleets of delivery trucks to protect.

On a crisp winter Sunday in June 1999, the faithful converge on an open field in Sekhukhuneland, singing, dancing, and shaking fists at the sky. Weapons are evident. Militant cries rend the air. It's just like a freedom rally in the apartheid era, save that today's slogan is "Forward with African Traditional Crime Prevention," and the song goes, "Rights are destroying the nation." One's mind begins to bend. One collars an old man in his Sunday best and asks why he's here.

"On my side, the problem was stolen cattle," says Mr. John Makapane. He lost eight before he gave up on the police and turned to Mapogo for salvation. Now, he says, if rustlers strike, his Mapogo connections are on the scene within fifteen minutes to hunt them down. And if you catch them? "We just work with the thieves so they'll tell us everything." And if they refuse to talk? "That is a secret," chuckles Mr. Makapane. "Just say it's a medicine, a black medicine."

An hour or so later, a pewter BMW with vaguely sinister smoked windows rolls into view, trailed by a "reaction force" of muscular heavies in gleaming new panel vans. The leader has come. Women start ululating. John Magolego steps out of his chariot, resplendent in an olive suit with gold cuff links and tie pin. As he takes the podium, an acolyte hails him as, "The man with the answer for all of Africa."

The speech that follows is Magolego's standard lament about falling standards, lack of respect, children who take guns to school, and laws that say it's a crime to take a rod to their "naughty" backsides. "All the talk in South Africa is of human rights," he says. "But we say, 'What about the rights of ordinary people?'" As always, he brings up the seminal thief bashing of November 1996 and its allegedly salubrious consequences for this area: crime has declined to almost nothing, or so he claims. "Up to today," he says, "we are still happy and nice." The message is that any community can emulate the feat if it just has the courage to fight back. "We don't want cowards," he cries. "We want strong men who are frightened of bugger-all!"

Magolego waits for the applause to subside, then moves into the concluding phase of his speech. "We must cling to our culture," he declares. "As Africanists we have the means of controlling crime. It is beautiful and good. We believe in the infliction of physical pain. It is the only way to solve the problem."

A sigh goes up from the crowd, as if they're yearning for something lost in the march toward democracy and industrialization, something deeper than the right to punish miscreants as they see fit. In all his speeches, Magolego seems to be groping toward a vision he can't quite articulate in English, other than to insist that the new order he proposes is "healthy" and "beautiful," capable of uniting Africans in "a very good warmth of being together." Whipping thieves is just a beginning. The end is a society where Africans live according to precepts rooted in their own culture and tradition.

But other Africans take a radically different view. Even as he speaks, thunderclouds are building over Mr. Magolego's head. Special teams of police and prosecutors are beavering away in distant cities, building criminal cases against Mapogo members. Magolego himself was recently investigated for treason and is soon to stand trial for murder. A prudent man might back down at this point, but Magolego remains defiant. "So long as there is crime," he thunders, "Mapogo will be active!" And so the gauntlet is cast down, and I go home thinking this man is either mad or insanely brave, because the forces ranged against him are invincible at present. In the longer run, it's hard to say, because John Magolego has raised the existential African question: What's the point of having a state if it's too weak and disorganized to protect anyone?

Academics who ponder such things maintain that the primal function of any state is to arbitrate internal conflicts via its monopoly on the use of violence and to protect its subjects from external enemies. Indeed, that's how the idea arose in the first place—warlords or kings or barbarian chiefs struck covenants with their vassals, trading promises of protection for the right to impose taxes, raise armies, and so on. From such primitive beginnings arose the modern nation-state, which European imperialists attempted to impose on Africa in the nineteenth century. But the graft has not taken, and countries created by white men at the Berlin Conference of 1885 are everywhere teetering on the edge of chaos.

So what do you do if you live in Africa and thieves make off with your cattle? Tiny (and anomalously rich) Botswana has an efficient Western-style judicial system but even there traditional courts hold sway outside the cities. Much the same is true in Namibia and a few other countries, but traditional authority, usually imposed by village councils and their hereditary chiefs or kings, is the only authority across vast swathes of Africa. Peasant farmers under Mount Kilimanjaro set lion traps for Masai cattle raiders. Kenyans beat pickpockets to death in market places. Tanzanians reportedly burned 256 witches and thieves last year. Nigeria's Bakassi Boys vigilantes carried out nearly a thousand executions in the same period. And now the contagion has spread to South Africa, omen of a weakening state.

Nelson Mandela and his socialist allies came to power with some advanced ideas about crime, which they attributed largely to poverty and capitalist exploitation. If they thought about policing at all, it was in the context of curbing the abuses of racist white lawmen who knocked suspects around, extracted confessions under torture, and hanged those found guilty of murder. Hence South Africa's new constitution, possibly the most liberal on the planet: legal aid, the right to remain silent, new evidentiary rules that favor defendants, massive sanctions against police use of force, and no capital punishment. The aim was a British-style force of gender-sensitive Bobbies, cautioning drunkards and helping pensioners across busy roads. The result was a fiasco. Bull cops quit the force rather than face emasculation. Those who remained grew demoralized. Courts gridlocked. Criminals grew bolder. Tormented beyond endurance, ordinary people started executing petty thieves on street corners.

The Mapogos of Sekhukhuneland are possibly South Africa's largest vigilante group, but the Islamic fundamentalists of People Against Gangsterism and Drugs (PAGAD) are more deadly, responsible for hundreds of pipe bombings and shootings over the past four years. Masifunisane and Unit 50 operate in Xhosa territory, hunting cattle rustlers with automatic weapons. The Fist consists of urban white hard-liners who dress in black and harass drug dealers and hookers. Every tribal area has traditional courts, and most townships have vigilante contingents whose outrages are legion and daily: four criminal suspects butchered here, six there, child molesters frog-marched naked through the streets, rapists flogged at train stations, petty thieves strung up from lampposts, an alleged murderer bailed out of jail by his neighbors purely for the pleasure of burning him alive.

These incidents are now so common that they no longer make headlines unless there's an unusual angle. Consider: a rapist attacks a woman in Alexandra Township near Johannesburg. A few days later, he's spotted in the street and set upon by members of a ladies church choir, who beat him for several hours, cut off his penis, and toss it into the back of the ambulance that comes to take him away. When they hear that the severed member has been reattached by surgeons, the church ladies—all of whom give their names to the papers—profess outrage. "We should have made a fire and barbecued it," they say.

The rage that drives ordinary people to such extremes underscores Magolego's point: the state is failing its people. He says he gets five to ten calls a week from crime victims desperate to be saved or protected or delivered from evil. "I have left my business," he says. "Now I am fishing people." Last week he was in Pretoria and Cape Town, laying the groundwork for new branches. Tomorrow he's addressing white farmers in the Free State. Right now, he's sitting in his car outside a grimy café on the border between South Africa and the tiny mountain kingdom of Lesotho, wondering exactly what he's doing here.

The call came from the Majaka Thata United Taxi Association, an agglomeration of very large black men in dark glasses. They are at odds with the upstarts of the Manyatseng Taxi Association, who have opened a rival rank and are "stealing" Majaka Thata's passengers. The established taximen want to put the upstarts out of business, but whenever they go down to sort them out, they are confronted by armed policemen who appear to be in league with the other side. Outgunned, they are looking for allies in what might turn at any moment into a shooting war, but it's not Mr. Magolego's scene. He doesn't like guns, and besides, this isn't crime, just a skirmish for market share in the action-adventure world of South African capitalism.

So he bids farewell to the taxi bosses and heads for the car, a bodygaurd snapping into formation at each shoulder. Tsepo wears a pistol on either hip. China isn't showing any metal, but he tells me that he could kill me with his bare hands if he had to; trained in East Germany, Vietnam, France, and Cuba, he was a member of Mandela's security detail until a few months back. They pile into the BMW and hit the road, about which Mr. Magolego has some observations.

"You will note," he says, "that the tar carrying traffic into Lesotho is much lighter than the tar that goes in the other direction. This tells me that trucks enter fully loaded, but come out empty. That country has no exports, no industry, no agriculture, nothing." The moral of the story is that Lesotho has become a basket case after three decades of chaotic independence, and that a similar fate awaits South Africa unless crime is crushed. "Our economy is going already," he says. "Many shops are half-empty. Tourists don't come. We are on the brink of dying or surviving."

Right now, we're also hungry, so we stop off in a small town to get something to eat. Magolego orders a spinach *trammezini* and a nice pot of tea and admonishes me for calling him a vigilante. "I am calling all journalists to order," he says. "You make it sound as if Mapogo lacks direction and discipline." Furthermore, he adds, he has no time for people who tell him that two wrongs don't make a right. "It's a rotten idea," he says. "I want to dismantle it." He's about to do so when his cell phone rings. It's a newspaper reporter, asking why he imagines he can tackle big-city crime syndicates with just a whip in his hand. They'll kill you, says the journalist. "We are dying anyway," Magolego replies. "Is it not better to die in struggle?"

With that, he dabs his lips with a napkin and calls for the bill. "As leader," he observes on the way out, "I am in the most vulnerable position. But I'm not afraid of death. People will remember my efforts, and God is behind me." An hour later, he's in the town of Virginia, attending yet another taxi squabble. The following morning, he's at the local farmers' association, admonishing slack-jawed Afrikaners to stand together and defend themselves.

The Mapogo road show is a pleasure to watch—part crusade, part political campaign, and part guerrilla theater. Arriving in a new town, Magolego lurks in his car, projecting an aura of power and mystery from behind those tinted black windows, timing his entrance for maximum impact. The bodyguards proceed him into the meeting and take up positions on either side of the podium. Finally, the leader steps into the spotlight, windmilling his arms, widening his eyes in comic displays of indignation, spinning great skeins of home truth, half-truth, and hyperbole. To hear him talk, criminality has been all but wiped out in provinces where his movement is strongest. All that's necessary, he sometimes suggests, is to sign up, pay your membership fee, and slap some terror-inducing Mapogo stickers on your garden gate. Everyone knows it's not quite that simple but they warm to him anyway, chuckling at his pithy rural metaphors.

The country is a cockroach-infested kitchen, he tells audience after audience. The government is trying to sweep up with a rake instead of a broom, and since this is obviously ineffectual, it is a patriot's duty to help out. In order to help, you need information. To get information, you sometimes have to apply pressure, or, as he puts it, "If you want to get water from a sponge, you must squeeze." Once you have information, you apply "medicine" with the four-foot snake lying before him on the table, a weapon of intriguing provenance.

In ancient times, it was the Persian *chambok*, which became the sjambok of Java and Sumatra, and was, in turn, brought to Africa by Malay slaves and bequeathed to the Boers, who once cut similar whips from rhino hide. These days, it's just a tapering length of extruded plastic, but applied with force it raises weals, cuts skin, and inflicts terrible pain. Hundreds, possibly thousands, of criminal suspects have tasted this pain, and Magolego argues that it was good for both themselves and society.

"I abhor the death penalty," he says one night. We're in a steak house in the mining town of Welkom, discussing his concept of justice, which is African justice, imposed on the spot under the supervision of elders, with the chastised thief reintegrated into the community, not cast into a dungeon while his family starves. "As Africans, we're not happy to see a man sentenced to life imprisonment or death. If he can receive some strokes, he can stop his nonsense and he'll be a very good man. I'm basically clinging to corporal punishment. I'm very proud of what we are doing."

It's midwinter, and Mr. Magolego is coming down with the flu. He's ordered a hot whiskey to ease his symptoms, and his mood is expansive. It seems a good time to pose a critical question: if you genuinely believe a nation can flog its way to paradise, what will it look like once we get there? Mister M. lowers his cup and grows misty-eyed. "If we can just stop crime," he says, "with the passage of time, good things will flow. The economy will improve, reconciliation will be completed, there will be good relations between nations. People will be kind and helpful. We will protect one another, love one another, feel for one another. There will be a very good warmth of being together."

Pardon me, but I was touched. John Magolego may be a charlatan in some respects, riddled with vanity and hubris, but he has a dream, and dreams are in short supply on this troubled continent. But his idealism has a dark side, and it, too, must be considered.

We're in a restaurant in Pietersburg, which lies on the Great North Road to Cairo, talking to a portly man in a three-piece suit about his night of hell. A former Bantustan official, Alfred Puleng Mashiane got lucky a few years ago, picked up some government tractors on the cheap, started a plowing service, and parlayed the profits into a "bar lounge" on a dusty plain in a remote area called Doringdraai. A distant uncle owned a similar drinking spot nearby, and it soon became clear that there was too little custom to keep both men happy. Next thing, vigilantes showed up on Mashiane's doorstep and informed him that he was wanted for questioning. He was taken to his rival's business premises to confront his accusers: six terrified teenagers who claimed they'd sold him a stolen TV set. Mashiane was protesting his innocence when his uncle snapped, "Assault this man! We didn't call you to come here and play!"

At this, the vigilantes stripped him naked, tied a rope around his ankles, and strung him upside down from a tree. "Then they took sjamboks and came to me. All thirty-seven of them assaulted me while I was hanging there. On my face, my body, my genitals. Those who had guns were instructed to shoot into the ground around my head." The beating continued for hours. Mashiane fainted when they cut him down. When he came to, his uncle was distributing free liquor to the exhausted vigilantes—reward for a job well done. "All this revolves around jealousy," says Mashiane. "My relatives were trying to frame me so I'd be killed by this group."

It very nearly came to that. He fishes in his briefcase for a set of photographs taken soon after the ordeal. Every inch of his body is scarred. A tooth has snapped. He tore off all his fingernails in his desperate attempts to defend himself. The shots of his buttocks are particularly gruesome. After an hour or two of steady beating, the flesh turns soft and pulpy, and each stroke cleaves red meat down to white bone. As we recoiled in horror, Mashiane chuckled and told us what they'd done to one of his alleged accomplices. "They went to Pretoria to catch him. They slit his scrotum, pressed his testicles out, threw him in the boot of a BMW, and brought him back."

Mapogo denied responsibility for this particular atrocity, but stories told by confirmed Mapogo victims are often equally disturbing. A crime takes place in a village. Gossipers point fingers. The vigilantes are called in and, next thing, hooded men are pounding on the door in the dead of night, dragging suspects away for "questioning." Protesting your innocence is futile, because criminals are expected to do that anyway. Your family calls an ambulance as soon as you're taken, because they know that in an hour or three you'll come crawling out of the bush naked and bleeding, and that you might die unless you get to a hospital quickly.

It would be easier to overlook such cruelty if guilt was beyond doubt, but it seldom is. It is true that criminals lie, but it is also true that mobs are prone to fits of unreason and easily manipulated. One Mapogo victim felt he'd been singled out because he'd served in the ANC's guerrilla army, not necessarily a recommendation in the eyes of tribal conservatives. Another claimed he'd been set up by a malicious ex-wife. Several spoke of business or love rivalries. Mr. John Ledwaba drew an absolute blank. The vigilantes just told him he was a cattle thief and started thrashing. After three hours of torture, he stopped protesting, but swears he has no idea why he was attacked. "Personal grudges or maybe even jealousy," he said. "In my mind, I still can't come to grips with it."

This interview was one of several set up by a brave man named Dan Madiba. The earnest, bespectacled young schoolteacher contacted Ledwaba on our behalf and accompanied us to the rendezvous outside a Catholic mission. As we spoke, some Mapogo members were drinking beer in the yard of a shop across the way, watching us suspiciously. Their movement's two-headed tiger insignia hung on the mission's fence. They clearly regarded Madiba as a traitor and I was worried that there might be a reckoning after we left. Madiba shrugged off the danger. "I am obsessed that these vigilantes should not exist in any way," he said.

Madiba's case against Magolego and his henchmen is the classic Western one—justice should be blind and impartial, a judicious weighing of contested claims in deference to the doctrine of *audi alteram partum*, hear the other side. As a humanist, Madiba is appalled by the ongoing rape of this principle in his community, and as a leftist he finds the vigilantes politically repugnant, dismissing them as a gang of tribal reactionaries who should be suppressed at all costs. "If only the government could just ban them," he said.

After the interview, Madiba took us to his family compound, an airy complex of mud-brick buildings that commanded a breathtaking view of gaunt mountains and tawny savannah. His wife served tea while Dan juggled a gurgling baby and talked about the sort of society he'd like to live in, sounding curiously like Magolego in his more subdued moments. He also wants peace, brotherhood, and good order, and he's the last to defend the anarchic status quo. He just believes that the ANC's Western-style anticrime policies are the best remedy, and that given enough money and time they will work.

The best counterargument is John Magolego's own murder case, which provides a near-perfect illustration of the failures of South Africa's criminal justice system. The charges date back to the great thief bashing of November 1996, when two suspects were beaten to death. Magolego and eight others were charged the very next week. If the justice system had worked efficiently, Mapogo might have died in its infancy. Instead, the suspects were released on bail and carried on with their crusade, creating an impression of impunity. The police investigation was lethargic and incompetent, resulting in a docket so full of holes that the case was eventually thrown out of court. By then, almost two years had elapsed, and Mapogo had grown into a national force with tens of thousands of members.

Indeed, John Magolego might never have come to trial if the ruling African National Congress had not grown uneasy about his growing popularity. There was an election in the offing, and the ANC feared it might be vulnerable to attack for its inept handling of the crime crisis. The crackdown gathered urgency as the 1999 election neared. All cases involving Mapogo members were pulled out of sleepy rural police stations and reinvestigated by crack big-city Murder and Robbery Squads. Around 250 Mapogo members were arrested. A special team of prosecutors was appointed to try Mapogo cases in a special Mapogo court. Magolego himself was briefly investigated for treason, and his 1996 murder charges were resurrected.

Magolego claims that he is being crucified for daring to speak truth to power, and he has a point: South African criminals are seldom pursued with such vigor. On the other hand, two men were beaten to death. As this article went to press, Magolego was about to stand trial, and martyrdom was in the offing.

But even if he loses his freedom, a legacy of sorts is already taking shape. Apparently shaken by the vigilante backlash, President Thabo Mbeki's government is finally making tough noises about crime. The last police minister sounded like a left-wing social worker, constantly wringing his anguished hands and simpering about suspects' rights. The new one says criminals are "scum" who will be "mercilessly" dealt with. Several ANC politicians have spoken of reviving traditional courts, once dismissed as relics of feudalism, and the influential Black Lawyers Association wants the entire judicial system restructured on the grounds that it is "alien," slow, and "doesn't hold African values sacred."

And that, of course, is John Magolego's point exactly. It might be a bitter consolation, but when the dust settles, the strong man from Sekhukhuneland may turn out to have had the answer all along.

—Esquire, 1999

Postscript: At the ensuing trial, witnesses failed to identify John Magolego as one of their attackers, and he was acquitted of murder. His vigilante movement has since faded in the public eye, but his legacy persists in the strangest way.

In the run-up to South Africa's 2009 general election, ANC presidential candidate Jacob Zuma made some extraordinary speeches to rural African audiences, saying that children should be brought up "to fear God and respect their elders," that schoolgirls who became pregnant should be sent to special institutions, and that criminals should be "made to talk to the police."

In an interview, I noted that white liberals found these statements disturbing, and asked Zuma to comment. His response spoke of a profound yearning for a lost Africa where people had "the great and loving heart" to take care of orphans and the aged in their own homes, and where there was no need for prisons because miscreants were punished in other ways—fined cattle, whipped, or, in extremis, put to death. "White liberals think you are backward if you exercise your culture," he said. "I truly believe we were more holy before whites came."

This was an outcome I would never have predicted—the ANC's leader sounding much like John Magolego in his heyday. Zuma didn't say anything about "a very good warmth of being together," but I could swear it was implicit in his affable demeanor.

When he came to power a few weeks later, State President Zuma appointed a police commissioner whose slogan was "Shoot to kill."

REPORT FROM PLANET MBEKI

It seems a wonder that I have any friends at all, given the abuse they have endured over the years. After a drink or two, any mention of the African National Congress's "struggle for democracy" always gets me ranting about the slavish pro-Moscow stance the ANC assumed during its decades of exile. "People who saw the Soviet Union or Cuba as models for a free South Africa were not true democrats," I'd say. "They were Red Fascists who wanted to put all of us into the Gulag." Someone at the table would inevitably challenge my analysis, usually citing one of the stellar foreign liberals (often Joseph Lelyveld et al.) who portrayed the ANC as a band of innocuous black liberals who just wanted to establish a democracy like Thomas Jefferson's. At this point, I'd go apoplectic, but I could never quite sustain my case. I am therefore deeply grateful to Mark Gevisser for settling the issue in my favor.

I'd like to dedicate this essay to my ex-wife, a fiery (as they say) Latin American who looked a bit like Bianca Jagger and had similarly leftish politics. The Contessa (for that is what I called her) was educated at Brandeis and cut her political teeth on the Left Bank of Paris, where she dated a fashionably radical "tankie" (one who yearned to see Soviet tanks trundling down the Champs Élysées) and was peripherally involved with an underground Marxist group called Action Directe. She wasn't exactly a Marxist herself but would argue spiritedly

45

on behalf of Castro and Ortega and saw the Soviet Union as an essentially benign country that should be judged on its good intentions (a chicken in every pot and so on) rather than its dismal record of oppression, subversion, incompetence, and mass murder.

Why did this glamorous and civilized creature marry a Boer whose idea of a good time was discussing the radically anti-Soviet books of Jean-François Revel (*The Totalitarian Temptation*) and Bernard-Henri Lévy (*Barbarism with a Human Face*)? I guess she enjoyed fighting as much as I did. We fought for years before she lost patience and filed for divorce on the grounds that "the parties argue continuously." This was true. We got so good at it that I eventually took to sketching the argument she was about to make before she'd actually made it, in the interest of saving time and getting to the point quicker. This drove the Contessa mad. "Stop it!" she'd shout. "You're putting words in my mouth and distorting the context out of all recognition!"

I offer this as a sort of truth-in-journalism disclosure because I am about to pull a similar move on Mark Gevisser, author of *The Dream Deferred*, the groundbreaking biography of President Thabo Mbeki. Before I do Mr. Gevisser the dirty, it seems only fair to acknowledge that his book is a very good one, offering some staggering insights into the forces that shaped our enigmatic president.

I particularly enjoyed the opening movements, in which Gevisser sketches the life and times of Mbeki's forebears, ineffably civilized African Victorians who owned land, qualified for the vote, and schooled their offspring to become lawyers, mathematicians, and classical composers. His maternal grandfather, Jacane Moerane, was even a settler of sorts, sent into darkest Africa by foreign powers (the Basotho king and the Paris Evangelical Mission Society) to colonize territory on the western fringe of the Xhosa empire. Jacane built a forbidding stone mansion that looked out over hundreds of acres of lush pasture on which grazed a herd of 130 prize dairy cattle. Almost but not quite as grand was the homestead of Skelewu Mbeki, a headman of the Mfengu people, who fought for Queen Victoria in the frontier wars of the nineteenth century and were rewarded with grants of land in the buffer zone between anxious white farmers and the barbarous tribesmen of the Xhosa hinterland.

The Moeranes and Mbekis were devout Christians, so it was entirely natural that their children Govan and Epainette should become Communists. The Contessa would never concede the link, but as I saw it, even a cursory reading of Milan Kundera revealed that the state of "lyrical delirium" experienced by Marxist converts was closely akin to the bliss on offer in Christian churches: both were redemptive faiths, neither was entirely rational, and both murdered scores of millions in pursuit of their respective utopias. Govan Mbeki was a particularly earnest convert, turning his back on a Durban teaching career and dragging his young wife off to a remote corner of the Transkei to found a cooperative trading store. Their dream, says Gevisser, was to uplift the peasantry and bring light to a place of darkness. In other words, they were missionaries.

And so it came to pass that Thabo Mbeki was born on the cusp of a kingdom he didn't quite understand and never felt part of: the kingdom of the *amaqaba*, the raw Xhosa peasantry. The Mbekis did not mix, as it were. They took a dim view of feudal tribal structures and did not perform traditional rites or send their eldest son to circumcision school. Indeed, says Gevisser, the scholarly young Thabo was usually to be found in his father's study, imbibing revolutionary doctrines, while his mother ran the cooperative. Sadly, it failed to prosper, and by the time Thabo was ten, his father had returned to the city to pursue a career as a journalist and agitator.

Thabo did his A-levels in 1961, and fled the country a year later, one of twenty-five young students deployed by the ANC to acquire skills and begin the arduous task of rebuilding the recently banned movement in exile. This is the official version, at any rate. One of Thabo's comrades, Vincent Mahali, told Gevisser that only seven of the fugitives were committed ANC activists, the rest being nonaligned civilians who wanted only to escape apartheid and get an education. Alas, poor Mahali: he wound up in the Soviet Union, "where he found the Stalinist strictures of his new environment even more oppressive than apartheid." Thabo was more fortunate: as an ANC blue blood and a bright lad besides, he was deployed to the University of Sussex, an experimental left-wing campus where nutty professors gave lectures on subjects about which they knew nothing, in order to "liberate ourselves and the students."

According to Gevisser, Thabo was initially miffed to find himself at this harebrained institution rather than Oxford or Cambridge, but he eventually settled down and spent five magical years studying economics and doing what students do—drinking, partying, listening to jazz, and sleeping with girls newly liberated by the advent of the Pill. In Gevisser's account, young Thabo was something of a lady-killer, his allure hugely enhanced by the mystique of the revolutionary engaged in dashing underground work for a fashionable cause. The president-to-be organized anti-apartheid marches, boycotted South African oranges, and led a delegation to a youth conference in East Germany, where he was photographed demonstrating the gum-boot dance and the *kwela*.

These photographs are a crushing blow to those who joke of Mbeki as the stiffest man in Africa. He was a beautiful young man: lean, lithe, starry-eyed, and very sexy (buy the book, you'll see). Gevisser says these pictures hold a special poignancy for him, for it was the last time in years, perhaps ever, that his subject would look free and happy. The Sussex idyll was drawing to a close, and Thabo was about to vanish into the dark Stalinist maw of the ANC underground.

I must stress that I am not even paraphrasing Gevisser here; he's a sweetie who would never dream of saying anything unkind about fellow leftists. Indeed, he'll be appalled to think his fastidious prose should inspire such an uncouth conclusion, but I can't help myself: the ANC in exile was a Stalinist organization and anyone who says otherwise is flat wrong. During the Cold War, the ANC's liberal supporters took their cues from apologists like Thomas Karis, an influential commentator who repeatedly assured Americans that only three of the thirty leaders on the ANC's national executive were Reds, with the balance made up of hymn-singing Uncle Toms and bourgeois democrats. Karis was a useful idiot. Also wrong was the journal *Africa Confidential*, whose seemingly authoritative sources claimed the true number was twelve. The Boers in Pretoria charged that twenty-three of the top thirty were Communists, but nobody took them seriously and they were off the mark anyway:

according to Gevisser, ANC records reveal that all but one of the potentates who sat on the movement's national executive in the seventies were secretly members of the Communist Party.

This is a staggering revelation. You have to be a Cold Warrior to get the joke, so I won't belabor it here, but I will say this: unless you have some sort of understanding of what it meant to be a disciplined Communist in the era of Soviet hegemony, you have no hope of understanding Mbeki. His courage will be invisible to you, and his triumphs will seem as nothing. Even his present political problems will remain opaque, because they, too, are rooted in the ANC's Sovietist genetic code and best understood as the latest phase of an ideological battle that's been under way for decades.

Thanks to Gevisser, we can even pinpoint the very first skirmish. It took place on April 14, 1967, when police were called to a Moscow youth hostel to save Thabo from a beating at the hands of drunken comrades who accused him of being some sort of counterrevolutionary double agent.

According to Gevisser, the ANC's hard-liners disliked Mbeki from the outset. They saw him as an arrogant toff whose nepotistic connections got him goodies (a scholarship to Sussex and a seat on the national executive) undreamed of for the rank and file, who were mostly stuck in grim Russian institutions or forlorn African military camps. They also resented his tweedy, English squire style, his fondness for the better things (good whiskey and debonair suits), and his reluctance to go on active service with MK, the ANC's military wing. In years to come, they would add a much more serious grievance: Thabo was not securely committed to the quasi-religious doctrines of the South African Communist Party, or SACP.

Liberals like the aforementioned Thomas Karis would say this proves their point: the ANC was actually a broadly social democratic movement, full of non-Communists dedicated to fostering Western-style freedoms. Not so: everyone important in the ANC was a Communist, including Thabo himself. According to Gevisser, the ANC's Swedish backers were shocked to hear that the suave, apparently freethinking Thabo Mbeki was secretly in league with Moscow's troglodytes. Same applies to the legions of white South African business and political leaders who succumbed to Thabo's charm in the talks-about-talks phase of the 1980s. Thabo invariably presented himself to outsiders as a liberal who cherished all the freedoms they themselves held dear, but there is no way he would have said the same things at a meeting of the SACP's politburo. Are you mad? They would have shot him.

Gevisser asked Mbeki when his faith in Communism began to waver and got a vague answer about the discontent displayed by an apparatchik who guided Mbeki and his wife around East Germany in the 1980s. As Gevisser says, there was something "oddly disingenuous and not entirely credible" about this, given that Mbeki had been visiting the Soviet bloc since the sixties and knew all about its food queues, drabness, and suffocating security apparatus. It seems more likely that his disenchantment began as early as 1978, when he got into a very nasty scrape in Lusaka.

Having lived in the West, Mbeki understood the power of the media and the ease with which it could be manipulated. He therefore urged his boss, Oliver Tambo, to allow the U.S. television network CBS to make a documentary about the ANC's "Battle for South Africa." As Thabo anticipated, the resulting film was a huge propaganda coup, with the ANC coming off as the good guys and the Boers as McCarthyite bigots. But the hard-liners were too rigid to understand this. All they knew was that Thabo was talking to the enemy, and next thing, the ANC's dreaded security service—Mbokodo, the grinding stone—had listed him as a CIA agent and put watchers on his trail. In that dark period, says Gevisser, Mbeki often sought refuge in the home of a friend who got the impression that he feared he was about to be assassinated.

Gevisser will probably say that I am laying undue emphasis on this incident and spinning it for my own devious ends. This is true, but I have justification: he thinks his book is about Mbeki's role in apartheid's downfall, but between the lines, it's actually the story of one man's brave and lonely struggle to outwit Communist hard-liners and drag the ANC into the modern era.

In this, Mbeki's chief antagonist was Joe Slovo, the white ideologue generally credited with authorship of the ANC's metastrategy, which called for a two-stage ending to the South African struggle—a "national democratic revolution," followed by a second revolution in which the Marxist-Leninist vanguard took power. According to Gevisser, Slovo and Mbeki's antipathy came to a head in 1982, when Slovo announced that he intended to become chairman of the Communist Party. Mbeki disapproved, pointing out that in terms of the movement's two-stage revolutionary theory, the boss of the Communist Party would ultimately become the president of South Africa, and he doubted that the African masses were ready to accept a white ruler.

Slovo was outraged, describing Thabo's position as "inflammatory" and "dangerously racist" and ordering him to appear before the SACP's politburo, an organ so deeply secret that most comrades weren't even aware of its existence. Mbeki ducked the confrontation, but he was disciplined in absentia and Slovo had his way. On the day of his investiture as SACP chairman, Thabo turned to a sidekick and said, "That's the end of the party."

And so it was, in the long run. Over the years, Mbeki had made himself indispensable to ANC president Oliver Tambo, one of the few senior leaders who never joined the Communist conspiracy. He'd also concluded that the armed struggle was a hopeless affair, and that it was time to start looking toward a negotiated settlement. With Tambo's blessing, Mbeki started meeting anyone with influence. SACP hardliners like Joe Slovo and Chris Hani were deeply suspicious. As far as they were concerned, negotiations were fine, so long as the object was to lull the enemy into lowering his guard. But they suspected—correctly as it turns out—that Mbeki was negotiating in earnest, and that was heresy.

Luckily, Mbeki was a convincing dissembler, capable of proceeding straight from a meeting in which he assured Pretoria that the ANC was ready to negotiate, to a Communist Party conclave where he drafted a resolution calling for "seizure of power" through "mass insurrection."

Asked about such duplicity, Mbeki told Gevisser, "Some people were hostile to negotiation. They saw it as selling out, treachery." His solution was to feign belief in the military option while pursuing more promising initiatives behind Slovo's and Hani's backs. By 1988, he and the Stalinists were living on different planets. When the Soviets asked about prospects for the future, Chris Hani warned them to expect another ten years of armed struggle. Mbeki said, "We'll be home by 1990." He was right on target. The year was barely forty days old when F. W. de Klerk freed Mandela and invited exiled ANC leaders to come home and hammer out a peace deal.

By the time the hard-liners' jets touched down on South African soil, the Berlin Wall had fallen and Communism as we knew it was dying. It was a time of agony for true believers. Chris Hani staggered dazed and blinking into the media spotlight, uttering robotic lines about the "glorious" Bolshevik revolution of October 1917. Joe Slovo presented himself as a born-again democrat, but when Moscow hard-liners attempted to overthrow the reformer Gorbachev and restore Communist dictatorship, his party sent the plotters a premature message of congratulation.

Such men were loath to see Mbeki walk off with the laurels, so they staged a "palace coup" in 1991, axing Thabo's then-ally Jacob Zuma as ANC intelligence chief and toppling Mbeki from his lofty post as head of negotiations. With Cyril Ramaphosa as their point man, they proceeded to play what Gevisser calls "an intensely dangerous game of brinkmanship," taking up positions they knew would force a breakdown of peace talks and then launching a campaign of "rolling mass action," with uncontrollable crowds replacing Soviet tanks as the weapon that would finally crush the Boers and usher in the socialist millennium.

Thabo warned that this was a foolish course, but no one listened. "I was alone," he told Gevisser. "I was alone." And Thabo was right; the anticipated crowds failed to materialize, the enemy stood firm, and the hard-liners learned their lesson: talk was the only way. Beyond that point, the revolutionaries faded away, and we achieved a happy ending.

Or did we?

Mark Gevisser's book launch at Wits Great Hall was an extraordinary event, not least because of the crowd it drew. It was like a who's who of Johannesburg's intelligentsia, and their presence spoke volumes about our fascination with the inscrutable and unfathomable Mbeki. The audience was thirsting for insight, but I knew nobody would mention what Gevisser calls "the two-ton Russian bear" in the room with us. We heard learned talk about history, revolutionary idealism, and psychoanalytic paradigms, but not a word about Communism. That's because South Africa's chattering classes are rather like my beloved ex-wife: they think it is bad form even to mention the ANC's long love affair with left-wing totalitarianism.

I have a wise friend who says, "Truth has its own sound; we know it when we hear it." I have read all the major books about South Africa's transition, and most rang false to me, largely because their authors believed (or pretended to believe) that the Communist plot was a bogeyman conjured up by Pretoria's evil racists. Gevisser is the first to put the Red Faith at center stage, and that's why his book stands head and shoulders above its rivals.

In a way, it's a pity that Gevisser doesn't share my dim view of the Reds, or my glee at the manner in which Mbeki outwitted them, because it could have turned his biography into a thriller. For him, it is more a case of Thabo good, Stalinists good, too, with rival factions pursuing "parallel paths" to a similar end. This evenhandedness saps his narrative of drama and contributes to its exhausting length, but still, he has put the truth on the table, and succeeded in what he set out to do: "give Mbeki his rightful place as the primary architect of post-apartheid South Africa."

I closed *The Dream Deferred* feeling great admiration for Thabo Mbeki. He had the courage to confront the Sovietists who controlled the ANC, and the brains to see that negotiation was necessary and inevitable. Once in power, he turned his back on failed socialist nostrums and pursued economic policies he knew would make him unpopular with his own constituency and vulnerable to attacks from the left. Willingness to court unpopularity is the only true test of a politician's integrity, and by that reckoning Mbeki is a great man.

Which is not to say he's not riddled with flaws. My opinion, for whatever it's worth, is that the president is something of a megalomaniac, driven by a vision he's never been able to share. In the bad old days of Red hegemony, it would have got him shot as a traitor. More recently, he had to watch his words for fear of instigating precisely the sort of left-wing backlash now unfolding inside the ANC. The Mbeki vision is what you see when you walk out your front door: a bourgeois democracy with free speech, free markets, a fairly healthy capitalist economy, and the emerging trappings of an African welfare state, with twelve million of the poorest poor receiving grants from the state.

I suspect Mbeki expects us to say thank you and beg him to stay on forever as our philosopher-king. Instead, we moan about his autocratic style, refuse to forgive his AIDS dissidence and the arms deal, trash his judgment as regards Zimbabwe, and denounce his handling of corruption scandals. Being a megalomaniac who struggles to distinguish between himself and the state, Mbeki interprets all this as proof of a racist counterrevolutionary plot and reacts accordingly, lashing out at imaginary enemies, using the state's security apparatus against political opponents, and generally spreading poison in our society.

Unfortunately, these recent developments are not covered in *The Dream Deferred*. One gets the impression that Gevisser had excellent inside sources on the rise of Thabo Mbeki, but once he entered the presidency the doors closed, and now you might as well ask me what goes on in the presidential brain. If you want to know how we got here, Gevisser's book is the one to read. But if you want to know where we're going . . .

—*Empire*, January 2008

PART TWO
CULTURE

IN THE JUNGLE

First the Zulu man made the magic. Then the white man made the money. This is the secret history of popular music, as told through the long, twisted saga of one amazing melody.

Once upon a time, a long time ago, a small miracle took place in the brain of a man named Solomon Linda. It was 1939, and he was standing in front of a microphone in the only recording studio in black Africa when it happened. He hadn't composed the melody or written it down or anything. He just opened his mouth and out it came, a haunting skein of fifteen notes that flowed down the wires and into a trembling stylus that cut tiny grooves into a spinning block of beeswax, which was taken to England and turned into a record that became a very big hit in that part of Africa.

Later, the song took flight and landed in America, where it mutated into a truly immortal pop epiphany that soared to the top of the charts everywhere, again and again, returning every decade or so under different names and guises. Navajo Indians sing it at powwows. The British know it as the theme tune of a popular Web site. Phish performs it live. It has been recorded by artists as diverse as R.E.M. and Glen Campbell, Brian Eno and Chet Atkins, the Nylons and Muzak schlockmeister Bert Kaempfert. The New Zealand army band turned it into a march. England's 1986 World Cup soccer squad did a parody. Hollywood put it in *Ace Ventura: Pet Detective*. It has logged nearly three centuries of continuous radio airplay in the U.S. alone. It is the most famous melody ever to emerge from Africa, a tune that has penetrated so deep into the human consciousness, over so many generations, that one can truly say, here is a song the whole world knows.

Its epic transcultural saga is also in a way the story of popular music, which limped pale-skinned and anemic into the twentieth century but danced out the other side, vastly invigorated by transfusions of ragtime and rap, jazz, blues, and soul, all of whose bloodlines run back to Africa via slave ships and plantations and ghettos. It was in the nature of this transaction that black men gave more than they got, and were often robbed outright. This one's for Solomon Linda then, a Zulu who wrote a melody that earned untold millions for white men but died so poor that his widow couldn't afford a stone for his grave. Let's take it from the top, as they say in the trade.

A story about music

This is an African yarn, but it begins with an unlikely friendship between an aristocratic British imperialist and a world-famous American Negro. Sir Henry Brougham Loch is a rising star of the British Colonial Office. Orpheus McAdoo is the leader of the celebrated Virginia Jubilee Singers, a combo that specializes in syncopated spirituals. The dudes met during McAdoo's triumphant tour of Australia in the 1880s. When Sir Henry becomes governor of the Cape Colony a few years later, it occurs to him that Orpheus might find it interesting to visit. Next thing, McAdoo and his troupe are on the road in South Africa, playing to slack-jawed crowds in dusty villages and mining towns.

This American music is a revelation to "civilized natives," hitherto forced to wear starched collars and sing horrible dirges under the direction of dour white missionaries. Mr. McAdoo is a stern old Bible thumper, to be sure, but there's a subversive rhythmic intensity in his music, a primordial stirring of funk and soul. Africans have never heard such a thing. The tour turns into a five-year epic. Wherever Orpheus goes, "jubilee" outfits spring up in his wake and spread the glad tidings, which eventually penetrate even the loneliest outposts of civilization.

One such place is Gordon Memorial School, perched on the rim of a wild valley called Msinga, which lies in the Zulu heartland, about three hundred miles southeast of Johannesburg. Among the half-naked herd boys who drift through the mission is a rangy kid called Solomon Linda, born 1909, who gets hooked on the Orpheus-inspired syncopation thing and works bits of it into the Zulu songs he and his friends sing at weddings and feasts.

In the mid-1930s Linda and his friends shake off the dust and cow shit and take the train to Johannesburg, city of gold, where they move into slums and become kitchen boys and factory hands. Life is initially very perplexing. Solly keeps his eyes open and transmutes what he sees into songs that he and his homeboys perform a cappella on weekends. He has songs about work, songs about crime, songs about how banks rob you by giving you paper in exchange for real money, songs about how rudely the whites treat you when you go to get your pass stamped. People like the music. Solly and his friends develop a following. Within two years, they've turned themselves into a very cool urban act that wears pinstriped suits, bowler hats, and dandy two-tone shoes. They've become Solomon Linda and the Evening Birds, inventors of a music that will later become known as *isicathamiya*, arising from the warning cry *"Cathoza, bafana"*—tread carefully, boys.

These were Zulus, you see, and their traditional dancing was punctuated by mighty foot stompings that, when done in unison, literally made the earth tremble. This was fine in the bush, but if you stomped the same way in town you smashed wooden floors, cracked cement, and sometimes broke your feet, so the whole dance had to be restrained and moderated. Cognoscenti will recall Ladysmith Black Mambazo's feline and curiously fastidious movements on stage. That's treading carefully.

In any event, there were legions of careful treaders in South Africa's big cities, usually Zulu migrants whose Saturday nights were devoted to epic beer-fueled bacchanalias known as tea meetings. A tea meeting was part fashion show and part heroic contest between rival a cappella gladiators, with a stray white man pulled off the street to act as judge and a cow or goat as first prize. The local black bourgeoisie was mortified by these antics. Careful treaders were an embarrassment, widely decried for their "primitive" bawling and backward lyrics, which dwelled on such things as witchcraft, crime, and getting girls with love potions. They had names like the Naughty Boys or the Boiling Waters, and when World War II broke out, some started calling themselves mbombers, after the dive-bombing Stukas they'd seen on newsreels. Mbombers were by far the coolest and most dangerous black thing of their time.

Yes! Dangerous! Skeptics are referred to "Ngazula Emagumeni" (on Rounder CD 5025), an early Evening Birds track whose brain-rattling intensity flattens anything played or sung anywhere in the world at the time and thoroughly guts anyone who thinks of a cappella as smooth tunes for mellow people. The wild, rocking sound came from doubling the bass voices and pumping up their volume, an innovation that was largely Linda's, as was the high dressing style and the new dance moves. He was the Elvis Presley of his time and place, a shy, gangly thirty-year-old, so tall that he had to stoop as he passed through doorways. It's odd to imagine him singing soprano, but that was usually his gig in the group: he was the leader, the "controller," singing what Zulus called *fasipathi*, a bloodcurdling falsetto that a white man might render as first part.

The Evening Birds were spotted by a talent scout in 1938 and taken to the top of an office block in downtown Jo'burg, where they saw a machine that cut grooves into spinning discs of beeswax, and a lone microphone on the far side of a glass partition. This was the first recording studio in sub-Saharan Africa, shipped out from England by Eric Gallo, a jovial Italian who started out selling imported American hillbilly records to working-class Boers. Encouraged by strong sales, Gallo bought his own recording machine and started churning out covers of American tunes in local languages, first Afrikaans, then Zulu, Xhosa, and what have you.

Gallo's ally in this experiment was Griffiths Motsieloa, the country's first black producer, a slightly stiff and formal chap whose true interests were classical music and eisteddfodau, wherein polished African gentlemen entertained one another with speeches in high-falutin King's English. Motsieloa abhorred the boss's passion for cultural slumming, but what could he do? Gallo was determined to find a black audience for his product. When Afro-hillbilly failed to catch on, they decided to take a leap into the unknown and lay down some *isicathamiya*.

Solomon Linda and the Evening Birds cut several songs under Motsieloa's direction, but the one we're interested in was called "Mbube," Zulu for "the lion," recorded at their second session in 1939. It was a simple three-chord ditty with lyrics along the lines of "Lion! Ha! You're a lion!," supposedly inspired by an incident in the Birds' collective Zulu boyhood, when they chased lions that were stalking their father's cattle and managed to kill a cub in the process. The first take was a dud, the second likewise. Exasperated, Griffiths stuck his head into the corridor, dragooned some session cats—a pianist, guitarist, and banjo player—and tried again.

The third take almost collapsed at the outset as the unrehearsed musicians dithered and fished for the key, but once they started cooking the song was glory bound. "Mbube" wasn't the most remarkable tune, but there was something terribly compelling about the underlying chant, a dense meshing of low male voices above which Linda yodeled and howled for two minutes, mostly making it up as he went along. The third take was the great one, but it achieved immortality only in its dying seconds, when Linda took a deep breath, opened his mouth, and improvised the melody that the world now associates with these words:

In the jungle, the mighty jungle, the lion sleeps tonight.

Griffiths Motsieloa must have realized he'd captured something special, because that chunk of beeswax was shipped all the way to England, and shipped back in the form of ten-inch 78 rpm records that went on sale just as Hitler invaded Poland. Marketing was tricky because there was hardly any black radio in 1939, but the song went out on "the rediffusion," a landline that pumped music, news, and native affairs propaganda into certain black neighborhoods, and people began trickling into stores to ask for it. The trickle grew into a steady stream that just rolled on for years and years, necessitating so many repressings that the master ultimately disintegrated. By December 1948 "Mbube" had sold somewhere in the region of 100,000 copies, and Solomon Linda was a superstar in the world of Zulu migrants, the undefeated and undefeatable champion of hostel singing competitions.

Pete Seeger, on the other hand, was in a rather bad way. He was a banjo player living in a cold-water flat on MacDougal Street in Greenwich Village with a wife, two young children, and no money. A scion of wealthy New York radicals, he'd dropped out of Harvard ten years earlier and gone on the bum with his banjo on his back, learning hard-times songs for hard-hit people in the Hoovervilles, lumber camps, and coal mines of Depression America. In New York he joined a band with Woody Guthrie. They wore work shirts and jeans and wrote folk songs that championed the downtrodden common man in his struggle against capitalist bloodsuckers. Woody had a slogan on his guitar that said, "This machine kills fascists." Pete's banjo had a kinder, gentler variation: "This machine surrounds hate and forces it to surrender." He was a proto-hippie, save that he didn't smoke reefer or even drink beer.

Pete Seeger was also a pacifist, at least until Hitler invaded Russia. Scenting a capitalist plot to destroy what they saw as the brave Soviet socialist experiment, Pete and Woody turned gung ho overnight and started writing anti-Nazi war songs, an episode that made them briefly famous but quickly faded. After that it was into uniform and off to the front, where Pete played the banjo for bored GIs. Demobbed in '45, he returned to New York and got a gig of sorts in the public school system, teaching toddlers to warble the half-forgotten folk songs of their American heritage. It wasn't particularly glorious, the money was rotten, and atop of that he was sick in bed with a bad cold.

One day there was a knock on the door and lo, there stood his friend Alan Lomax, later to be hailed as "the father of World Music."

Alan and his dad, John, were already famous for their song-collecting forays into the parallel universe of rural black America, where they'd discovered giants like Muddy Waters and Leadbelly. Alan Lomax was presently working for Decca Records, where he'd just rescued a package of 78s sent from darkest Africa by a record company in the vain hope that someone might want to release them in America. They were about to be thrown away when Lomax intervened, thinking, God, Pete's the man for these.

And here they were—ten shellac 78s, one of which said "Mbube" on its label. Pete put it on his old Victrola and sat back. He was fascinated —there was something catchy about the underlying chant, and that wild, skirling falsetto was amazing.

"Golly," he said to himself, "I can sing that." So he got out pen and paper and started transcribing the song, but he couldn't catch the words through all the scratching and hissing. The Zulus were chanting, *uyimbube, uyimbube,* but to Pete it sounded like *awimboowee,* or maybe *awimoweh,* so that's how he wrote it down. A while later, he taught "Wimoweh" to the rest of his band, the Weavers, and it became, he says, "just about my favorite song to sing for the next forty years."

This was no great achievement, given that the Weavers' late-1940s' repertoire was full of dreck like "On Top of Old Smoky" and "Greensleeves." Old Pete will admit no such thing, but one senses that he was growing tired of cold-water flats and work shirts and wanted a proper career, as befitting a thirty-something father of two. He landed a job in TV, but someone fingered him as a dangerous radical and he lost it before it even started. After that, according to his biographer David King Dunaway, he fell into a depression that ended only when his band landed a gig at the Village Vanguard. Apparently determined to make the best possible impression, Pete allowed his wife to outfit the Weavers in matching blue corduroy jackets—a hitherto unimaginable concession to showbiz.

The pay was fifty a week plus free hamburgers, and the booking was for two weeks only, but something odd happened: crowds started coming. The gig was extended for a month, and then another. The Weavers' appeal was inexplicable to folk purists, who noted that most of their

songs had been around forever, in obscure versions by blacks and red-
necks who never had hits anywhere. What they failed to grasp was that
Seeger and his comrades had somehow managed to filter the stench of
poverty and pig shit out of the proletarian music and make it wholesome
and fun for Eisenhower-era squares. Six months later, the Weavers were
still at the Vanguard, drawing sellout crowds of fur-coated ladies and tux-
edoed refugees from the swell supper clubs of Times Square.

One such figure was Gordon Jenkins, a sallow jazz cat with a gig-
olo's mustache and a matinee idol's greased-back hairstyle. Jenkins
started out as Benny Goodman's arranger before scoring a huge hit in
his own right with an appalling piece of crap, "I'm Forever Blowing
Bubbles." Now he was Frank Sinatra's arranger, and the musical director at Decca Records. Jenkins loved the Weavers, returning night after
night, sometimes sitting through two consecutive shows. He wanted to
sign them up, but his bosses were dubious. It was only when Jenkins
offered to pay for the recording sessions himself that Decca capitu-
lated and gave the folkies a deal.

Their first recording came out in August 1950. It was "Goodnight,
Irene," an old love song they'd learned from their friend Leadbelly,
and it was an immediate click, in the parlance of the day. The B-side
was an Israeli hora called "Tzena, Tzena, Tzena," and it clicked, too.
So did "Roving Kind," a nineteenth-century folk ditty they released
that November, and even "On Top of Old Smoky," which hit number
two the following spring. The Weavers leapt from amateur hootenan-
nies to the stages of America's poshest nightspots and casinos. They
wore suits and ties, appeared on TV, rode around in limos, and pulled
down two grand a week. Chagrined and envious, their former comrades on the left started sniping at them in small magazines. "Can an
all-white group sing songs from Negro culture?" asked one.

The answer, of course, lay in the song Seeger called "Wimoweh."
His version was faithful to the Zulu original in almost all respects save
for the finger-popping rhythm, which is probably a bit white for some
tastes but not entirely offensive. The true test lay in the singing, and
here Seeger passed with flying colors, bawling and howling his heart
out, tearing up his vocal chords so badly that he was almost mute by

the time he reached seventy-five. Audiences were thunderstruck by his performance. "Wimoweh" was by far the most edgy and unsettling song in the Weavers' set, which is perhaps why they waited a year after their big breakthrough before recording it.

Like their earlier recordings, it took place with Gordon Jenkins presiding and an orchestra in attendance. Prior to this, Jenkins had been very subdued in his instrumental approach, adding just the occasional sting and the odd swirl of strings to the Weavers' cheery sing-alongs. Maybe he was growing bored, because his arrangement of "Wimoweh" was a motherfucker, a great Las Vegas-y explosion of big-band raunch that almost equaled the barbaric splendor of the Zulu original. Trombones blared. Trumpets screamed. Strings swooped and soared through Linda's miracle melody, the one invented on the immortal third take of 1939. And then Pete cut loose with all that hollering and screaming. It was a revolutionary departure from everything else the Weavers had ever done, but *Billboard* loved it, anointing it a "Pick of the Week." *Cash Box* said "might break." *Variety* said, "Terrific!"

But around this time *Variety* also said, "Scripter names five more H'wood Reds," and "Chaplin being investigated." It was January 1952, and America was engaged in a frenzied hunt for Reds under beds. The House Un-American Activities Committee was probing Hollywood. "Red Channels" had just published the names of artists with Commie connections. The American Legion was organizing a boycott of their movies. And in Washington, DC, someone called Harvey Matusow was talking to federal investigators.

Harvey was a weaselly little man who had once worked alongside Pete Seeger in Peoples' Artists, a reddish front that dispatched folk singers to entertain on picket lines and in union halls. Harvey had undergone a change of heart, though, and decided to tell all about his secret life in the Communist underground. On February 6, 1952, just as "Wimoweh" made its chart debut, he stepped up to a mike before the House Un-American Activities Committee and told one of the looniest tales of the entire McCarthy era. Evil Reds, he said, were "preying on the sexual weakness of American youth" to lure recruits into their dreaded movement. What's more, he was willing to name names of Communist Party members, among them three of the Weavers—including Pete Seeger.

The yellow press went ape shit. Reporters called the Ohio club where the Weavers were scheduled to play that night, demanding to know why the Yankee Inn was providing succor to the enemy. The Weavers' show was canned, and it was all downhill from there. Radio stations banned their records. TV appearances were canceled. "Wimoweh" plummeted from number six into oblivion. Nightclub owners wouldn't even talk to the Weavers' agents, and then Decca dropped them, too. By the end of the year, they'd packed it in, and Pete Seeger was back where he'd started, teaching folk songs to kids for a weekly pittance.

So the Weavers were dead, but "Wimoweh" lived on, bewitching jazz ace Jimmy Dorsey, who covered it in 1952, and the sultry Yma Sumac, whose cocktail lounge version caused a minor stir in the mid-1950s. Toward the end of the decade, it was included on . . . *from the Hungry I*, a monstrously big LP by the Kingston Trio that stayed on the charts for 178 weeks, peaking at number two. By now, almost everyone in America knew the basic refrain, so it would have come as no particular surprise to see four nice Jewish teenagers popping their fingers and going *ah-weem-oh-way, ah-weem-oh-way* on some Long Island beach in the summer of 1961.

The Tokens were clean-cut Brooklyn boys who had grown up listening to Alan Freed, Murray the K, and the dreamy teen stylings of Dion and the Belmonts and the Everly Brothers. Hank Medress and Jay Siegel met at Lincoln High, where they sang in a doo-wop quartet that briefly featured Neil Sedaka. Phil Margo was a budding drummer and piano player, also from Lincoln High, and Mitch Margo was his kid brother, age fourteen.

One presumes girls were cutting eyes in their direction, because the Tokens had recently been on TV's *American Bandstand,* decked out in double-breasted mohair suits with white shirts and purple ties, singing their surprise top twenty hit, "Tonight I Fell in Love."

And now they were moving toward even greater things. Barely out of high school, they'd landed a three-record deal with RCA Victor, with a $10,000 advance and a crack at working with Hugo Peretti and Luigi Creatore, ace producers of Jimmie Rodgers, Frankie Lymon, and many, many others. These guys worked with Elvis Presley, for God's sake. "This was big for us," said Phil Margo. "Very big."

The Tokens knew "Wimoweh" through their lead singer Jay, who'd learned it off an old Weavers album. It was one of the songs they sang when they auditioned for Huge and Luge, as Peretti and Creatore were known in the trade. The producers said, yeah, well, there's something there, but it's a bit weird, and besides, what's it about? Eating lions, said the Tokens. That's what some joker at the South African consulate had told them, at any rate: it was a Zulu hunting song with lyrics that went, "Hush, hush, if everyone's quiet, we'll have lion meat to eat tonight."

The producers presumably rolled their eyes. None of this got anyone anywhere in the era of *Shooby-doo, I love you*. They wanted to revamp the song, give it some intelligible lyrics, and a contemporary feel, so they sent for George David Weiss, a suave young dude in a navy-blue blazer, presently making a big name for himself in yesterday's music, writing orchestrations for Doris Day, Peggy Lee, and others of that sort. The Tokens took him for a hopeless square until they discovered that he'd also cowritten "Can't Help Falling in Love" for Elvis Presley. That changed everything.

So George Weiss took "Wimoweh" home with him and gave it a careful listen. A civilized chap with a Juilliard degree, he didn't much like the primitive bawling, but the underlying chant was okay and parts of the melody were very catchy. So he dismantled the song, excised all the hollering and screaming, and put the rest back together in a new way. The chant remained unchanged but the melody—Solomon Linda's miracle melody—moved to center stage, becoming the tune itself, to which the new words were sung: "In the jungle, the mighty jungle" and so on.

In years to come, Weiss was always a bit diffident about his revisions, describing them as "gimmicks," as if ashamed to be associated with so frothy a bit of pop nonsense. The Tokens say that's because he wrote nothing save thirty-three words of doggerel, but that's another lawsuit entirely. What concerns us here is the song's bloodline, and everyone agrees on that. "The Lion Sleeps Tonight" was a reworking of "Wimoweh," which was a copy of "Mbube." Solomon Linda was buried under several layers of pop-rock stylings, but you could still see him beneath the new song's slick surface, like a mastodon embalmed in a block of clear ice.

The song was recorded live in RCA's Manhattan studios on July 21, 1961, with an orchestra in attendance and some session players on guitar, drums, and bass. The percussionist muted his timpani, seeking that authentic "jungle drum" sound. A moonlighting opera singer named Anita Darian practiced her scales. Conductor Sammy Lowe tapped his baton, and off they went, three Tokens doing the *wimowehs* while Jay Siegel took the lead with his pure falsetto and Darian swooped and dove in the high heavens, singing the haunting countermelodies that were one of the song's great glories. Three takes (again), a bit of over-dubbing, and that was more or less that. Everyone went home, entirely blind to what they'd accomplished. The Tokens were mortified by the new lyrics, which struck them as un-teen and uncool. Hugo and Luigi were so uninterested that they did the final mix over the telephone, and RCA topped them all by issuing the song as the B-side of a hum-drum tune called "Tina," which sank like lead.

Weird, no? We're talking about a pop song so powerful that Brian Wilson had to pull off the road when he first heard it, totally overcome; a song that Carole King instantly pronounced "a motherfucker." But it might never have reached their ears if an obscure DJ named Dick Smith in Worcester, Massachusetts, hadn't flipped the Tokens' new turkey and given the B-side a listen. Smith said, "Holy shit, this is great," or words to that effect, so his station, WORC, put "The Lion Sleeps Tonight" on heavy rotation. The song broke out regionally, hit the national charts in November, and reached number one in four giant strides.

A month later, it was number one in England, too. By April 1962, it was number one all around the world, and heading for immortality.

Miriam Makeba sang her version at JFK's last birthday party, moments before Marilyn Monroe famously lisped, "Happy Birthday, Mister President." Apollo astronauts listened to it on the take-off pads at Cape Canaveral. It was covered by the Springfields, the Spinners, the Tremeloes, and Glen Campbell. In 1972, it returned to number three in a version by Robert John. Brian Eno recorded it in 1975.

In 1982, it was back at number one in the UK, this time performed by Tight Fit. R.E.M. did it, as did the Nylons and They Might Be Giants. Manu Dibango did a twist version. Some Germans turned it into heavy metal. A sample cropped up on a rap epic titled "Mash Up da Nation." Disney used the song in *The Lion King,* and then it got into the smash-hit musical of the same title. It's on the original Broadway cast recording, on dozens of kids' CDs with cuddly lions on their covers and an infinite variety of nostalgia compilations. It's more than sixty years old, and still it's everywhere.

What might all this represent in songwriter royalties and associated revenues? I put the question to lawyers around the world, and they scratched their heads. Around 160 recordings of three versions? Twelve movies? Five TV commercials and a smash hit musical? Ceaseless radio airplay in every corner of the planet? It was impossible to be sure, but no one blanched at $15 million dollars. Some said ten, some said twenty, but most felt that fifteen million was squarely in the ballpark.

Which raises an even more interesting question: What happened to all that loot?

A story about money

"It was a wonderful experience," said Larry Richmond, hereditary president of the Richmond Organization. It was two in the morning in Johannesburg and Larry was telling me about his company's "wonderful efforts" to make sure that justice was done for Solomon Linda. I wanted to hear everything, but we were on opposite sides of the planet, so I said, "Hold it right there, I'm coming to see you." I hung up, started packing, and a few days later I walked into the headquarters of TRO, a strangely quiet suite of offices in Manhattan.

The dusty old guitar in the waiting room was a relic of a long-gone era. Back in the 1940s, when TRO was young, eager songwriters streamed in here to audition their wares for Larry's dad, Howie, the firm's founder. If he liked the songs, he'd sign 'em up, transcribe 'em, and secure a copyright. Then he'd send song pluggers out to place the tunes with stars whose recordings would generate income for the composer and the publisher. At the same time, salesmen would be flogging the sheet music, while bean counters in the back office collected royalties and kept an eye out for unauthorized versions.

In its heyday, TRO was a music publishing empire that spanned the globe, but it was forced into decline by the advent of the savvy rock and roll accountants of the 1970s, who advised clients to publish themselves, which was fairly easy and almost doubled one's songwriting income, given that old-style publishers generally claimed 50 percent of royalties for their services. By 1999, TRO was little more than a crypt for fabulously valuable old copyrights, manned by a skeleton crew that licensed old songs for TV commercials or movies.

Larry Richmond was an amiable bloke in an open-necked shirt and beige slacks. We drank coffee and talked for an hour or two, mostly about social justice and TRO's commitment to the same. There were stories about Woody Guthrie and Pete Seeger, the famous radical troubadours in TRO's stable. There was a story about the hospital in India to which the Richmonds made generous donations. And finally, there were some elliptical remarks about Solomon Linda and TRO's noble attempts to make sure that he received his just dues. I was hoping Larry would give me a formal interview on the subject, but first I had to get some sleep. It was a mistake. By the time I'd recovered, Larry had changed his mind and retreated into the labyrinth of his voice-mail system, from which he would not emerge again.

So there I was in New York, with no one to talk to. I called music lawyers and record companies, angling for appointments that failed to materialize. I wandered into the offices of *Billboard* magazine, where a veteran journalist warned that I was wasting my time trying to find out what any song had ever earned and where the money had gone. But I'd come a long way, so I kept looking and, eventually, figured some of it out.

The story begins in 1939, when Solomon Linda was visited by angels in Africa's only recording studio. At the time, Jo'burg was a hick mining town where music deals were concluded according to trading principles as old as Moses: record companies bought recordings for whatever they thought the music might be worth in the marketplace; stars generally got several guineas for a session, unknowns got almost nothing. No one got royalties, and copyright was unknown. Solomon Linda didn't even get a contract. He walked out of that session with about ten shillings in his pocket, and the music thereafter belonged to the record company, with no further obligations to anyone. When "Mbube" became a local hit, the loot went to Eric Gallo, the playboy who owned the company. All Solomon Linda got was a menial job at the boss's packing plant, where he worked for the rest of his days.

When "Mbube" took flight and turned into the Weavers' hit "Wimoweh," Eric Gallo could have made a fortune if he had played his cards right. Instead, he struck a handshake deal with Larry Richmond's dad, trading "Mbube" to TRO in return for the dubious privilege of administering "Wimoweh" in such bush territories as South Africa and Rhodesia. Control of Solomon Linda's destiny thus passed into the hands of Howie Richmond and his faithful sidekick, one Albert Brackman.

Howie and Al shared an apartment in the 1930s, when they were ambitious young go-getters on Tin Pan Alley. Howie was tall and handsome, Al was short and fat, but otherwise they were blood brothers, with shared passions for nightlife and big-band jazz. After World War II, Howie worked as a song promoter before deciding to become a publisher in his own right. He says he found a catchy old music-hall number, had a pal write new lyrics, and placed the song with Guy Lombardo, who took it to number ten as "Hop Scotch Polka." Howie was on his way. Al joined up in 1949, and together they put a whole slew of novelty songs on the hit parade. Then they moved into the burgeoning folk music sector, where big opportunities were opening up for sharp guys with a shrewd understanding of copyright.

After all, what was a folk song? Who owned it? It was just out there, like a wild horse or a tract of virgin land on an unconquered continent. Fortune awaited the man bold enough to name himself as the composer of some ancient tune like, say, "Greensleeves." A certain Jessie Cavanaugh did exactly that in the early fifties, only it wasn't really Jessie at all—it was Howie Richmond under an alias. This was a common practice on Tin Pan Alley at the time, and it wasn't illegal. The object was to claim writer royalties on new versions of old songs that belonged to no one. The aliases seem to have been a way to avoid potential embarrassment, just in case word got out that Howard S. Richmond was presenting himself as the author of a madrigal from Shakespeare's day.

Much the same happened with "Frankie and Johnny," the hoary old frontier ballad, or "Roving Kind," a ribald ditty from the clipper-ship era. There's no way Al Brackman could really have written such songs, so when he filed royalty claims with the performing rights society BMI, he attributed the compositions to Albert Stanton, a fictitious tunesmith who often worked closely with the imaginary Mr. Cavanaugh, penning such standards as "John Henry" and "Michael Row the Boat Ashore." Cavanaugh even claimed credit for "Battle Hymn of the Republic," a feat eclipsed only by a certain Harold Leventhal, who accidentally copyrighted an obscure whatnot later taken as India's national anthem.

Leventhal started out as a gofer for Irving Berlin and wound up promoting concerts for Bob Dylan but, in between, he developed a serious crush on the Weavers. In 1949, he showed up at the Village Vanguard with an old friend in tow—Pete Kameron, a suave charmer who was scouting around an entree into showbiz. Leventhal performed some introductions, and Kameron became the Weavers' manager. Since all these players knew one another, it was natural that they should combine to take charge of the naive left-wingers' business affairs. Leventhal advised; Kameron handled bookings, negotiated with mob-linked nightclub owners, and tried to fend off the red-baiters. Howie and Al took on the publishing, arranging it so that Kameron owned a 50 percent stake. The Weavers sang the songs and cut the records, and together they sold around four million platters in eighteen months or so.

In the late 1940s, these men found themselves contemplating the fateful 78 rpm record from Africa and wondering exactly what manner of beast it could be. The label said "Mbube—by Solomon Linda and the Evening Birds," but at the time, it was not copyrighted anywhere. Anything not copyrighted was a wild horse, strictly speaking, and wild horses in the Weavers' repertoire were usually attributed to one Paul Campbell. The Weavers' version of "Hush, Little Baby" was a Paul Campbell composition, for instance. The same was true of "Rock Island Line" and "Kisses Sweeter than Wine," tunes the folkies had learned off Leadbelly and reworked in their own style.

On the surface of things, Paul Campbell appeared to be one of the most successful songwriters of the era but, of course, the name was just another alias used to claim royalties on songs from the public domain. "Mbube" wasn't public domain at all, but it was the next best thing— an uncopyrighted song owned by an obscure foreign record label that had shown absolutely no interest in protecting Solomon Linda's rights as a writer. So the Zulu's song was tossed in among the Weavers' wild horses and released as "Wimoweh," by Paul Campbell.

As the song found its fans, money started rolling in. Every record sale triggered a mechanical royalty. Every radio play counted as a performance, which also required payment, and there was always the hope that someone might take out a "synch license" to use the tune in a movie or TV ad. Al, Howie, and Pete Kameron divided the standard publisher's 50 percent among themselves and distributed the other half to the writers—or, in this case, adapters: Pete Seeger and the Weavers. Solomon Linda was entitled to nothing.

This didn't sit well with Seeger, who openly acknowledged Linda as the true author of "Wimoweh" and felt he should get the money. Indeed, he'd been hassling his publishers for months to find a way of paying the Zulu.

"Originally they were going to send the royalties to Gallo," Seeger recalls. "I said, 'Don't do that, because Linda won't get a penny.'"

Anti-apartheid activists put Seeger in touch with a Johannesburg law-yer, who set forth into the forbidden townships to find Solomon Linda. Once contact was established, Seeger sent the Zulu a $1,000 check, and instructed his publisher to do the same with all future payments.

He was still bragging about it fifty years later. "I never got author's royalties on 'Wimoweh,'" Seeger says. "Right from '51 or '52, I under-stood that the money was going to Linda. I assumed they were keep-ing the publisher's 50 percent and sending the rest."

Unfortunately, Linda's family maintains that the money only ar-rived years later, and even then, it was nothing like the full writer's share Seeger was hoping to bestow. We'll revisit this conundrum in short order, but first, let's follow the further adventures of "Wimoweh," which fell into the hands of RCA producers Hugo and Luigi, by way of the Tokens, in the summer of 1961. In addition to being ace producers and buddies of Elvis Presley, these men were also wild-horse breakers of the very first rank. They'd put their brand on a whole herd of them—"Pop Goes the Weasel," "First Noël," you name it. They even had "Grand March from Aida," a smash hit for Giuseppe Verdi in the 1870s.

As seasoned pros, these guys would have checked out the "Wimoweh" composer of record—Paul Campbell—and discovered that he was an alias and that his oeuvre consisted largely of folk songs from previous centuries. They leapt to a seemingly obvious conclu-sion: "Wimoweh" was based on an old African folk song that didn't belong to anyone. As such, it was fair game, so they summoned George Weiss, turned "Wimoweh" into "The Lion Sleeps Tonight," and sent it out into the world as a Weiss/Peretti/Creatore composition. They did exactly the same thing a few months later with "The Click Song," a Xhosa tune popularized in America by Miriam Makeba: Weiss cooked up some more doggerel about jungle drums and love-lorn maidens, the Tokens sang it, and it landed in record stores as "B'wanina," another "original composition" by the same trio.

But they had made a mistake. "The Click Song" was indeed a wild horse that had been roaming Africa for centuries, but "Wimoweh" was the subject of a U.S. copyright, and "Wimoweh" was clearly the lion song's progenitor. When "The Lion Sleeps Tonight" began playing on

America's radios, Howie Richmond instantly recognized its bloodline and howled with outrage. He set his lawyers on the Tokens and their allies, and what could they say? It must have been deeply embarrassing. On the other hand, Howie was on first-name terms with Hugo and Luigi and deeply respectful of George Weiss's talents. Howie was thus willing to forget the whole thing—provided the publishing rights to "Lion" came back to him.

Within a week there was a letter acknowledging infringement on Howie's desk, and urgent settlement talks were under way. Why urgent? Because "The Lion Sleeps Tonight" was soaring up the charts and the Weiss/Peretti/Creatore cabal was desperate to avoid a dispute that might abort its trajectory. This put Richmond and Brackman in a position to dictate almost any terms they pleased. Pete Seeger says he had informed them that he didn't feel entitled to composer royalties and would prefer any benefits to flow to Solomon Linda, author of the underlying "Mbube." If they'd seen fit, Richmond and Brackman could have forced Luigi, Hugo, and Weiss to share their spoils with the Zulu. But they had no legal obligations toward Linda, and besides, taking a hard line might have soured an important business relationship. So they allowed three men they were later to describe as "plagiarists" to walk away with 100 percent of the writer royalties on a song that originated in Solomon Linda's brain.

And why not? It was no skin off their backs. TRO received the full 50 percent publisher's cut. Huge and Luge and Weiss were happy. The only person who lost out was Linda, who wasn't even mentioned: the new copyright described "Lion" as "based on a song by Paul Campbell."

The paperwork was finalized on December 18, 1961, just as the song commenced its conquest of the world's hit parades. It was number one in the States on Christmas Day, and reached South Africa two months later, just in time to bring a wan smile to the face of a dying Solomon Linda. He'd been ailing since 1959, when he lost control of his bowels and collapsed onstage. Doctors diagnosed kidney disease, but his family suspected witchcraft.

If true, this would make Linda a victim of his own success. Sure, he was nothing in the world of white men, but "Mbube" made him a

75

legend in the Zulu subculture, and to be a legend among "the people of heaven" was a pretty fine destiny in some respects. Strangers hailed him on the streets, bought him drinks in shebeens. He was in constant demand for personal appearances and earned enough to afford some sharp suits, a second bride, and a wind-up gramophone for the kinfolk in mud huts back in Msinga.

A thousand bucks from Pete Seeger aside, most of his money came from the uproarious all-night song contests, which remain a vital part of urban Zulu social life to this day. Most weekends, Solly and the Evening Birds would hire a car and sally forth to do battle in distant towns, and they always came back victorious. Competitors tried everything, including potions, to make their voices hoarse and high like Linda's, but nothing worked. The aging homeboys would take the stage and work themselves into such transports of ecstasy that tears started streaming down Solly's face, at which point the audience would go wild and the Evening Birds would once again walk off with first prize—sometimes a trophy, sometimes money, sometimes a cow that they slaughtered as the sun came up, and roasted and shared with their fans. Blinded by the resulting adulation, Linda wasn't particularly perturbed when his song mutated into "The Lion Sleeps Tonight" and raced to the top of the world's hit parades.

"He was happy," said his daughter Fildah. "He didn't know he was supposed to get something."

Fildah is Linda's oldest surviving child, a radiant woman who wears beads in her hair and a goatskin bangle on her right wrist, the mark of a *sangoma*, or witch doctor. Her sister Elizabeth works as a nurse in a government clinic but she announced, giggling, that she was a *sangoma*, too. A third daughter, Delphi, had just had surgery for arthritis, but she was also using ancestral medicine under her sisters' direction—a plant called *umhlabelo*, apparently. Elizabeth thought a water snake might be useful, too, and wondered where she could obtain such a thing. They lived in an urban slum but were deeply Zulu people, down to the cattle horns on the roof above the kitchen door—relics of sacrifices to the spirits of their ancestors. Only Elizabeth spoke fluent English, but even she didn't flinch at the talk of witchcraft.

Their aunt, Mrs. Beauty Madiba, was the one who brought it up. A sweet old lady in her Sunday best, she remembered meeting Linda in the late 1940s, when he started to court her sister Regina. The singer was at the peak of his career at the time, and he had no trouble raising the ten cattle their father was asking as the bride price. The wedding feast took place in 1949, and Regina went to live in Johannesburg. Beauty joined her a few years later and had a ringside seat when Linda was brought down by dark forces. "People were jealous, because all the time, he won," she explained. "They said, 'We will get you.' So they bewitched him."

Elizabeth muttered something about renal failure, but even she had to acknowledge there was something odd about the way her father's disease refused to respond to treatment. He grew so sick that he had to stop singing. By the time "The Lion Sleeps Tonight" was released, he was in and out of the hospital constantly, and on October 8, 1962, he died.

Everyone sighed. Rival a cappella groups were to blame, growled Victor Madondo, a burly old warrior whose father sang alto in the Evening Birds. "They were happy, because now they could go forward nicely."

But they went nowhere. Linda was the one whose influence lived on, becoming so pervasive that all Zulu male choral singing came to be called "Mbube music." Ethnomusicologists dug up the early Birds recordings, and Linda was posthumously elevated to godhead—"one of the great figures in black South African music," according to Professor Veit Erlmann of the University of Texas. Latter-day Mbube stars like Ladysmith Black Mambazo sent gifts to this very house when they made it big, a tribute to the spirit of a man they venerated. And then I came along asking questions about money.

It soon became clear that Linda's daughters had no understanding of music publishing and related arcana. All they knew was that "people did something with our father's song outside," and that monies were occasionally deposited in their joint bank account by mysterious entities they could not name. I asked to see documents, but they had none, and they were deeply confused as to the size and purpose of the payments. "Mister Tucker is helping us," they said. "Mister Tucker knows everything."

Raymond Tucker is a white lawyer with offices in a grand old colonial mansion on the outskirts of Jo'burg's decaying downtown. On the phone, he explained that intermediaries had contacted him on Pete Seeger's behalf some decades back, asking him to act as a conduit for payments to Linda's widow. Tucker was honored to help out, he said. As we spoke, he flipped through his files, assuring me that royalty payments were "pretty regular, with proper accounting," and that everything was "totally and absolutely aboveboard."

Solomon's daughters didn't contest this, but they rejected Seeger's claim that royalties had been flowing through the Tucker channel since the 1950s. According to their recollections, their father's 1962 death was a catastrophe that left the family destitute. Their mother, Regina, was an illiterate peasant with no job and six children to feed. She illegally brewed and sold African beer to make ends meet. Her girls went to school barefoot, took notes on cracked bits of slate, and went to bed hungry. Critical Zulu death rites went unperformed for years, because the family was too poor to pay a *sangoma* to officiate.

"This house, it was bare bricks," says Elizabeth. "No ceiling, no plaster, no furniture, just one stool and one coal stove." Her eldest brother left school and started working, but he was murdered by gangsters. Her second brother became the breadwinner, only to die in an accident, whereupon Delphi took a job in a factory to keep the family going. "There was suffering here at home," says Elizabeth. She is adamant that the mysterious money "from outside" started arriving only much later, perhaps around 1980. That's when they erected a tombstone for their father, who had rested in a pauper's grave since 1962. That's how they remembered.

I asked Tucker if I could see his files, but he balked, citing his clients' confidentiality. I obtained a letter from the daughters and called to discuss it, but Tucker slammed the phone down, so I wrote a note, pointing out that the daughters were legally and morally entitled to information. In response came a series of letters accusing me of misrepresenting myself as a "white knight," when I was clearly just a devious muckraker intent on "writing an article for your own gain." "I have absolutely no intention of cooperating with a journalist of your type," he wrote.

Defeated on that front, I sent an e-mail to Larry Richmond, asking him to clarify the size and nature of TRO's payments to Linda's family. "It will take some time to review your letter," he wrote back. "I hope to get back to you in due course." Months passed but nothing happened, so I appealed to Harold Leventhal, the grandfatherly figure who had once managed the Weavers' affairs. "You're in a void," he said, sounding sympathetic. "All you can do is describe it, or you'll never finish your story." A wise man would have heeded his advice, but I plodded onward until someone took pity and provided me with a few key documents. Ambiguities remained, but at least I found out why the publishers and their cronies were so coy about making disclosures: it looked as if Linda's family was receiving 12.5 percent of "Wimoweh" royalties, and around 1 percent of the much larger revenues generated by "The Lion Sleeps Tonight."

The payments on "Lion" were coming out of "performance royalties," jargon for the bucks generated when a song is broadcast. The sums in question averaged around $275 a quarter in the early 1990s, but who are we to raise eyebrows? Solomon's family was desperate and grateful for the smallest blessing. The money "from outside" enabled his widow to feed her children and educate the two youngest, Elizabeth and Adelaide. After Regina's death in 1990, Raymond Tucker set up a joint bank account for the daughters in which small sums of money continued to materialize—never much, but enough to build a tin shack in their backyard and rent it out for extra money, and even enough to start a little shop at the front gate. In American terms, their poverty remained appalling, but in their own estimation this was a happy ending—until I showed up and told them what might have been.

The annals of a curious lawsuit

It's November 1991 and we're in a bland conference room in the American Arbitration Association's New York headquarters. At the head of a long table sit three veteran copyright lawyers who will act as judges in these proceedings. Ranged before them are the warring parties: the entire cast of the 1961 "Lion Sleeps Tonight" plagiarism contretemps, either in person or legally represented.

Hugo Perretti died a few years back, but fortune has smiled hugely on the rest of the guys since last we saw them. Howie Richmond published the Rolling Stones and Pink Floyd for a while and is now rich beyond wild imaginings. His sidekick Al Brackman (who got 10 percent of all Howie's deals) is rich, too; puttering around in boats on weekends and wintering at his second home near San Diego. Luigi Creatore has retired to Florida on the proceeds of his many hit records, and George Weiss is a successful composer of movie scores and musicals. So why are they cooped up here, flanked by lawyers? It's another long story.

In the fall of 1989, just as the initial copyright on "The Lion Sleeps Tonight" was about to expire, Howie and Al were notified that George Weiss and his fellow writers wanted a handsome bonus. Failing this, they'd renew the "Lion" copyright in their own names and thereafter publish the song themselves, thus cutting Howie and Al out entirely. The publishers were incensed, pointing out that "Lion" would never have existed if they hadn't allowed Weiss and Company to "plagiarize" the underlying music. To which the "Lion" team responded by asking a single question: How can you accuse us of stealing something you gave us in 1961? The fight went to court in 1990 and wound up in this arbitration months later—two rival groups of rich white Americans squabbling over ownership of the most famous melody ever to emerge from Africa.

The music industry is riveted, because these men are pillars of the showbiz establishment. Al sits on the board of the Music Publishers Association. Howie founded the Songwriters Hall of Fame. George Weiss is president of the Songwriters Guild of America and a tireless champion of downtrodden tunesmiths. As such, he can't possibly say that "The Lion Sleeps Tonight" infringes on the work of a fellow composer, so he doesn't. Sure, he says, we "threw the music together" using a "few themes from this Weavers record," but so what? Weiss said he'd been told that "Wimoweh" was just Pete Seeger's interpretation of "an old thing from Africa," so they hadn't really plagiarized anyone. To prove his point, Weiss produces the liner notes of an old

Miriam Makeba record in which "Mbube" is described as "a familiar Zulu song about a lion hunt."

TRO counters by presenting a yellowing affidavit in which Solomon Linda swears that "Mbube" was wholly original. At this juncture Weiss backs down, saying, in essence, Gee, sorry, all this is news to me, and the hearing moves on to the real issue, which is the validity of the 1961 contract between TRO and the "Lion" trio. Drawn up in a spirit of incestuous back scratching, the contract allows the Weiss parties free use of "Wimoweh" and "Mbube" in "The Lion Sleeps Tonight," with no royalty provisions for the author of the underlying songs. The judges seem to find it a bit curious that TRO should now start shouting. "Hold on! Our own contract's inaccurate!"

Apparently worried that they might not be taken seriously, the men from TRO develop a sudden and barely explicable concern for Solomon's descendants. "The defendants seek to deprive Mr. Linda's family of royalties," cries Larry Richmond, directing the brunt of his attack at George Weiss. The president of the Songwriters Guild should be "protecting the poor families of songwriters," Larry declares, not robbing them. Stung by these accusations, the Weiss parties say that if they win the case they'll give a share to Solomon's estate. The TRO boys then raise the ante, declaring that the family is rightfully entitled to up to a half of "Lion"'s enormous spoils.

Amazing, no? If TRO had enforced such a distribution from the outset, Solomon's daughters might have been millionaires, but nobody had informed them that this dispute was taking place, so there was no one to laugh (or cry) on their behalf.

The arbitrators weren't very impressed, either—they awarded "The Lion Sleeps Tonight" to Weiss and Company, with the proviso that they send "10 percent of writers' performance royalties" to Soweto. The order came into effect on January 1, 1992, just as the song set forth on a new cycle of popularity. That very year, a new recording rose to the top of the Japanese hit parade. Pow woW's version made number one in France in 1993. Then someone at Disney wrote a cute little scene in which cartoon animals prance hand-in-hand through a forest glade, singing, "In the jungle, the mighty jungle . . ." The song had been used in at least nine earlier movies, but *The Lion King* became a supernova. Every kid on the planet had to have the video and the vast array of CDs that went with it. George Weiss could barely contain his glee. "The song leads a magical life," he told a reporter. "It's been a hit eight or nine times but never like this. It's going wild!" The great composer came across as a diffident fellow, somewhat bemused by his enormous good fortune. "The way all this happened was destiny," he said. "It was mysterious, it was beautiful. I have to say God smiled at me."

I was hoping to talk to Weiss about God and Solomon Linda, but his lawyer said he was out of town and unavailable. On the other hand, he was visible in the *New York Times* Sunday magazine, which had just run a six-page spread about his amazing retreat in rural New Jersey. I drove out to Oldwick and found the place—an eighteenth-century farmhouse in a deer-filled glade, with a pool and a recording studio in the outbuildings—but Weiss wasn't there. Maybe he was in Santa Fe, where he maintains a hacienda. Or in Cabo San Lucas, Mexico, where he and his wife were building a house on a bluff overlooking the sea. Defeated yet again, I returned to my hotel and wrote him a letter. Weiss faxed back, saying he was "distressed" to hear that Solomon had been shabbily treated in the past. "As you can see," he continued, "none of that was our doing. While we had no legal obligation to Mr. Linda whatsoever, when we gained control of our song, we did what we thought was correct and equitable so that his family could share in the profits."

A nice gesture, to be sure, but what did "Lion" earn in the nineties? A million dollars? Two? Three? Ten? And what trickled down to Soweto? Judging from tattered scraps of paper in the daughters' possession, 10 percent of writer's performance royalties amounted to about $12,000 over the decade. Handwritten and unsigned, the notes purported to be royalty statements but there was no detailed breakdown of the song's overall earnings, and Weiss's business people declined to provide one, despite several requests. Twelve grand was nice money in Soweto terms, but split several ways it changed little or nothing. Solomon Linda's house still had no ceilings, and it was like an oven under the African summer sun. Plaster flaked off the walls outside; toddlers squalled underfoot; three radios blared simultaneously.

Fourteen people were living there, sleeping on floors for the most part, washing at an outdoor tap. Only Elizabeth was working, and when she moved out, most of the furniture went with her.

The last time I visited, in January, the kitchen was bare save for six pots and a lone Formica table. Linda's youngest daughter, Adelaide, lay swooning under greasy bedclothes, gravely ill from an infection she was too poor to have properly treated. A distant relative wandered around in an alcoholic stupor, waving a pair of garden shears and singing snatches of "Mbube." Elizabeth put her hands to her temples and said, "Really, we are not coping."

All the sisters were there: Fildah, with her *sangoma*'s headdress swathed in a bright red scarf; Elizabeth and Delphi in their best clothes; Adelaide, swaying back and forth on a chair, dazed, sweat pouring down her gaunt cheekbones. I'd come to report back to them on my adventures in the mysterious overseas, bringing a pile of legal papers that I did my best to explain. I told them about Paul Campbell, the fictitious entity who seemed to have collected big money that might otherwise have come their way, and about Larry Richmond, who wept crocodile tears on their behalf in a legal proceeding that might have changed their destiny if only they'd been aware of it. And finally I showed them the letter in which George Weiss assured me that his underlings were depositing a "correct and equitable" share into the bank account of their mother, "Mrs. Linda," who had been dead and buried for a decade.

The daughters had never heard of any of these foreigners but they had a shrewd idea of why all this had happened. "It's because our father didn't attend school," Elizabeth said. "He was just signing everything they said he must sign. Maybe he was signing many papers." Everyone sighed, and that was that.

In which a moral is considered

Once upon a time, a long time ago, a Zulu man stepped up to a microphone and improvised a melody that earned in the region of $15 million. That Solomon Linda got almost none of it was probably inevitable. He was a black man in white-ruled South Africa, but his American peers fared little better. Robert Johnson's contribution to the blues went largely unrewarded. Leadbelly lost half of his publishing to his white "patrons." DJ Alan Freed refused to play Chuck Berry's "Maybellene" until he was given a songwriter's cut. Led Zeppelin's "Whole Lotta Love" was nicked off Willie Dixon. All musicians were minnows in the pop-music food chain, but blacks were most vulnerable, and Solomon Linda, an illiterate migrant from a wild and backward place, was totally defenseless against sophisticated predators.

Which is not to say that he was cheated. On the contrary, all the deals were perfectly legal. No one forced Linda to sell "Mbube" to Eric Gallo for ten shillings, and if Gallo turned around and traded it at a profit, so what? It belonged to him. The good old boys of TRO were perfectly entitled to rename the song, adapt it as they pleased, and allocate the royalties to nonexistent entities. After all, they were its owners. Linda was legally entitled to nothing. The fact that he got anything at all seemed to show that the bosses were not without pity.

So I sat down and wrote long letters to George Weiss and Larry Richmond, distancing myself from pious moralists who might see them as sharks and even suggesting a line of reasoning they might take. "The only thing worse than exploitation," I mused, "is not being exploited at all." And then I enumerated all the good things old Solomon gained from making up the most famous melody that ever emerged from Africa: ten shillings, a big reputation, adulation and lionization, several cool suits, a wind-up gramophone, a check from Pete Seeger, and a trickle of royalties that had spared his daughters from absolute penury.

"All told," I concluded, "there is a case to be made against the idea that Solomon Linda was a victim of injustice."

I sat back and waited for someone to make it.

—*Rolling Stone*, May 2000

Postscript: As this article was going to press, Howie Richmond got back to me, saying he wanted to accept responsibility for some "gross errors." The blame for this "tragic situation," he continued, lay with the long-dead Gallo Records executive who'd replied to the New Yorkers' initial 1951 query about the legal status of "Mbube." Alec Delmont said something along the lines of, "It's a traditional Zulu song, but it belongs to us."

It's hard to say what Delmont was up to. It's possible that he didn't understand the legal meaning of "traditional," using it as synonym for rural. It is also possible that Delmont foolishly imagined he'd hit on a way to avoid awkward questions. After all, if "Mbube" was traditional, Solomon Linda wasn't entitled to composer royalties and nobody could object if Delmont's company kept the proceeds of the envisioned Weavers recording for themselves.

Either way, Gallo Records had made a blunder from which it would never recover. The instant Howie Richmond and company saw the word "traditional," they thought, Aha, another wild horse; we can adapt this one as we please. When the Jo'burg boys realized what was happening, they hastily reversed themselves, but it was too late: the New Yorkers just shrugged off their attempts to recast "Mbube" as an original composition.

As it happens, Gallo had irrefutable proof of this contention in its vaults—all three acetates recorded during the fateful 1939 session. Played consecutively, they showed beyond all doubt that the miracle melody was Solomon Linda's creation. But forty years would pass before archivist Rob Allingham rediscovered these treasures. Back in 1951, the Gallo boys thought their case was unwinnable, so they settled for the right to administer "Wimoweh" in territories like Northern Rhodesia and Portuguese East Africa and grumbled their way out of the picture.

But anyway, Howie Richmond's heart seemed to be in the right place. A week or so later, I received a call from Linda's daughter Elizabeth, who said thugs had barged into her house a few nights earlier, terrorized her family at gunpoint, and looted her possessions. Her front door was still hanging off its hinges, so she couldn't leave home to check out a rumor she'd heard from her bank. I investigated on her behalf and called back an hour later. "Money is pouring into your bank account from America," I said. "Nearly $15,000 in the last ten days." At the time, currency speculators were making a run on the rand, so the total came close to R150,000, a mountain of cash for someone in Elizabeth's position. She said nothing for the longest time. I couldn't be sure, but I think she was crying.

The windfall arose from the use of "Wimoweh" in a U.S. TV commercial for a hotel chain. Some of the money had initially gone to Pete Seeger, who'd turned it back. It seemed he'd been receiving royalties on the song all along. "I just found out," he told me on the phone. "I didn't know." Seeger and his publishers later agreed to cede all future royalties from "Wimoweh" to Linda's family. That left unresolved the far greater earnings of "The Lion Sleeps Tonight."

After the *Rolling Stone* article was published, I introduced Linda's daughters to a young Johannesburg lawyer named Hanro Friedrich, who took up their case. Hanro convinced Gallo Records to finance some research by Dr. Owen Dean, Johannesburg's leading copyright lawyer. Dean spotted an obscure clause in the Imperial Copyright Act of 1911 that offered a cause of action, and the South African government agreed to finance litigation. One morning in 2005, the world woke up to hear that Dr. Dean had taken Donald Duck and Mickey Mouse hostage. Or more accurately: that he'd attached Disney's trademarks on the grounds that the giant American corporation was making unauthorized use of Solomon Linda's music in *The Lion King* and its many lucrative spinoffs.

Dean's ploy had the desired effect. Disney had no stomach for an embarrassing court case, so it brought pressure to bear on George Weiss and his partners. In 2006, the parties reached an out-of-court settlement, the precise terms of which remain secret. Let's just say it involved a lot of money, even after legal fees, and that it included a provision entitling Linda's daughters to a reasonable share of the future earnings of "The Lion Sleeps Tonight." The daughters traded their *sangoma* braids for fashionable hairpieces, bought cars for crash-prone sons, and commenced a turbulent but no doubt pleasurable adjustment to life in the middle classes.

THE BEAUTIFUL
AND THE DAMNED

I didn't take South Africa's 1993 peace talks very seriously, in part because I doubted that our politicians could control their followers even if they really wanted to. Also, I'd been watching Yugoslavia degenerate into an orgy of ethnic butchery. Those Muslims, Serbs, and Croats were very civilized, at least in relation to us. They looked alike and had a language in common. Decades of authoritarian socialism had flattened the class differences between them. But when the crunch came, they fell on each other like animals. If Yugoslavs couldn't check their slide into race war, what hope had we? There was none, as far as I could see.

So I failed to join in the general rejoicing when politicians announced that they'd agreed on an interim constitution and set a date for free elections. On the other hand, I wasn't above clutching at straws, and the optimistic shift in the nation's mood was entirely agreeable. Also, it was summer, and a free trip to Sun City seemed just the thing.

Friday, November 26, 1993: not a red-letter day in South Africa, exactly, but sandwiched between several of them. Last week, negotiators signed off on a constitution that's supposed to bring us peace. Yesterday, U.S. sanctions were repealed and now the sky above us is dark with flying investors. Next week, the last white parliament convenes to vote itself into oblivion and after that it's all aboard for free elections, *uhuru*, and State President Mandela. The long dark epoch of apartheid is finally ending and all I can say, being white, is hallelujah! Liberation from guilt! Redistribution of responsibility! The freedom to board a private plane, fly off to King Sol's regal hog trough, and not feel in the least shit about it. I think I'm going to love the new South Africa.

The plane is a ten-seat turbo prop, laid on by Sol Kerzner's hotel and casino conglomerate: Sun International. It takes off from Midrand Airport, hops over Hartebeesport Dam, and sets down on the bushveld airstrip near Sun City. The sun is hot, the veld is green, and my heart is full, but my friend the Botanist is feeling a bit queasy. She has a past, you understand. She used to edit the feminist journal *Spare Rib* and owns an entire library of weighty feminist tomes. In the 1970s, she demonstrated against Mrs. Julia Morley's grotesque cattle show, so she's conflicted about being a guest at Miss World 1993.

The last beauty contest I attended was in Johannesburg City Hall in 1972 or thereabouts. The girls came on one by one and did their go-go dancing bikini thing. Then they were all brought back on stage and the winner chosen by acclamation. The emcee walked down the line, holding his hand over the head of each contestant and yelling, "Let's hear it for Sandra! Let's hear it for Debbie!" Pretty girls drew lewd cheers, which was gratifying, I dare say, but plain ones with plumpish thighs were booed and hissed and humiliated so horribly that I bled for them, but that was long ago, when I was a callow left-winger who believed quite passionately in tearing down what was and replacing it all with something cleaner and brighter and better. Now I just go with the flow, which carries me into a Sun International mini-bus, through the portals of Sun City casino, and up to the summit of a nearby hill, where an astonishing sight awaits: a tumble of ancient, weathered ruins, rising from the savannah like the set of some wildly improbable Hollywood movie.

A turbaned Nubian in flowing robes steps forward to greet us. Another Nubian takes my luggage and leads me through the massive wooden gates and into the Palace, where the air is filled with the perfumes of Arabia. Water drips off ancient stone masonry. Rivers leap from the rock and flow away into mysterious underground passages. You pass through a hall the size of a cathedral and under the shadow of a rampaging bull elephant. Then a door opens before you and the bellboy says, "Sir, your suite."

The Palace, as you have no doubt gathered, is a grand hotel. The bellboy is about eighteen and he just loves his job. He shows you how to work the TV, the safe, and the wooden ceiling fan. He draws your attention to the silver bowl full of luscious fruits and bonbons, the rich bathrobes in the closet, the French champagne in the minibar. He draws back the drapes to offer a view of the magical ruins below—the Temple of Courage, the Gong of the Sun Lion, the Royal Arena. A dark green lake lies at the foot of the valley and, all around, tawny hills rise into a blazing blue sky. All this splendor and the bellboy's alone to display. He turns, bursting with pride, and says, "Isn't it wonderful?"

Well, yes, it is. I came willing to be facetious, but this spectacle defeats me: all the clever remarks in the back of my mind suddenly seem so blindingly obvious as to sound stupid. So, the truth then: the Palace of the Lost City is magnificent. Completed in 1993 at a cost of almost $350 million, it is situated somewhat precariously in Bophuthatswana, one of the tribal republics created by apartheid. Until a year or two ago, we used to crack jokes about Bop's so-called independence and the tragicomic pronouncements of its strongman, Chief Lucas Mangope, but we're not laughing much anymore. Mangope is refusing to rejoin a united South Africa and knuckle under to Nelson Mandela. And Mandela, for his part, is threatening to send in the tanks if Mangope refuses to come to heel. But we don't want to talk about that, do we? Nah, it's too depressing.

Let's instead pop the cap on a Perrier and sit down to read the official Miss World press kit. Hmm. One gathers that it's a caring, sharing event these days, gender sensitive and politically progressive. The girls—sorry, women—are judged less on their bodies and faces than on their intellect, personality, and commitment to fighting AIDS, saving the planet, or whatever. What's more, proceeds from this year's ticket sales are going to feed starving black children, and Variety Club International is getting a rake-off from the satellite TV fees. In short, we're going to preen and pose, ogle flesh, sip Veuve Clicquot, and benefit the previously disadvantaged. Gee whiz. I can't wait.

But first, we must pay tribute to King Sol, the man who made all this possible.

Friday, 12:30 pm. I'm sitting on the terrace under crumbling buttresses and ancient copper domes talking to Sol Kerzner, schlockmeister, schmoozer, mensch, tycoon. I love this man. He's one of the all-time great white South Africans, a schlemiel from Bez Valley who grew up with almost nothing, and now look at him, lounging on the terrace in Gucci loafers, drawling in a fake American accent, master of an international empire of resort hotels and casinos. Sol's spent most of the past two days talking to foreign media and I am curious as to the drift of their questions. "Tell me," I say, "do they still think you're a moral leper?"

Poor Sol. He's so used to being reviled and spat upon for making a buck off the back of apartheid that he automatically assumes I'm challenging the morality of doing business in the Bantustans. He's five minutes into a justificatory monologue before I can stop him. I tune him, relax my bro. Relax. Nobody cares anymore. We've buried the hatchet. The revolution has been postponed. Let's talk about girls, man. Let's talk about the Miss World competition. Let's talk about this press release from the ANC's Women's League, which strongly objects to "the reduction of women to objects of beauty," and accuses you of complicity in "ongoing gender oppression."

"There's nothing wrong with a beautiful girl," says Sol, and nothing wrong with staging a contest that celebrates beauty, especially if your heart is pure, as is his. He is at pains to stress that he is not staging this beauty pageant because he's into beauty pageants *per se*. He is doing it for promotion—not just for himself or Sun International, but for all of us, for the nation. "Around 700 million people will be watching," he says. "They're going to see Cape Town, game reserves, beaches. The exposure is incredible." In theory, a certain percentage of these international TV viewers will rush to South Africa, clutching fistfuls of hard currency, at least some of which will trickle down to the hard-done-by masses.

All this is offered somewhat shamefacedly, as if to concede that the staging of beauty pageants cannot really be justified in its own terms. And I'm sitting there thinking, Hey, Sol, wise up! This is the new South Africa! You're being Mau-Mau'd by a tiny cabal of over-educated feminist mission girls! Forget the Women's League! South Africa's black masses are massively into beauty pageants. There were seven beauty pageants *in Soweto alone* last weekend. Seven! Country-wide, there may have been as many as fifty, for all I know. We're talking serious commitment to beauty pageant culture here. We're talking about a country in which the oppressed African majority has exacted the right to give bossy Euro-feminists the finger and hold as many beauty pageants as it pleases! You're a hero, Sol! You're finally doing right by black people!

Yes? No? On balance, no. Sol seems to think I'm a bit cracked, so I toss him a normal question about the Palace.

How did it happen, Sol? I mean, when did the inspiration actually inspire you? It was January 1990, he says, a week or two before Nelson walked to freedom. There was a certain madness in the air, a sense that the worst was over and that the good times were about to roll. Addled with optimism, King Sol stood on a barren hillside in the bushveld of Bophuthatswana and said, here shall arise a ziggurat, a Xanadu, a plea-sure dome to which pilgrims will stream from all corners of the planet. He summoned his minions and bade them begin. "Whatever you do," he told them, "it has to be African."

And lo, here it is; the Lost City, an instant ruin, celebrating the African authentic: African murals designed in Italy, African artwork conceived in LA, and the music of Dead White Men, performed in the great vaulted tea lounge by the Soweto String Quartet. It's magnifi-cent! I love it!

Unfortunately, it costs almost $300 a night, way beyond the reach of 98 percent of South Africans. Only foreigners can afford such prices and most of them are too scared to come here on account of the terrible violence they see on TV—mobs ransacking cities, burning buildings, burning each other. But we really don't want to go into that, do we? Nah. We want to laze in the sun all afternoon, preparing for the evening's rigors.

Friday, 6:00 pm. We're in the Superbowl, Sun City's 7,000-seat auditorium. The Miss World logo is suspended above the stage, upon which a dress rehearsal is unfolding. Eighty-one strong young women with well-developed intellects are teetering around in knock-me-down-and-fuck-me pumps, trailing choking clouds of perfume and hairspray, trying out their Little Bo Beep speeches in the microphone. "Hi, I'm Miss Indonesia! If I become Miss World, I will work for world peace!" Or, "I'm Miss Paraguay, and I'm seriously worried about the rain forests." Whales are mentioned, along with the poor, the orphaned, and the maimed. Charmain Naidoo and I are giggling. We're writing it all down dutifully, but we're giggling. Wouldn't you?

Charmain works for the local *Sunday Times,* "the largest newspaper in Africa." She's been here all week, keeping tabs on celebrities. She has a pretty shrewd idea of who's been sleeping with whom and doing which drugs in what quantity, and it's all absolutely fascinating. Not to you, maybe, but Charmain and I are survivors of the brutal celebrity drought inflicted on South Africa by apartheid. We spent our youths reading about foreign celebrities in magazines, listening to their records, and watching their movies, but they never set foot in our pariah state. In my teens, the only rock stars who showed up to be adulated were Barclay James Harvest, who were boring, and the Byrds, who were by then so far gone on acid that they could barely tune their guitars.

But now . . . now the skies have opened and it's raining celebrities: Joan Collins, Jerry Hall, Yasmin Le Bon, Ursula Andress, La Toya Jackson, Phil Collins, and Elton John are on their way and there are at least ten world-class celebrities here already, including Twiggy, Christie Brinkley, Lou Gosset Junior, Pierce Brosnan, and George Benson. Charmain sighs. She's had a mild crush on George Benson for the last decade. Yesterday he materialized before her in an elevator doorway. He smiled. He stepped inside. She was so excited she could barely breathe. The door closed and by the time they reached the ground floor, Charmain had formed a close relationship with a boil on the back of Benson's neck. "It's weird," she says. "You spend your whole life dreaming about these people, but when you see them up close they are so ordinary and frail. In a way I wish they'd just stayed pictures on the wall."

Friday, 10:00 pm. The Botanist and I are in the casino, contemplating a thousand myriad reflections of ourselves in the mirrored walls. We're losing heavily, but we're not crying. We are watching a bronzed bloke with gold chains throwing money away at a roulette table. He signs a check, buys a mountain of chips, and carpets the bottom third of the table—five grand on a single turn of the wheel. *Whirr,* click, he loses it all. He clicks his fingers for the floor manager, signs another check, and repeats the procedure, again, and again. He drops $15,000 before our eyes. "Agh," he says, "it's only paper and plastic."

Friday, 10:30 pm. The media center is deserted. The hacks have filed, the phone banks are silent, and there is no sign of Miss South Africa, the lovely Jacqui Mofokeng of Soweto. I had an appointment to interview her here, but I tarried too long at the gaming tables and Jacqui has retired to her beauty sleep. Alas, alas. I was so looking forward to a stimulating discussion of beauty pageant politics, South Africa–style.

Everything in this country is a zone of intense political/racial conflict, even the humdrum world of beauty pageants. For years, the Miss South Africa contest was dominated by Aryan blondes, and black girls weren't even allowed to enter. This odious color bar was done away with in the late 1980s, but the title still went to the sort of girl who'd appeal to your average white male moron—if not a blonde, then a light-skinned quadroon with straight hair and an aqualine nose. Full-blooded Africans still did not feature. This was not fair. It would not do, not in a country where 80 percent of the population is African and passionate about beauty pageants.

The distressed cries of all the disenfranchised Miss Afro Paragons and Miss Benetton Sowetos were heard in high places, and Mandela's ANC brought pressure to bear on the sponsors of the Miss South Africa pageant. These days, one does not argue with the ANC. One cuts a deal. In public, we were told that the capitalists had agreed to set up a fund to foster beauty pageant culture among the previously oppressed, but some claimed there was a secret codicil to the agreement: the next Miss South Africa would be a full-blooded African. Enter Jacqui Mofokeng, who won the coveted title seven months ago. The instant the crown descended on her head, white racists yelled, "Fix!" Some accused the sponsors of deferring to the ANC and rigging the outcome. Others called radio talk shows and said, "How can you call her a beauty queen? She's got thick lips and a flat nose."

I wanted to tell Jacqui how sordid I found all this, and how ashamed I was for my fellow white South Africans. I wanted to tell her that I for one found her extremely sexy, but perhaps it's as well that I blew the opportunity, because she would probably have slapped me. Jacqui's a feminist who takes no shit. Just yesterday, she almost ripped the head off a British TV presenter who used the phrase "glitz and tits" in her presence. The poor English girl was reportedly reduced to tears.

Jacqui and I went to the same school, incidentally, a rather expensive private establishment called Woodmead. In my day, Woodmead was whites-only, but it was integrated in the late seventies, in bold defiance of apartheid. Now it's predominantly black and widely regarded as a model of racial harmony and integration. The headmistress's office was petrol-bombed by rioting students the other day, but we don't want to go into that, do we? Nah, fuck it. Let's party.

Midnight. The lobster is done for, the salmon are skeletal, and the Veuve Clicquots lie upside down and dead in ice buckets. The massed hacks, having hogged, are partying in the courtyard under that statue of a towering elephant. And in their midst . . . Grace Jones! Grace Jones, in person at Sun City! It's amazing. Grace seems to be a very good sport. She lifted the skirt of a prim local TV newsreader to see what sort of panties she was wearing, if any. She did lewd dances with Sweden's Marcus Schenkenberg, "the highest-paid male model in the world." She commandeered a mike in the discotheque last night and got fans to join her in a hypnotic chant of "Sex! Sex! Sex!" She'll talk to anyone, kiss anyone, dance with anyone—pimply teenagers, obscure locals, even waiters.

Tonight she's dancing with Christina, King Sol's present paramour. They're doing a very stylish semi-Latin shimmy to the music of George Benson, who's jamming with the cocktail band. After a song or two, George wipes the sweat from his brow and yields the spotlight to the Soweto String Quartet, four scholarly African gentlemen in evening dress who usually play chamber music in the tea lounge. Tonight, however . . . tonight they're letting their hair down. Tonight they're playing *mbaqanga*, or township jive, the bass and cello sawing out repetitive three-chord phrases while the violins cut loose with wild solos. They're so good they bring tears to my eyes.

Ah, this country, this country. It's pathetically fucked up for most part, but tonight I survey the jiving racial all-sorts, and an outrageous idea takes root in my brain: maybe we really can do it; synthesize rich and poor, black and white, Europe and Africa, and create something so blindingly lovely that the rest of you fall back in awe and dismay. Maybe Bill Clinton's right. Maybe we are living in the midst of a miracle. Or maybe it's just a surfeit of champagne.

Saturday, November 27. The Big Day dawns hot and blue. I wake to find a newsletter stuck under my door announcing the results of an overnight poll of the press corps. Odds-on favorite to win the crown is Miss Puerto Rico, with Misses Italy, Chile, and Sweden hot on her trail—all blonde Aryans, you'll note, or golden-skinned Latinate Barbie dolls.

Sipho "Hotstix" Mabuse is ensconced in a corner of the vast dining emporium with his wife and children, eating eggs Benedict. Sipho is a pop star, inventor of a cool sound generally known as Soweto bubble gum. His wife, Chichi, is part owner of the local franchise for a line of American cosmetics called Black Like Me. Their little girls are very cute numbers with cornrowed hair and missing front teeth.

Sipho says, "Sit down," so we do, and soon he's telling us about the bad old days, when it was dangerous to be black and beautiful in small South African towns. Once he was beaten senseless for urinating in a whites-only pissoir at a service station. Another time, he and his sidemen were attacked by white thugs and then arrested by white police when they dared defend themselves. Sipho laughs, but the incident left scars on his face, and barely concealed hurt and rage in his heart.

The food is fine, but the talk leaves the Botanist upset and confused. She was just growing to like the new South Africa when Sipho started rubbing her nose in the grim realities of the old. "God," she says, "this country is exhausting. You change your mind all the time." About what? Well, about Nelson Mandela, for instance. The Botanist regards Mandela as a man of enormous moral gravity, one of the most noble figures of the twentieth century. She was, therefore, shocked and appalled to see the pictures of him in this morning's paper, resplendent in a penguin suit, opening the new Dunhill boutique in exclusive Sandton. "I'm so disillusioned," she says. "I never thought he'd stoop to that."

Ja, well. Depends were you stand, I suppose. Myself, I'm elated to see Madiba schmoozing with bankers and captains of the industry. Three years ago he was threatening to nationalize everything and plunge us in the antediluvian grayness of total socialist paralysis. I think an interest in luxury leather goods and fine tobaccos is entirely suitable in a future head of state.

Saturday, 6:00 pm. Excitement is mounting. On distant continents, 700 million viewers are glued to their TV screens. The live audience is streaming down carpets and taking seats in the Superbowl. I survey the crowd and wince for the ANC Women's League, whose righteous denunciations of this gender-oppressive cattle show have clearly gone unheeded. At least a quarter of the seats are occupied by the members of the oppressed masses—sleek, gleaming Sowetans and Nigerians and Zairians in the tribal finery of modern Africa, which is to say, suits by Armani, frocks by YSL or Dior.

One of them is Wally Serote, head of the ANC's Arts and Culture Department and widely regarded as Minister of Culture in waiting. A few years ago, Comrade Serote was briefly notorious for writing a poem in which he speculated about how it would feel to pour gasoline on white children and set them on fire. Now here he is in a tuxedo, living it up with the bourgeois pigs. God, I adore the new South Africa. All our sacred cows are keeling over, legs in the air. Nelson Mandela opens boutiques! Apartheid cabinet ministers marry colored girls! White women anoint a black former "terrorist" (Tokyo Sexwale) "sexiest politician in the nation"! Anything goes. I mean, *Peter Mokaba is here tonight!* Peter Mokaba, boss of the ANC's ultramilitant Youth League! Last time I saw him he was on a podium, chanting "Shoot the Boers!" Now it's, "All youth to battle! All youth to the front line! Forward to the Superbowl!"

Trumpets blare, music swells, and a dancin', prancin' New Orleans–style marchin' band appears, followed by a forest of waving pennants and banners and scores of glamorous misses. Around the auditorium they come, so close I can almost touch them, not that I would dare.

They seem to fall into three fairly distinct categories. Girls from rich white countries slouch along halfheartedly, as if to say, I'm not really into this, you know, I'm much too hip to take it seriously but there's a lot of money at stake and who knows, maybe I'll wind up a supermodel or something. Girls from the Afro-Asian bloc, on the other hand, carry themselves with a potentially tragic solemnity. One imagines them in humble apartments in overcrowded tropical cities, offering their best profile to the mirror, practicing that smile, that walk, that wave. And finally, there are the Latin Americans, who are simply and splendidly sluttish. Their heads are haloed by great fans of ostrich feathers. Their dresses are slit almost to the armpit. Some are virtually naked. What rare pleasure it is to sit within touching distance of such creatures, admiring their intellects and strong personalities.

After the march-past it's all downhill. Ghastly inspirational songs are sung, insipid homilies delivered. Pierce Brosnan of *Remington Steele* fame pulls some names out of a hat, and seventy-one losers exit left. Cut to commercial. A few minutes later, there is another winnowing. Miss South Africa makes it into the final five, causing me to be overcome by visions of the glory that is about to descend on our old school. Sadly, it is not to be. Miss Philippines comes third, Jacqui Mofokeng is runner-up, and the crown goes to Miss Jamaica, a TV presenter from Kingston. A clean sweep for the third world, please note, with not one of the media favorites showing. Feminists might be on to something when they complain that the media are dominated by Eurocentric males who harbor secret prejudices against the exotic.

Saturday, 10:00 pm, and the Coronation Ball is commencing. We're sharing a table with three inscrutable Mayans from *Vogue* Mexico and a tabloid reporter from Fleet Street, aflush with liquor and clearly confused by the "authentically African" ambience of his surroundings. He claims to have a scoop, the hottest story of the entire week. "I've filed already," he whispers conspiratorially, "so I'll share it with you. It happened in a town called Krugersdorp, that's K-R-U-G-E-R-S-D-O-R-P . . ." He proceeds to tell a harrowing story about two unfortunate Chinese, waylaid en route to Miss World by carnivores. "It happened yesterday," he whispers. "That's why there were two empty front-row seats at the pageant."

Poor fellow. Krugersdorp is a suburb. The last predators there were shot circa 1860. Someone's pulled his leg right off, but who am I to intervene? I hold my tongue and the story appears in the next day's *Sunday People*: "Miss World Fans Eaten By Lions."

Sunday, 4:00 am. The Botanist and I are rolling home, our pockets bulging with swag—two thousand dollars, count 'em, the consequence of a lucky streak at the blackjack and roulette tables. Poor old Sol Kerzner. We drink his booze, eat his lobsters, sleep in his beds, pose mocking questions in an interview, and then cash in our chips and take his money home. Must be tough to own a casino.

Sunday, November 28, early afternoon. I am drifting on an inner tube through an ancient stone canyon, created eighteen months ago by one of Sol's cunning landscape architects. The maw of a tunnel gapes before me. I sail over an artificial waterfall and into pitch-black freefall. An eternity later, the sun explodes above my head and I splash down on a designer-made blue lagoon. In the distance, girls in bikinis are sipping daiquiris on a designer beach, in the shade of designer palm trees. Something goes *whoosh* in the wall behind me and a tall wave rushes forward, clearly man-made in its curling blue perfection. I strike out, catch it before it breaks, and bodysurf into the concrete shallows. Ah, yes, the sweet life in the Valley of Waves, the Lost City's own Tahiti.

The Botanist is sitting on the beach, reading the Sunday papers. Each front page features the dusky lovelies Miss Jamaica and Miss South Africa arm in arm like sisters, flashing blinding smiles. Do we really want to turn the page and examine the horrors that lie within? Nah, not really. South Africa's politicians might be embracing like brothers, but their followers are still attacking police stations, butchering each other in squatter camps, and, in the case of the white right wing, plotting to resist black rule with guns, terror bombs, and heavy weapons. Who wants to read such things? Not I. One loses stomach, eventually. One shrugs and turns to the business pages, where optimism reigns.

The stock market is booming. A new elite is coming into being. Former revolutionaries are moving into boardrooms. Almost 70 percent of white capitalists now back Mandela. The men in suits say we're heading for a happy ending, that countless jobs will soon materialize, along with houses for the homeless, food for the hungry, and hope for the teeming millions of utterly wretched. Who knows, maybe they're right. Maybe it'll all come true. And maybe it's just a fantasy, like this place.

—Esquire, February 1994

Postscript: By the time this piece hit the newsstands, South Africa's political factions were tearing one another apart in the worst bloodletting we'd ever seen, and the pessimism evident in my cynical asides seemed entirely prescient. Ninety days later, Nelson Mandela came to power in a miraculously peaceful election, and I wound up looking, as was so often the case, like an idiot.

GREAT WHITE HYENA

"This is a goer," declares Deon du Plessis. It's Sunday afternoon, and the Great White Hyena is presiding over a news conference in the Johannesburg offices of the *Daily Sun,* the largest daily in Africa. Mr. du Plessis is publisher and part owner of this august organ. Seated before him are his editor, Themba Khumalo, an amiable Zulu in a baseball cap, and a cheerful menagerie of subs and hacks. Some weeks ago, they ran a story slugged, "Dark Secrets of Crime Terror!," which revealed that unscrupulous *sangomas* or witch doctors were charging up to R100,000 for magical potions (almost) guaranteed to render robbers invisible to police. Now fate has delivered a follow-up in the form of two criminals caught at a Soweto roadblock with nineteen stolen speed-point machines in their boot and a bag of supernatural goodies dangling from their rearview mirror. There are photographs, too. "I like it," says Deon. "This is front page."

It's also a cue for a bout of reminiscing about similar stories, of which the paper has carried many. "Penetrated by a python" featured a woman ravished by a snake that came out of the toilet. "Raped by a Gorilla" told the story of an evil *inyanga* who conjured a giant apelike creature to punish a lady who had spurned his love proposals. Deon was particularly fond of the one about a tree with magical penis-enlarging powers. "A woman from Skukuza revealed to us that if you put your dick in one of this tree's pods, it would grow as the pod grew," he says. "Next thing, the National Parks Board rang us saying every tree in the area was shaking. An endless stream of *Sun* readers had gone there to stick their members into pods."

Mr. du Plessis confesses that he acquired such a pod for his own use, but that it had not proved efficacious. This prompts rewrite man Denis Smith, formerly of Paddington, to recall a story about "stuff in a bottle" that was "supposed to give you a permanent hard-on" but instead rendered a *Sun* editor unconscious for four days. By now everyone in the room is incapacitated with laughter. The Great White Hyena wipes tears from his left eye (the right is presently covered with a piratical eye patch necessitated by eye surgery) and says, "What the fuck are they going to make of this in England?"

More to the point—what will they make of it at Rhodes University, where journalism professor Guy Berger wages war against South Africa's rising tide of journalistic barbarism? Berger would regard this conference as thunderous confirmation of his charges against tabloids, and in a way he's right: it is a carnival of thought crime. On the other hand, one gets the sense that Du Plessis enjoys playing the bad boy. Either way, it would be remiss to dismiss Du Plessis as a joker, because he's the central figure in a tabloid revolution that has shaken corporate monoliths, lured three million virgin readers into the newspaper market, and triggered a furious battle around questions of national identity.

Left-wingers portray South Africa as a painfully politically correct society, imbued with gender sensitivities and what have you. The *Daily Sun* suggests otherwise. It is conservative, at least to the extent that it supports old-fashioned family values and clamors for tough law enforcement. Gay rights make it a bit queasy, and it does not like illegal immigrants who come here to steal our jobs and defile our women. And finally, it is respectful of the cult of ancestor worship and frequently carries stories about miracles and magic. This cocktail has proved enormously popular. Founded in July 2002, the *Daily Sun* now sells 500,000 copies on a good day, utterly dwarfing all competitors.

Several ironies lurk hereabouts. Eleven years ago, when Nelson Mandela came to power, South Africa boasted a dozen or so English-language dailies, all owned by white media conglomerates and deemed to be in dire need of transformation. Within five years, almost all these titles had new owners (often black), new editors (almost always black), and a new ideology—billows of soft-left waffle about women's rights, human rights, gender issues, and cultural diversity. Reading these papers became an ordeal for some, but we bore it because this was supposedly what the black masses wanted. Only they didn't, as it turns out. Circulations stagnated. Pundits blamed the Internet, but Deon du Plessis knew better.

Du Plessis is the sort of Boer that the English have been caricaturing for centuries: a jovial giant with thighs like tree trunks and a great raw slab of a face. He likes guns and big game hunting. He eats and drinks to excess, tells dirty jokes, swears. His car license plates read, "Beast1," and his business philosophy comes from Conan the Barbarian: "Find the enemy, crush him, and hear the lamentations of the women." He and his heiress wife are famous for their outrageous parties. A friend was at one such when gunfire broke out in the back-yard. Drunk and bored, Deon was shooting up the shrubbery with a shotgun. On another occasion, trolling for marlin in the Indian Ocean, he came across a boatload of "wily orientals" fishing illegally in SA territorial waters. He drew his long-barreled .44 magnum and charged, crying, "Fuck emperor! Fuck emperor wife!" through a bullhorn.

Until 1999 or thereabouts, Du Plessis was a senior executive at Independent Newspapers, the local arm of Irish press baron Tony O'Reilly's empire. It was not a happy relationship. Tony's South African acolytes tended to be blow-dried metrosexuals with delicate manners and carefully manicured PC opinions. Du Plessis was a rough ex–war correspondent with a rock 'n' roll attitude toward journalism and vivid views about almost everything, including "the man in the blue overall." This mythic African hero is a skilled black worker with money in his pocket. He's a home owner, thanks to government sub-sidies. He's saving to buy a car, and even has enough money to go on holiday, an unthinkable prospect for his parents. "I like the man in the blue overall," says Du Plessis. "He's optimistic and positive-minded. He's going places."

Du Plessis wanted to launch a tabloid for Blue Overall Man, but O'Reilly turned him down, allegedly on the advice of minions who whispered that the Boer was totally out of touch with the mood of black South Africa. Whereupon the Great White Hyena resigned and started pounding pavements with his business plan. Banks turned him down, Rupert Murdoch's organization likewise, but he eventually secured the backing of Media 24, an Afrikaans media conglomerate with holdings in eastern Europe and China. The first *Daily Sun* appeared on the streets in July 2002, and the rest is history. Today, Du Plessis's paper sells more than all O'Reilly's titles put together.

"The opposition are not happy bunnies," says Du Plessis. He attributes his success to hard work, good timing, and absolutely loyalty to Blue Overall Man, a statue of whom stands in the *Daily Sun*'s foyer. Okay, it's a shop window mannequin rather than a statue, but you get the picture. "The guy in the blue overall comes first," says Du Plessis. "If a story doesn't amuse him or serve his interests, it doesn't go in."

A second Blue Overall Man sits outside the hyena's glass-walled office, grinning broadly as he plows through a back issue. Interestingly, says Du Plessis, Blue Overall Man isn't really interested in scandal about celebrities, so the paper's front page is mercifully free of these. Also absent are bare-breasted Page 3 girls (Blue Overall Man finds them offensive), presidential speeches, and analysis of government policy. A *Sun* story is about the everyday travails of ordinary people. Domestic squabbles. Struggling to get the children educated. Battling to get lazy politicians to do their duty. Falling victim to crime or striking back against criminals. "We call it people's justice and it's a rough thing," says Du Plessis. "Mobs turning on suspects and setting them on fire. The police don't come, so people take the law into their own hands." Another category that resonates is stories about "strong women who refuse to be pushed around," and witchcraft stories are routine.

This formula reduces the *Sun*'s critics to apoplexy. Joe Thloloe, a past chairman of the National Editors' Forum, charges that Du Plessis's paper "exhibits contempt for black South Africans." University professors complain about "brainless perpetuation of stereotypes." Mathatha Tsedu, editor of the broadsheet *City Press,* opines that nobody really believes the guff that appears in the *Daily Sun,* and journalism professor Berger excoriates the paper for its "caricatural content" and "crass archetypal narratives." Berger urges the *Sun* to publish more, rather than less, celebrity gossip, on the grounds that such stories at least offer a "more upwardly mobile representation" of black South Africa.

What's interesting about this criticism is that most of it emerges from the leftist elite that led the campaign to transform and democratize apartheid media. It galls them beyond endurance to see black people lining up to buy the *Daily Sun,* but as former human rights commissioner Rhoda Kadalie says, they have only themselves to blame. "The tabloids are a reaction against politically correct newspapers," she says.

"I don't really give a shit about critics," says *Sun* editor Themba Khumalo, aka Bra TK. "If Soweto said, 'Bra TK, you're screwing up,' I would listen. But not some uptight academic." Khumalo can afford to be dismissive, because he and Du Plessis are walking on water these days, buoyed up by a triumph that might be unique in the annals of journalism: the *Daily Sun* is so popular that readers are known to sell used copies to neighbors at half price. It employs three typists to record tip-offs and accolades from fans. The volume of incoming calls is such that it sometimes causes the switchboard to crash.

The other day, Khumalo announced that his paper was planning to raise its cover price to R1.40 and asked readers what they thought. Back came a flood of letters—"thousands," says Khumalo—endorsing the move. "Upping the price is normal," they said. "Let's support the People's Paper." "Go ahead, Bra Themba! Your hard work deserves reward." One lamented declining standards of TV news coverage, adding that "I am left only with the *Daily Sun* to console me." Some went so far as to suggest that an even steeper price rise would be acceptable.

These letters read like a tabloid story to me. I ask Du Plessis if they were fabricated. "No," he says, "they really love us. The day we raised our price, circulation went up 10 to 17 percent, depending on the area."

We proceed to a slightly more thoughtful discussion about the paper's critics, who charge inter alia that the *Daily Sun* simply ignores the great issues of the day. "It's true," he says. "We don't do traditional politics. We do real politics. Real politics is shit flowing past your front door because the municipality won't fix the sewerage. It's workmen leaving open holes for kids to fall into. It's police ignoring calls for help. Last year, every day, we did a thing called the Hall of Shame. Every day, we invited people to send us details of government failing them, then published the names and addresses of those responsible. I think that campaign contributed to the emphasis Mbeki's government is now placing on local government delivery, and that's where the rubber hits the proverbial road. Don't say we're not political."

He also bridles at suggestions that it is racist to air stories about magic and ancestral spirits. "I'm not going to slag off these beliefs," he says. "We once carried a picture of a bed on a roof in the township of Mangaung. The owner insisted that he woke up there. His neighbors told our reporter there was a white horse hanging around, and that the horse and the removal of the bed were connected by magic. Are we supposed to go to Mangaung and tell people they're talking shit? I'm not going to do any such thing. We'll report it as it was told to us."

With that, he blows an ear-splitting blast on a *vuvuzela*, summoning the troops to daily conference. On the agenda this afternoon we have "Three Die in East Cape Road Horror" (an ordinary traffic accident story) and "Sex Maniac Flattened!," the tale of a would-be rapist who tried to jump a woman on a crowded station platform and was beaten to a pulp for his trouble. Next up is the tale of Fikiwe Godo, whose Eastern Cape home was invaded by a swarm of killer bees. A *sangoma*, Nogazi Ntoni, informed Mrs. Godo that the bees had been sent by her ancestors, who were upset because the family had failed to perform certain rituals. The *sangoma* advised the Godos to slaughter a cow to appease the spirits, then presented them with a bill for R3,000. The Godo family did as instructed, but the bees refused to leave, and when they asked for their money back, the *sangoma* said, "Sorry, I spent it on booze." Whereupon the angry family dumped buckets of cold water on her head.

This latter detail causes great perplexity. Normally, an offender in this position would be thrashed or worse. "They should come to Diepsloot for lessons," quips editor Khumalo, referring to a township famed for do-it-yourself law enforcement. There is also a dispute about the headline, occasioned by a sub who suggests something along the lines of "Evil Ancestors Send Killer Bees." "Never!," thunders the Great White Hyena. "This is not the *Surbiton Times*! This is Africa! Ancestors are never evil!" Bees, on the other hand, are fair game, so the gathering eventually settles on "Cursed by Evil Bees!"

In a few hours, "Cursed by Evil Bees!" will be on the newsstands, battling for attention against an array of imitators. Du Plessis's partners in Media 24 have launched *Die Son*, a national tabloid in Afrikaans. The *Sowetan*, which suffered a catastrophic drop in circulation after the *Daily Sun* appeared, has fired the self-regarding editors who presided over its decline and returned to the mass-market battlefield. Broadsheets have been forced to brighten their news holes, and Tony O'Reilly's newspaper group has launched The *Voice*, a racy Cape Town tabloid edited by an Irishman named Karl Brophy. One gathers that Mr. Brophy simply cannot believe the stories one gets here—mystery, magic, Jesus appearing in people's bathrooms, and man-eating sharks in the surrounding seas. (The latter gave rise to the immortal headline "Great Sharks Eat Whites.") A friend who used to work for him says Brophy believes he has died and gone to tabloid heaven.

And so we come to the moral of the story. According to *Media* magazine, the tabloids have added 1.3 million to the combined circulation of SA dailies. Since readership per copy is very high, this translates into five million readers, some three million of whom were reading nothing a few years ago. That's an awful lot of readers, and an awesome degree of influence. Does President Mbeki lie awake at night worrying about it? Is he haunted by memories of British Labur prime minister Jim Callaghan, cast into the wilderness in 1979 after Rupert Murdoch's mass-market tabloids convinced the working class it was okay to vote Tory?

Deon du Plessis defers these questions to Blue Overall Man, saying that the *Daily Sun* will be guided by his interests and desires. As for political parties, they seem curiously indifferent; according to Du Plessis, the only politician who has come courting his endorsement is Patricia de Lille, and she didn't get it. But watch this space; Jim Callaghan also believed the tabloids were neutral, only to wake up one morning with a knife in his back.

So there you have it. A once stagnant newspaper market has turned into a "thunderdome" (Khumalo's phrase). Intellectual snobs are beside themselves, but I am rather enjoying the spectacle. Missionaries, Marxists, and Great White Masters have always sought to feed South Africa's natives what they thought was good for them. It's nice to see Blue Overall Man at last spitting out their tepid medicine.

—*Spectator,* December 2005

JEWISH BLUES
IN DARKEST AFRICA

*W*hat follows is a labor of love writ-
ten at the behest of Benjy Mudie, a record guy who spent his youth following
the same Jo'burg longhair rock bands as I. Decades later, he called to say he
was planning to reissue a certain seminal LP on his Fresh label, and would I
please write some liner notes.

I was fourteen when it happened. Life in the white suburbs was
a hell of boredom and conformity. The Beatles were banned on state
radio and haircut regulations were merciless, but help was on its way.
They came from the north in the summer of 1969, armed with axes
and Scarab amps, long hair streaming behind them, and proceeded to
slay the youth of the nation with an arsenal of murderous blues-rock
tunes, synchronized foot stomping, and, on a good night, maniacal
writhing in advanced states of rock 'n' roll transfiguration. The masses
roared. The establishment was shaken. They were the biggest thing
our small world had ever seen, our Led Zeppelin, our Black Sabbath,
maybe even our Rolling Stones. They were the Otis Waygood Blues
Band, and this is their story.

It begins in 1964 or so, at a Jewish youth camp in what was then Rhodesia. Rob and Alan Zipper were from Bulawayo, where their dad had a clothes shop. Ivor Rubenstein was Alan's best mate, and Leigh Sagar was the local butcher's son. All these boys were budding musicians. Alan and Ivor had a little "Fenders and footsteps" band that played Shadows covers at talent competitions, and Rob was into folk. They considered themselves pretty cool until they met Benny Miller, who was all of sixteen and sported such unheard-of trappings as a denim jacket and Beatles-length hair. Benny had an older sister who'd introduced him to some way-out music, and when he picked up his guitar, the Bulawayo boys were staggered: he was playing the blues, making that axe sing and cry like a Negro.

How did the music of black American pain and suffering find its way to the rebel colony of Rhodesia, soon to become a breakaway state under the leadership of prime minister Ian Smith, who vowed to preserve white rule for another five centuries? It's a long story, and it begins in Chicago in the 1940s and '50s, where blues cats like Howlin' Wolf and Sonny Boy Williamson cut 78s that eventually found their way into the hands of young British enthusiasts like John Mayall and Eric Clapton, who covered the songs in their early sessions and always cited the bluesmen as their gurus. Word of this eventually penetrated Rhodesia and sent Benny scrambling after the real stuff, which he found on Pye Records' Blues Series, volumes one through six. Which is how a nice Jewish boy came to be playing the blues around a campfire in Africa. The Bulawayo contingent reached for their own guitars, and thus began a band that evolved over several years into Otis Waygood.

In its earliest incarnation, the band was built around Benny Miller, who remains, says Rob Zipper, "one of the best guitarists I've ever heard." Rob himself sang, and played the blues harp and sax. His younger brother Alan was on bass. Bulawayo homeboys Ivor and Leigh were on drums and rhythm respectively, and flautist Martin Jackson completed the lineup. Their manager, Andy Vaughan, was the dude who observed that if you scrambled the name of a famous elevator manufacturer you came up with a moniker that sounded authentically black American: Otis Waygood. Rob thought it was pretty witty. Ivor said, "Ja, and lifts can be pretty heavy, too." And so the Otis Waygood Blues Band came into being.

By now, it was 1969, and the older cats were students at the University College of Rhodesia, earnest young men, seriously involved in the struggle against racial bigotry, prejudice, and short hair. By day they were student activists, by night they played teen dances. Their repertoire consisted of blues standards and James Brown grooves, and they were getting better and better. They landed a Saturday afternoon gig at a bar called Les Discotheque. Crowds started coming. When Rob stood up to talk at student meetings, he was drowned out by cries of "You're Late Miss Kate."

"Miss Kate" was the band's signature tune, an old Deefore/Hitzfield number that they played at a bone-crunching volume and frantic pace. Toward the end of 1969, Otis were asked to perform "Miss Kate" on state TV. The boys obliged with a display of sneering insolence and hip-thrusting sexuality that provoked indignation from your average Rhodesian. These chaps are outrageous, they cried. They have "golliwog hair" and bad manners! They go into the locations and play for natives! They aren't proper Rhodies!

Indeed they weren't, which is why they were planning to leave the country as soon as they could. Rob graduated at the end of 1969. He was supposed to be the first to go, but it was summer and the boys were young and wild and someone came up with the idea of driving to Cape Town. Benny Miller thought it was a blind move, and refused to come. But the rest were game, so they loaded their amps into a battered old Volkswagen Kombi and set off across Africa to seek their fortune.

South of the Limpopo River, they entered a country in which a minor social revolution was brewing. In the West, the hippie movement had already peaked, but South Africa was always a few years behind the times, and this was our summer of love. Communes were springing up in the white suburbs. Acid had made its debut. Cape Town's Green Point Stadium was a great milling of stoned longhairs, come to attend an event billed as "the largest pop festival south of and since the Isle of Wight." It was also a competition, with the winner in line for a three-month residency at a local hotel. Otis Waygood arrived too late to compete, but impresario Selwyn Miller gave them a fifteen-minute slot as consolation—2 pm on a burning December afternoon.

The audience was half asleep when they took the stage. Twelve bars into the set, they were on their feet. By the end of the first song, they were "freaking out," according to reports in the next morning's papers. By the time the band got around to "Fever," fans were attacking the security fence, and Rob got so carried away that he leapt off the ten-foot-high stage and almost killed himself. "That's when it all started," he says. Otis made the next day's papers and went on to become the "underground" sensation of 1969's Christmas holiday season, drawing sell-out crowds wherever they played.

In South Africa, this was the big time, and it lasted barely three weeks. The holidays ended, the tourists departed, and that was that: the rock heroes had to pack their gear and go back home. As fate would have it, however, their Kombi broke down in Johannesburg, and they wound up gigging at a club called Electric Circus to raise money for a valve job. One night, after a particularly sweaty set, a slender blond guy came backstage and said, "I'm going to turn you into the biggest thing South Africa has ever seen."

This was Clive Calder, who went on to become a rock billionaire, owner of the world's largest independent music company. Back then he was a lightie of twenty-four, just starting out in the record business. His rap was inspirational. He said he'd just returned from Europe, where he'd watched the moguls break Grand Funk Railroad. Maintained he was capable of doing the same thing with Otis Waygood and that, together, they would conquer the planet. The white bluesboys signed on the dotted line, and Clive Calder's career began.

The album you're holding in your hand was recorded over two days in Jo'burg's EMI studios in March 1970, with Calder producing and playing piano on several tracks. Laid down in haste on an old four-track machine, it is less a work of art than a talisman to transport you back to sweaty little clubs in the early days of Otis Waygood's reign as

South Africa's premier live group. Rob would brace himself in a splay-legged rock hero stance, tilt his head sideways, close his eyes, and bellow as if his life depended on it. As the spirit took them, the sidemen would break into a frenzied bowing motion, bending double over their guitars on every beat, like a row of longhaired rabbis dovening madly at some blues-rock shrine. By the time they got to "Fever," with its electrifying climactic foot stomp, the audience was pulverized. "It was like having your senses worked over with a baseball bat," said one critic.

Critics were somewhat less taken with the untitled LP's blank black cover. "We were copying the Beatles," explains Alan Zipper. "They'd just done *The White Album*, so we thought we'd do a black album." It was released in May 1970, and Calder immediately put Otis Waygood on the road to back it. His plan was to broaden the band's fan base to the point where kids in the smallest town were clamoring for the record, and that meant playing everywhere—Kroonstad, Klerksdorp, Witbank, you name it; towns where longhairs had never been seen before.

"In those smaller towns we were like aliens from outer space," says drummer Ivor. "I remember driving into places with a motorcycle cop in front and another behind, just sort of forewarning the town, 'Here they come.'" Intrigued by Calder's hype, rural whites turned out in droves to see the longhaired weirdos. "It was amazing," says Ivor. "Calder had the journalists eating out of his hand. Everything you opened was just Otis."

The boys in the band were pretty straight when they arrived in South Africa, but youths everywhere were storming heaven on hallucinogenics, and pretty soon Otis Waygood was doing it, too. By now they were living in an old house in the suburbs of Jo'burg, a sort of headquarters with mattresses strewn across the bare floors and a family of twenty hippies sitting down for communal meals. The acid metaphysicians of Abstract Truth crashed there for weeks on end. Freedom's Children were regular guests, along with Soweto stars like Kippie Moeketsi and Julian Bahula. Everyone would get high and jam in the soundproofed garage. Otis's music began to evolve in a direction presaged by the three bonus tracks that conclude this album. The riffs grew darker and heavier. Elements of free jazz and white noise crept in. Songs like "You Can Do (Part I)" were eerie, unnerving excursions into regions of the psyche where only the brave dared tread. Flautist Martin Jackson made the trip once too often, suffered a "spiritual crisis," and quit the band at the height of its success.

His replacement was Harry Poulus, the pale Greek god of keyboards, recruited from the ruins of Freedom's Children. Harry was a useful guy to have around in several respects: he was an enormously talented musician and a Zen mechanic to boot, capable of diagnosing the ailments of the band's worn-out Kombi just by remaining silent and centered and meditating on the problem until a solution revealed itself. With his help, the band recorded two more albums in quick succession (*Simply Otis Waygood* and *Ten Light Claps and a Scream*) and continued its epic trek through platteland towns, coastal resorts, and open-air festivals. They finished 1970 where they started—special guests at the grand finale of Cape Town's annual Battle of the Bands. The audience wouldn't let them off the stage. Rob worked himself into such a state of James Brownian exhaustion that he had to be carried off in the end. "Whether you accept it or not," wrote critic Peter Feldman, "1970 was their year."

After that, it was all downhill in a way. There were only so many heads in South Africa, and by the end of 1970, they'd all bought an Otis LP and seen the band live several times. Beyond a certain point, Otis could only go around in circles. Worse yet, conservatives were growing intolerant of longhaired social deviance. National Party MPs complained that rock music was rotting the nation's moral fiber. Rightwing students invaded a pop festival where Otis was playing and gave several participants an involuntary haircut. "We had police coming to the house every second night," says Ivor, "or guys with crewcuts and denim jackets saying, 'Hey, man, the car's broken down, can we sleep here?' They always planted weed in the toilets, but we always found it before they busted us."

By March 1971, the day of reckoning was drawing nigh. Describing drug abuse as a "national emergency," the Minister of Police announced a crackdown that included mandatory (and very long) prison sentences for drug possession. At the same time, various armies started breathing down Otis Waygood's neck. When the South African Defence Force informed Ivor that he was liable for military service, the boys sneaked back into Rhodesia, only to find Rhodesian army call-up papers waiting for them at their parents' homes. "Ian Smith despised us," says Ivor. "They wanted to make an example of us, so we basically escaped." At the time, international airlines weren't supposed to land in Rhodesia because of sanctions. But there was a Jo'burg–Paris flight that made an unofficial stop in Salisbury. The boys boarded it and vanished.

Back in Jo'burg, we were bereft. Friends and I started a tribute band that played garage parties, our every lick, pose, and song copied off Otis, but that petered out in a year or two, and we were left with nothing but their records and vague rumors from a distant hemisphere. Otis were alive and well in Amsterdam. Later, they were spotted in England, transmogrified into a white reggae band that played the deeply underground blacks-only heavy dub circuit. Later still, they became Immigrant, a multiracial outfit that did a few gigs at the Rock Garden or the Palladium. But it never quite came together again, and the band disintegrated at the end of the 1970s.

Martin Jackson never made it back to the real world. He was last seen drifting around Salisbury in 1974, wild-eyed and tangle-haired, with a huge cross painted on his back. Harry Poulos stepped off a building, another casualty of an era whose mad intensity made a reversion to the ordinary almost unbearable. Leigh Sagar is a barrister in London. The Zipper brothers are also living in the UK: Rob is an architect and Alan runs a recording studio. Ivor Rubenstein returned to Bulawayo, where he manufactures hats.

As for Benny Miller, the nice Jewish boy who started it all, he's still in Harare, wryly amused by the extraordinary adventure he missed by ducking out of that fateful trip to Cape Town. He still plays guitar in sixties nostalgia bands and produces African music for a living.

—Fresh Records liner notes, 1999

Postscript: It strikes me on rereading that I underplayed the most interesting aspect of this story.

Let's start with a quiz: who made the most money out of pop music in the twentieth century? Most people would say the Beatles, or Elvis, or Michael Jackson. All wrong. Frank Sinatra maybe? Andrew Lloyd Webber? The Stones? Unfortunately not. In all likelihood, the winner was Clive Calder, the fast-talking young hustler who walked into Otis Waygood's dressing room in January 1970, promising to make them as big as Grand Funk Railroad and Led Zeppelin.

Clive Calder was born and raised in Johannesburg's northern suburbs. The white blues boys from Rhodesia were his first venture as a showbiz manager. When they folded, he signed an array of mixed-race boys with bell-bottoms and Afros (Richard Jon Smith and Jonathan Butler among others) in a far-sighted but ultimately futile attempt to create an African Michael Jackson. In 1977 or thereabouts, he moved to London, where one of his first signings was Sir Bob Geldoff's Boomtown Rats. One thing led to another and by the time Calder sold his Zomba empire to the German company BMG, circa 2001, he had the world's three biggest-selling teen pop stars (Britney Spears, the Backstreet Boys, and N'Sync) under contract, along with most of America's seminal rap singers and countless thousands of songwriters. The Germans paid three billion dollars for Calder's business. If Calder was the sole shareholder, as is widely presumed, his cashing-out bonus dwarfs all other contenders.

Unfortunately, we can't be sure, because Zomba was privately held and Calder himself is a reclusive Howard Hughes–like figure, rumored to be riddled with germ phobias and mysterious allergies, and totally invisible in the media. *Rolling Stone* once commissioned me to do a story about him and his sometime partner, a country boy named Robert John "Mutt" Lange, who learned his chops as a session cat on Springbok Radio's "Springbok Hits" series, a long-running enterprise that issued note-for-note cover versions of international hits that cost less than half of the genuine article.

The training served its purpose, and Mutt went on to become one of the twentieth century's most successful songwriters and producers, churning out hits galore for AC/DC, Def Leppard, and his wife, Shania Twain, among many others. But Mutt was also a recluse who never gave interviews. I suspect he and Calder were worried that journalists would discover their South African background and start asking awkward questions about apartheid. Whatever the truth, Mutt and Clive liked being invisible, and they were sufficiently rich and powerful to keep it that way.

The sale of Clive's Zomba/Jive empire to BMG was big news for business editors in Europe and America. They ransacked the world for photographs of the mysterious South African and were staggered to find that none existed. Nor was he willing to pose for one. The story ran without a picture, even in the *New York Times*.

Odd to think that it all began in Sandringham, Johannesburg. One Friday night in 1970, my pimply teenaged friends and I hitchhiked across the city to see Otis performing at the Electric Circus. I have a dim memory of a slender, pixielike young man manning the ticket booth. His hair was blond, collar-length, and cut just so. He was wearing smart casuals, including a navy-blue blazer. He didn't drink, dance, or smoke dope but seemed pretty glamorous anyway. That was Clive Calder. It was the closest I ever got to him.

PART THREE
DISEASE

THE BODY COUNT

My friend Michelle, a left-wing literary critic, argues that all claims to truth are spurious. "The mere fact of chosing what facts you report, and what weight you attach to them, reduces all journalism to just another form of fiction," she declares.

This sounds dubious, but Michelle has a point in at least one regard: the facts you leave out are often at least as telling as those you set down on the page. So then: the truth about this story. When Rolling Stone asked for a piece about the inside and untold story of President Thabo Mbeki's descent into AIDS madness, I did not accept because I was interested in the subject. I accepted because I wanted to strike a blow at State President Thabo Mbeki.

There was a time when the image Mbeki projected struck me as quite appealing: all those tweed jackets and single-malt whiskeys and earnest undergraduate probings of the larger significance of almost everything. By the time Rolling Stone called, the enchantment had faded. I would have attacked Mbeki for nothing, but this American magazine was offering me a small fortune to exercise my disgruntlement on the presidential person, and I could scarcely believe my luck. I'd been struggling for years to get naive and idealistic Americans to publish anything even vaguely negative about the South African situation. Now they were offering me serious money to sever the presidential head and serve it up on an elegant literary platter. I said, Great, I'm your man.

Unfortunately, the facts as I found them failed to justify Mbeki's decapitation, so I veered off on a tangent that fell way outside Rolling Stone's *brief, with consequences that will dog me to my grave. What follows is a letter to* Rolling Stone *commissioning editor Bill Tonelli, written in December 2000.*

Yo, Bill—

You will be saddened to hear that Adelaide Ntsele has died. As you may recall, she featured briefly in my article a year ago about the long, twisted history of "The Lion Sleeps Tonight," which was based on a melody composed by her father, Solomon Linda. While I interviewed her sisters about the life and times of their father, Adelaide was swooning feverishly under greasy blankets in the next room. She got up from her sickbed to have her picture taken. She was so weak she could barely stand, but she wanted to be in your magazine.

I took her to the hospital afterward. We sat in emergency for a long time, waiting for attention. Her sister Elizabeth was there, too. She's a nurse. She looked at Adelaide's hospital card and grew very quiet. Later, she told me there was a secret code on it indicating that Adelaide had lit up an AIDS test. Atop that she had TB and a gynecological condition that required surgery. The operation had already been postponed repeatedly. To Elizabeth, it looked like the doctors had decided, Well, this one's had it, she'll die anyway, just let it happen. And so it did.

A year ago, the funeral scene would have written itself. I would have described the kindly old pastor, the sad African singing, the giant iron pots on fires for the ritual good-bye feast. I would have mentioned the eerie absence of any reference to AIDS in the eulogies, made some rote observation about the denial it betokened. I would have scanned the faces of mourners, trying to pick out the one in five who were carriers of the virus that put Adelaide in her coffin, withered and shriveled like a child. And in the end I would have turned sadly away, lamenting a society that allowed a thirty-seven-year-old woman to die because she couldn't afford the drugs available to rich white people.

Instead, I spent the ceremony thinking about viral antigens, cell-wall particles, heterophil cross-reactions, and other mysteries of what Sowetans call H.I. Vilakazi, the scourge of the deadly three letters. Midway through the proceedings, the pastor broke my reverie: perhaps the visitors would like to say something? I rose to my feet, straightened my tie, and prepared to speak my mind, but courage failed me, so I mumbled a few platitudes instead. "It is a heartbreak that Adelaide was taken so young," I said. "She bore terrible suffering with enormous dignity. We will always remember her as she appears in that picture," I concluded, nodding toward a framed portrait of a wistful young woman with huge doe eyes and cheekbones like Marlene Dietrich's. Adelaide wanted to be a model. She never made it. I extended my condolences to the family and sat down again.

It wasn't the eulogy Adelaide deserved, but then it wasn't the right time or place for a great cry of rage and confusion either. But now the mourning is done, and there are things that must be said. Unfortunately, I'm not sure you'll want to hear them.

Africa's era of megadeath dawned in the fall of 1983, when the superintendent of a hospital in what was then Zaire sent a communique to American health investigators, informing them that a mysterious disease had broken out among his patients. At the time, the United States was convulsed by its own weird health crisis. Large numbers of gay men were coming down with an unknown disease of extraordinary virulence. Scientists called it GRID, an acroynym for Gay-related Immune Disease, which, in turn, prompted conservatives and televangelists to call it God's vengeance on sinners. American researchers were thus intrigued to learn that a similar syndrome had been observed among heterosexuals in Africa. A posse of seasoned disease cowboys was convened and sent forth to investigate.

On October 18, 1983, they walked into Kinshasa's Mama Yemo Hospital, led by Dr. Peter Piot, age thirty-four, a Belgian who had been to Mama Yemo years earlier, investigating the first outbreak of Ebola fever. A change was immediately apparent. "In 1976, there were hardly any young adults there except for traffic accidents in orthopedic wards," Piot told the *Washington Post*. "Suddenly— boom—I walked in and saw all these young men and women, ema- ciated, dying." Improvised blood tests tests confirmed Piot's first impression—the mysterious new disease was present in Africa, and its victims were heterosexual. The human immunodeficiency virus itself was identified a year later, and in Africa it turned up wherever researchers looked for it—in 80 percent of Nairobi prostitutes, 32 percent of Ugandan truck drivers, and 45 percent of hospitalized Rwandese children. Worse yet, it seemed to be spreading very rap- idly. Epidemiologists plotted figures on graphs, drew lines linking the data points, and gaped in horror. The epidemic curve peaked in the stratosphere. Scores, maybe hundreds of millions, would die unless something was done.

These prophecies transformed the destiny of AIDS. In 1983, it was a fairly rare disease, confined largely to the gay and heroin- using subcultures in the West. Now it was reclassed as a threat to all humanity. "We stand nakedly before a pandemic as mortal as any there has ever been," World Health Organization chief Halfdan Mahler told a press conference in 1987. Western gov- ernments heeded his anguished appeal for action. Billions were invested in education and prevention campaigns. AIDS research started expanding "as rapidly as we could absorb money and people." AIDS organizations sprang up all across Africa—570 of them in Zimbabwe, a thousand in South Africa, 1,300 in Uganda. By 2000, global spending on AIDS had risen to around $35 billion a year, and activists were urging the commitment of billions more, largely to counter the apocalypse in Africa, where 22 million were said to carry the virus, and 14 million to have died.

And this is about where I entered the picture—July 2000, three months after President Thabo Mbeki announced that he

intended to convene a panel of scientists and professors to reex-
amine the relationship (if any) between the HI virus and AIDS.
Mbeki never actually said AIDS doesn't exist, but his actions
forced the question, and the implications were mind-bending.
South Africa was said to have more HIV infections (4.2 million)
than any other country on the planet, and the death toll was
reportedly rising daily. As the truth sank in, disbelief turned to
derision.

"Ludicrous," said the *Washington Post.*

"Off his rocker," said the *Spectator.*

"A degree of open-mindedness is fine," said *Newsday.* "But
sometimes you can be so open-minded your brains fall out."

The whole world laughed, and I rubbed my hands with glee:
South Africa was back on the world's front pages for the first time
since the fall of apartheid; fortune awaited the man of action. I
went to see Dr. Bob, a friend who also happens to be an AIDS
epidemiologist of international stature. He was so dismayed by
what he called the "genocidal stupidity" of Mbeki's AIDS initiative that he'd left work and gone home, where I found him
slumped in depression. "Hey Bob," I said, "snap out of it. Let's
make a deal." And so we did: he'd talk, I'd type, and together
we'd write the inside story of Thabo Mbeki's AIDS fiasco. All that
remained was to doff the hat to journalistic objectivity and briefly
consider the evidence that had led our leader astray.

According to newspaper reports, Mbeki had gleaned most of
it on the Web, so I revved up the laptop and followed him into
the virtual underworld of AIDS heresy, where renegade scientists
maintain Web sites dedicated to the notion that AIDS is a hoax
dreamed up by a diabolical alliance of pharmaceutical companies
and "fascist" academics whose only interest is enriching themselves. I visited four such sites, noted what they had to say, and
then turned to rival Web sites maintained by universities and
governments, which offered crushing rebuttals to same. Can't say
I understood everything, because the science was impenetrable,
but here's a rough sketch of the battlefield.

Let's look at AIDS from an African point of view. Imagine yourself in a mud hut, or maybe a tin shack on the outskirts of some sprawling city. There's sewage in the streets, and refuse removal is nonexistent. Flies and mosquitoes abound, and your drinking water is probably contaminated with feces. You and your children are sickly, undernourished, and stalked by diseases for which you're unlikely to receive proper treatment. Worse yet, these diseases are mutating, becoming more virulent and drug resistant. Minor scourges like infectious diarrhea and pneumonia barely respond to antibiotics. Malaria shrugs off treatment with chloroquine, often the only drug available to poor Africans. Some strains of TB—Africa's other great killer—have become virtually incurable. Now, atop all of this, there is AIDS, the most terrifying and deadly scourge of all.

According to what you hear on the radio, AIDS is caused by a tiny virus that lurks unseen in the blood for many years, only to emerge in deep disguise: a disease whose symptoms are other diseases, like TB, for instance. Or pneumonia. Or running stomach. These diseases are not new, which is why some of your neighbors are skeptical, maintaining that AIDS actually stands for "American Idea for Discouraging Sex." Others say nonsense, the scientists are right, we're all going to die unless we use condoms. But condoms cost money and you have none, so you just sigh and hope for the best.

Then one day you get a cough that won't go away, and start shedding weight at an alarming rate. You know these symptoms. In the past, you could take some pills and they would go away. But the medicines don't work anymore. You get sicker and sicker. You wind up in the AIDS ward.

The orthodox scientists, if they could see you, would say your immune system has been destroyed by the HI virus, allowing the TB (or whatever) to run riot. The AIDS dissidents who've captured Mbeki's ear would say, No way—the virus is a harmless creature that just happens to accompany immune-system breakdown caused by other factors—in this case, a lifetime of exposure to hunger and tropical pathogens.

Incensed by this nonsense, the orthodoxy whistles up a truck-load of studies from all over Africa showing that HIV-positive hospital patients die at astronomical rates relative to their HIV-negative counterparts. The dissidents are unimpressed. This proves nothing, they say. You claim this man is sick because he's HIV-positive. We say he's HIV-positive *because* he's sick. Either way, we agree on the outcome: hospital patients who carry the virus are very sick people, so of course they're more likely to die.

The orthodoxy grits its teeth. The dissidents are vastly out-numbered, but they're resolute and pugnacious and their ranks include a Nobel laureate (Kary Mullis) who says orthodox AIDS theory is so riddled with errors that anyone who believes it is "so stupid they deserve to be pitied." I won't even attempt to sum-marize Mullis's argument, because I didn't understand it. The rebuttals were equally incomprehensible, so I figured the best way to settle Mullis and Mbeki's hash was to show that AIDS has caused a massive increase in African mortality, which is of course the truth as we know it: 22 million Africans infected, according to the most recent reports, and 14 million already dead. If those numbers were accurate, Mbeki was guilty as charged. So I set out to confirm the death toll. Just that. I thought it would be easy. I picked up the phone. It was my first mistake.

There was a time when I imagined medical research as an ideal-ized endeavor, carried out by scientists interested only in truth. Up close, it turns out to be much like any other human enter-prise, riven with envy, ambition, and the standard jockeying for position. Labs and universities depend on grants, and grant making is fickle, subject to the vagaries of politics and intellec-tual fashion, and prone to favor scientists whose work grips the popular imagination. Every disease has champions who gather data and hype the threat they pose. The cancer fighters will tell you that their crisis is deepening and more research money is urgently needed. Those doing battle with malaria make similar pronouncements, as do those working on TB, and so on and so on. If all their claims are added together, says public health expert Christopher Murray, you wind up with a theoretical global death toll that "exceeds the number of humans who die annually by two- to threefold."

Malaria is said to kill two to three million humans a year, but malaria research gets about $1 for every $50 going to AIDS. Tuberculosis (1.7 million victims a year) is similarly sidelined, to the extent that there were no new TB drugs in development at all as of 1998. AIDS, on the other hand, is totally replete, employing an estimated 100,000 scientists, sociologists, epidemiologists, caregivers, counselors, peer educators, and stagers of condom jamborees. Furthermore, the level of funding grows daily as foundations, governments, and philanthropists like Bill Gates enter the field, unnerved by the bad news, which usually arrives in the form of articles describing AIDS as a "merciless plague" of "biblical virulence," as *Time* recently phrased it, causing "terrible depredation" among the world's poorest people.

These stories originate in Africa but the statistics that support them emanate from the suburbs of Geneva, Switzerland, where the World Health Organization has its headquarters. Technically employed by the United Nations, WHO officials are the world's disease police, dedicated to eradicating illness and fostering development. They crusade against old scourges, raise the alarm against new ones, fight epidemics, and dispense grants and expertise to poor countries. In conjunction with UNAIDS (the Joint United Nations Program on HIV/AIDS, based on the same Geneva campus), the WHO also collects and disseminates information about the AIDS pandemic.

In the West, this is a fairly simple matter: every new AIDS case is scientifically verified and reported to health authorities, who inform the disease police in Geneva. But most AIDS occurs in Africa,

where hospitals are thinly spread, understaffed, and often bereft
of the laboratory equipment necessary to confirm HIV infections.
How do you track an epidemic under these conditions? In 1985, the
WHO asked experts to hammer out a simple description of AIDS
that would enable bush doctors to recognize it and start counting
cases but the outcome was a fiasco—partly because doctors struggled to diagnose the disease with the naked eye, but also because
this reporting system produced nothing like the tidal wave of cases
anticipated. It was abandoned in 1988 and replaced by an alternative on which Africa's AIDS statistics are now "primarily" based.

The system works like this. On any given morning, anywhere in Africa, you'll find crowds of expectant mothers lining up outside government prenatal clinics: they've come for a
routine checkup that includes the drawing of a blood sample to
test for syphilis. AIDS researchers realized that serum left over
after this procedure could be a rich source of information on the
spread of HIV. So they set up a system whereby once a year,
AIDS researchers descend on selected clinics, remove the left-
over blood samples, and screen them for traces of the HI virus.
The results are forwarded to Geneva and fed into a computer
model that transmutes them into statistics. If so many pregnant
women are HIV-positive, then a certain percentage of all adults
and children are presumed to be infected, too. And if that many
people are infected, some percentage of them are presumed to
have died. Hence, when UNAIDS says 14 million Africans have
succumbed to AIDS, it does not mean that 14 million bodies have
been counted. It means that 14 million people linked via tortu-
ous mathematical models to women who tested positive in one
of those annual antenatal surveys are presumed to have died in
Africa's great unknown.

You can theorize at will about the rest of Africa and nobody
will ever be the wiser, but South Africa is different—a semi-
industrialized country with a respected statistical service. "South
Africa," says UNAIDS consultant Ian Timaeus, of whom more
later, "is the only country in sub-Saharan Africa where sufficient

deaths are routinely registered to attempt to produce national estimates of mortality from this source." He adds that "coverage is far from complete," but there's enough of it to be useful—around eight out of ten deaths are registered in South Africa, according to Timaeus, compared to about one in one hundred elsewhere below the Sahara.

It therefore seemed that checking the number of registered deaths in South Africa was the surest way of assessing the statistics from Geneva, so I dug out the figures. Geneva's computer models said that AIDS deaths had surged from 80,000-odd in 1996 to 250,000 in 1999. But no such rise was discernible in registered deaths, which went from 327,822 to 351,281 over roughly the same period. The discrepancy was so large that I wrote to Statistics SA to make absolutely sure I had understood these numbers correctly. An official answered in the affirmative,[1] and at that exact moment my story was in trouble. Geneva's figures reflected catastrophe. Pretoria's didn't. Between these extremes lay a gray area populated by local actuaries who privately muttered that the Geneva figures were far too high, but so what? They don't make the running in this debate. The figures you see in your newspapers come from Geneva, and they couldn't be substantiated.

But you don't want to hear all this, do you? Nor did I. It spoiled the plot, so I tried to ignore it. If it was indeed true that very large numbers of South Africans were dying, the nation's coffin makers had to be laboring hard to keep pace with growing demand. I called two entrepreneurs who'd been in the news in the mid-1990s for inventing cheap coffins made of recycled materials, anticipating a killing in the coming death boom. Oddly, they'd both gone out of business. "People weren't interested," said a dejected Mr. Rob Whyte. "They wanted coffins made of real wood."

So I called the real wood dudes, three industrialists who manufactured coffins on an assembly-line basis for the national

---

1. This is accurate, but the official failed to warn me that the death toll would rise somewhat as late registrations trickled in.

market. "It's quiet," said Kurt Lammerding of GNG Pine Products. "Very quiet. We aren't feeling anything at all." His competitors concurred—business was dead, so to speak. In fact, said Joe Alberts of Poliflora, it was so bad that smaller outfits were going bankrupt. I checked, and lo: two of the four coffin factories listed in Johannesburg's Yellow Pages had recently gone under, and one of the survivors maintained that the plague was a "moneymaking racket" aimed at extorting charity from the gullible. "It's a fact," said Mr. A. B. Schwegman of B&A Coffins. "If you go on what you read in the papers, we should be overwhelmed, but there's nothing. So what's going on? You tell me."

I couldn't, although I suspected it might have something to do with race. The big-time coffin firms were all white-owned, and they said South Africa's death business had undergone major changes since the downfall of apartheid in 1994, with unlicensed backyard funeral parlors mushrooming in black townships. They couldn't discount the possibility that these pirate outfits were scoring their coffins from obscure black business in places like Soweto. The only one they knew of was Mmabatho Coffins, but when I called, the phone just rang because it had gone bankrupt, too. Weird, no? According to a July 2000 news report, South Africa's death rate has almost doubled in the past decade. "These aren't predictions," said the *Sunday Times*. "These are the facts." And if the facts were correct, someone, somewhere had to be prospering in the coffin trade.

Further inquiries led me to Johannesburg's derelict downtown, where an abandoned multistory parking garage has recently been transformed into a vast warren of carpentry workshops, each housing a black carpenter set up in business with government seed money. I wandered around searching for coffin makers, but there were only two. Eric Borman said business was good, but he was a master craftsman who made one or two deluxe caskets a week and seemed to resent the suggestion his customers were the sort of people who died of AIDS. For that, I'd have to talk to Penny. He pointed, and off I went, deeper and deeper into the maze. Penny's place was locked up and deserted. Inside, unsold coffins were stacked ceiling-high, and a forlorn "closed" sign hung on the wire.

At that moment, a forbidden thought entered my brain. This will sound crazy, but put yourself in my shoes. You live in Africa—okay, in the postcolonial twilight of Johannesburg's once-white suburbs, but still, as close to the AIDS front line as a honky can get. For years, experts tell you that the plague is marching down the continent, coming closer every year. By 1999, the newspapers are telling you that one in five people on your street is walking dead.

This has to be true, because it's coming from experts, so you start looking for evidence. Laston the gardener, at number 10, is suspiciously thin and has a hacking cough that won't go away. His wife Sacred has a rash on her face, and there seems to be something wrong with her latest baby. On the far side of the golf course, Mrs. Smith has just buried her beloved servant. Mr. Beresford's maid has just died, too. Your cousin Lennie knows someone who knows someone who owns a factory where all the workers are dying. Your newspapers are predicting that the economy will ultimately be crippled by AIDS, and that the education system might collapse because so many teachers are dying. But then you wind up staring into Penny's failed coffin workshop and you think, Jesus, maybe this is all a hallucination.

Is this possible? Hard to say. In my suburb, people's brains are so addled by death propaganda that we automatically assume that almost everyone who falls seriously ill or dies has AIDS, especially if they're young, poor, and black. But we don't really know, and nor do the sufferers themselves, because hardly anyone has been tested. "What's the point?" asks Laston, the ailing gardener. He knows there's no cure for AIDS, and no hope of obtaining life-extending antiretrovirals. As a playboy, with three wives back in Malawi and a mistress in Jo'burg, he knows he's at risk for the virus, but finding out would ruin whatever remains of his life, so he refrains. Last winter, he came down with a bad cough, and everyone said it was AIDS, but it wasn't—come summer, Laston got better. Then Stanley the bricklayer became our street's most likely AIDS case. Stanley maintained he had a heart condition, but behind his back everyone was whispering, "Oh, my God, it's AIDS." But was it? We had no idea. We were playing a macabre guessing game, driven by hysteria.

But you don't want to hear this either, do you? Nor did anyone else. Worried friends slipped newspaper clippings into my mailbox: cemetery overflows, hospitals overwhelmed, prison deaths up 585 percent. Each time I'd check out the evidence, but there was always a contributing factor that had gone entirely unmentioned, like cut-price cemetery plots, a TB epidemic in scandalously overcrowded jails, or government hospitals in a state of "irreversible decline." After months of this, even my mother lost patience. "Shaddup," she snapped. "They'll put you in a straitjacket." Mother knows best, but I just couldn't get those numbers out of my head: 327,822 registered deaths in 1996; 351,281 three years later. I called Dr. Bob, the AIDS epidemiologist, and said, Listen, I am beset by demons and heresies, can you not shrive me? So we had lunch, and I aired my doubts, whereupon he said, Fear not, I know of absolutes that will soothe your fevered brain. He pointed in the direction where truth lay, and I set out to find it.

And here we are on a hilltop on the equator, overlooking the spot where Africa's first recorded outbreak of AIDS took place. It's a village called Kasenyi, which lies on the border between Uganda and Tanzania, close to where the Kagera River flows into Lake Victoria. In 1979 or thereabouts, according to legend, a trader named Kainga Bweinda crossed the river in a canoe to sell his wares in Kasenyi. Business done, he bought some beers and relaxed in the company of a certain Maria, who lived in that house right there. Some time later, Maria fell victim to a wasting disease that refused to respond to any known medication, Western or tribal.

Not long after, a similar drama unfolded in Rukunyu, a fishing village on the Uganda side of the river. There, the first victim was a certain Regina, and the agent of infection was said to be a visitor from Kasenyi. In due course, several of Regina's friends contracted the wasting disease. Her neighbors cried foul, accusing Rukunyu of putting a hex on them. Kasenyi responded in kind. Soon, villagers on both banks of the river were discarding objects brought from the other side, believing them to be bewitched. But nothing helped. The contagion spread away to the next village, and then the next. By 1983, it was in all the cities on the western shore of Lake Victoria. The first scientists arrived on the scene in 1985, and by 1988, a disturbing picture had emerged. Around 30 percent of pregnant women in the lakeside town of Bukoba were HIV-infected. In Lyantonde, 150 miles northward, the equivalent figure among barmaids was 67 percent. In the venereal clinics of Kampala, every second patient was carrying the virus. Newspapers took to describing Lake Victoria as "the epicenter of the AIDS epidemic." Ugandan president Yoweri Museveni declared that "apocalypse" was imminent.

This prophecy was based largely on surveys among small groups of high-risk subjects. Many factors remained unknown— the true extent of infection in the general populace, the rate at which it was spreading, the speed with which it killed. To formulate an effective battle plan, AIDS researchers desperately needed more data in these areas. They cast around for a place to study, and lit on Masaka, Uganda, a ramshackle town just west of Lake Victoria and about 100 miles north of ground zero. In 1988, a Dutch epidemiologist named Daan Mulder was sent there to lay the groundwork for what would ultimately become the largest and most significant study of its kind in Africa. Just over 8 percent of Masaka's adults were HIV-infected—not particularly high in the African context, but there were other considerations making it a good place to study. Uganda's government welcomed the research effort. The region was politically stable, and there was an international airport three hours away. Mulder's funders (the

British Medical Research Council and the UK government) gave the go-ahead, and an epic mortality study commenced.

Assisted by an army of field workers, Mulder drew an imaginary line around fifteen villages and counted everyone inside it. Then he took blood from all those who were willing (8,833 out of 9,777 inhabitants), screened it for HIV infections, and sat back to see what happened. Every household was visited at least once a year, and every death was noted and entered into Mulder's database, along with the deceased's HIV status.

The first results were published five years later and, as Dr. Bob promised, they were devastating. The HIV-infected villagers of Masaka were dying at an astronomical rate. Young adults with the virus in their bloodstream were sixty times more likely to perish than their uninfected peers. Overall, HIV-related disease accounted for a staggering 42 percent of all deaths. The AIDS dissidents were crushed; HIV theory was vindicated. "If there are any left who do not accept this," commented the CDC, "their explanation of how HIV-seropositivity leads to death must be very curious indeed." Clearly, only a fool would second-guess such powerful evidence, so I just visited the villages where Mulder's work was done, verified Dr. Bob's account, and headed back to the airport, my story about Mbeki's stupidity back on track. But my flight was delayed, so I got to spend an hour or two in Uganda's statistics office, and what I found there changed everything.

In 1948, Uganda's British rulers attempted a rough census in Masaka district, and concluded that the death rate was "a minimum of twenty-five to thirty per thousand." A second census in 1959 put the figure at twenty-one per thousand. In 1969, it was eighteen per thousand. By 1991, it had fallen to sixteen per thousand. Enter Daan Mulder with his blood tests, massive funding, and armies of field workers. He counted every death over two years, and then five, and here is his conclusion: the crude death rate in Masaka, in the midst of a horrifying AIDS plague, was 14.6 per thousand—the lowest ever measured. At first glance, this is exactly the outcome a dissident would predict. Blood tests would pick out people whose immune systems were already failing. They would proceed to die in very large numbers, but the overall death rate would remain more or less normal. But you don't want to hear this, do you? Nor did I, so I was relieved to discover an alternative explanation.

Daan Mulder's work began at a time when Uganda was emerging from two decades of chaos and civil strife during which no one kept track of mortality trends. According to British statistician Andrew Nunn, one of Mulder's collaborators, disease-related death rates must have fallen to record lows in the seventies and then surged massively with the advent of AIDS around 1980. "By the time we entered the picture," says Nunn, "the regional epidemic had already hit a plateau."

Maybe so, but the same explanation doesn't wash in neighboring Tanzania, which embarked, in 1992, on a mortality study that dwarfed anything previously undertaken in Africa. Again funded by the British government and supported by scientists from the University of Liverpool, the Adult Morbidity and Mortality Project recruited 307,000 participants in various urban and rural settings, each of whom was visited at least once a year over the next three years and interrogated about recent deaths or disease. The final results were rather like Masaka's: AIDS (or what participants and analysts assumed was AIDS) was by far the leading cause of adult mortality, but the overall death rate was 13.6 per thousand—10 percent lower than the death rate measured in Tanzania's 1988 census, which was rated "close to 100 percent" by Professor Ian Timaeus, the regnant authority on African mortality in the AIDS era. When no one else could answer my questions, I turned to him.

"Professor Timaeus," I said, "this study appears to show that there was no increase in Tanzania's death rate in the darkest heart of the AIDS epidemic." Timaeus shrugged. "The survey covered only part of the country," he said. True, said I, but a fairly large part, with hundreds of thousands of participants. "But were they representative?" he countered. I had no idea. Timaeus smiled and said, "I think this is the more critical evidence."

Whereupon he produced a sheath of graphs and papers and laid them on a table. There was, he began, a "regrettable" lack of knowledge about mortality in Africa, attributable to inertia, donor indifference, and a crippling lack of recent data. These factors bedeviled the AIDS demographer, but Timaeus found several ways around them, most important of which was the so-called sibling history techique of mortality estimation. It works like this.

Every five years or so, researchers financed by the U.S. Agency for International Development conduct detailed health interviews with mothers in developing countries. Among the questions put to them are these: "How many children did your own mother have? How many are still alive? When did the others die?" Timaeus realized that close analysis of the answers would reveal trends that were failing to show up elsewhere. He set to work, and published the results the journal AIDS in 1998. "In just six years (1989–1995) in Uganda," he wrote, "men's death rates almost doubled, and women's death rates more than doubled." Similar horrors were revealed in Tanzania, where male deaths were up 80 percent in the same period.

Again this seemed to settle the matter, but again, there were complications. For one thing, Timaeus's findings of a massive rise in Ugandan mortality contradicted Daan Mulder's epic study, which eventually ran for seven years without detecting any rise in the death rate. The same is true of Tanzania's giant adult mortality survey: the death rate remained stable during the very period when Timaeus says it was surging.

How come? I found a possible answer in a paper coauthored by Kenneth Hill, the ace Johns Hopkins demographer who coinvented the sibling history technique back in 1984. Last year, after a worldwide evaluation, Hill and his team concluded that sibling histories were useless for the purpose to which Timaeus put them. As I understand it, the problem was "downward bias"—people remember recent deaths pretty clearly, but those that happened years back tend to fade. According to Hill and company, this usually leads to a false impression of rising mortality as you near the present, even in countries like Indonesia or Bolivia where there's little or no AIDS. In Namibia, for instance, the sibling history method detected a wildly improbable 156 percent rise in the fourteen years prior to 1992. "This lack of precision," said Hill's team, "precludes the use of these data for trend analysis."

"I don't agree," says Timaeus, who maintains that Hill and his collaborators must have got their math wrong. But this is not an argument he pursues with much vigor, because his own papers acknowledge that the sibling history method is "untried" and that the results it produces "could be partly or wholly spurious."

Weird, no? For years, I'd been reading about villages in the Lake Victoria region where nobody was left alive save babies and the aged, and where vast tracts of agricultural land had been abandoned by AIDS-stricken peasants. I assumed devastation on this scale would be visible from satellites, and asked NASA to please forward the pictures so I could use them against Mbeki. Now I don't know what to think. I struggle to believe science would make a mistake of the magnitude claimed by Mbeki's dissident friends. But I have deepening qualms about the scale of the thing.

I was living in Los Angeles in 1981, when the very first cases of GRID were detected. I knew men who were stricken, and sympathized with their desperation. They wanted government action, and suspected there would be little so long as AIDS could be dismissed as a scourge of queers, junkies, and Haitians. So they forged an alliance with powerful figures in science and the media and set forth to change perceptions, armed inter alia with potent slogans such as "AIDS is an equal-opportunity killer" and "AIDS threatens everyone." Madonna, Liz Taylor, and other stars were recruited to drive home the message to the straight masses: AIDS is coming after you, too.

These warnings were backed up by estimates such as this one, published in the *New England Journal of Medicine* in 1985: 1.76 million Americans are already HIV-infected, said researchers Spivak and Wormser, and the disease is rapidly spreading. Dr. Anthony Fauci, now head of the National Institute of Allergic and Infectious Diseases, prophesied that "three to five million Americans" would be HIV-positive within a decade. *Newsweek*'s figures in a 1987 article were twice as high. That same year Oprah Winfrey told the nation that "by 1990, one in five heterosexuals will be dead of AIDS."

As the hysteria intensified, challenging such certainties came to be dangerous. In 1988, New York City health commissioner Stephen C. Joseph reviewed the city's estimate of HIV infections, concluded that the number was inaccurate, and halved it from 400,000 to 200,000. His office was invaded by protesters, his life threatened. Demonstrators tailed him to meetings, chanting "Resign, resign!"

In hindsight, Dr. Joseph's reduced figure of 200,000 infections might actually have been an exaggeration, given that New York has recorded a total of 120,000 AIDS cases since the start of the epidemic. In 1997, the *Washington Post* reported that the true number of HIV infections in the United States in the mid-1980s was probably in the region of 450,000—one-quarter of the figure put forth by the *New England Journal of Medicine* at the time.

If the numbers could be gotten so wrong in America, what are we to make of infinitely more dire predictions in the developing world? In the early 1990s, experts announced that Thailand's AIDS epidemic was "moving with supersonic speed." It stalled at 2 percent. They said AIDS in India was about to explode "like a volcano," but infection levels there have yet to crest 1 percent. The only place where the apocalypse has materialized in its full and ghastly glory is in Geneva's computer models of the African pandemic.

Why Africa, and Africa only? I know a possible reason. Read on.

In many ways, the story of AIDS in Africa is a story of the gulf between rich and poor, the privileged and the wretched. Here's one way of calibrating the abyss.

Let's say you live in America, and you committed an indiscretion with drugs and needles or unprotected sex a few years back, and now find yourself plagued by ominous maladies that won't go away. Your doctor frowns and says you should have an AIDS test. She draws a blood sample and sends it to a laboratory, where it is subjected to an exploratory ELISA (enzyme-linked immunosorbent assay) test. The ELISA cannot detect the virus itself, only antibodies that mark its presence. If your blood contains such antibodies, the test will "light up," or change color, whereupon the lab tech will repeat the experiment. If the second ELISA lights up, too, he'll do a confirmatory test using the more sophisticated and expensive Western blot method. And if that confirms the infection, the CDC recommends that the entire procedure be repeated using a new blood sample, to put the outcome beyond all doubt.

In other words, we're talking six tests in all, doubly confirmed. Such a protocol is probably fail-safe, but as you draw away from the first world, health care standards decline and people grow poorer, meaning that confirmatory tests start falling away. In Johannesburg, for instance, a doctor in private practice will typically want three consecutive positive ELISAs before deciding that you are HIV-infected. But his counterpart in a cash-strapped government hospital has to settle for two ELISAS and, in some circumstances, only one. That's also the WHO's recommended protocol for pregnancy clinic surveys in countries like mine, where the HIV rate is above 10 percent.

In America, one ELISA means almost nothing. "Persons are positive only when they are repeatedly reactive by ELISA and confirmed by Western blot," says the CDC. In Africa, however, such precautions are deemed expensive and unnecessary, partly because HIV infections are so densely concentrated, but mostly because the blood tests are held to be virtually infallible.

How do we know? Because commercial HIV tests are evaluated by the WHO as they come onto the market. These safety checks involve a panel of several hundred blood samples from all

over the world. Some are HIV-positive, some aren't. The object
is to make sure new tests are capable of determining which are
which. Among the scores of brands evaluated over the years, a
handful have proved to be useless. But those manufactured by
established biotechnology corporations usually pass with flying
colors, typically scoring accuracy rates close to perfect.

In South Africa, such outcomes are often cited in furious
attacks on President Mbeki. "HIV tests such as the latest generation ELISA are now more than 99 percent accurate," opined the
weekly *Mail & Gaurdian*. "The tests have confidence levels of
99.9 percent," said Professor Malekgapuru Makgoba, head of the
Medical Research Council. Science had spoken, and science was
unanimous: the tests were fine, and Mbeki was an idiot, "trying to
be a *Boys' Own* basement lab hero of AIDS science."

It was a good line. I laughed, too, but there came a moment
when it ceased to be funny. The story begins in Brazil, in 1994.
Dr. Marise Fonseca is studying for an advanced degree in tropical medicine. Her professors at São Paulo university suspect that
HIV might have gained a foothold in the Amazon, so they send
Marise to do some testing in a tough gold-mining camp. Most of
her 184 subjects are in high AIDS risk categories—miners who
scorn condoms and girls who work in saloons or cabarets—so
it comes as no great surprise when twenty-one test positive or
borderline positive on at least one HIV ELISA. In other respects,
however, the results are inexplicable. A locally manufactured
ELISA says two subjects are positive. A British one fingers seven,
but different people in almost every case. The French test is all
over the place, declaring fourteen infected.

Clearly, something in the blood of these people is confusing
the tests, and the prime suspect is *plasmodium falciparum*, one of
the parasites that causes malaria: of the twenty-one subjects who
lit up the tests, sixteen have huge levels of malaria antibody in
their veins. Fonseca and her key collaborator, U.S. Army scientist Lorrin Pang, decide to try an experiment. They formulate
a preparation that absorbs malaria antibodies, treat the Amazon

139

samples, and repeat the tests on the blood thus cleansed. Suddenly 80 percent of the suspected HIV infections vanish.

Pang and Fonseca write up their results and submit to the *Lancet,* expecting shortly to become famous. Instead, it's the start of a bitter struggle to have their findings recognized. The *Lancet* says their paper is "not of interest," so they try the *Journal of Infectious Disease,* which farms it out to anonymous peer reviewers who say the data are too meager to support the conclusions. Pang and Fonseca concede the point and ask the WHO to finance further investigation.

Pang thinks he stands a good chance of getting funding because he's been a WHO consultant for nearly twenty years but he's turned down, and worse yet, or so he claims, warned that his line of inquiry is "inflammatory." This brings out the bulldog in him, and he resolves to publish or perish. He keeps revising the paper and resubmitting it to new journals, but peer reviewers always point out flaws and shoot it down. The impasse persists until May 2000, when Pang and Fonseca find a sympathetic ear at the Royal Society of Tropical Medicine, a venerable British institution that agrees to publish their findings as a "short report" in its journal. The response, according to the Royal Society's editor, is dead silence: no arguments, no rebuttals, no letters disputing the outcome or trashing their methods. In terms of scientific convention, this means the finding stands.

So what's a layman to make of this? If Pang and Fonseca's finding stands in Africa—and they are the first to concede that this remains uncertain—hundreds of millions might be at risk of testing falsely positive for HIV. I asked Luc Noel of the WHO's blood safety unit for his opinion. He wasn't aware of the Pang/Fonseca paper, but seemed surprised that anyone should take such claims seriously. He handed me a booklet detailing the outcome of the WHO's evaluation of commercial ELISAs. In it, I found two of the three tests that Fonseca deployed in the Amazon—the very ones that went haywire: second- and third-generation kits manufactured in Britain and France, respectively. One was rated 97 percent accurate, the other 98 percent.

But these levels of near-perfection are the end result of a process that involves as many as five confirmatory tests. What happens if you use just one or two, like Fonseca? And what if your subjects are Africans whose immune systems are typically, as UNAIDS head Peter Piot once phrased it, in a state of "chronic activation" check as a result of "chronic exposure" to hunger and tropical pathogens?

I found an answer of sorts at the Uganda Virus Research Institute, possibly Africa's greatest citadel of HIV studies. Perched on a hilltop overlooking Lake Victoria and generously funded by the British government, the UVRI is a many-splendored institution with great glories to its name. It employs two hundred scientists and support personnel, runs an array of advanced AIDS studies, tests experimental drugs, labors to produce an AIDS vaccine, and has generated hundreds of scientific papers over the past decade. It also publishes an annual report. I found a copy of the latest edition on a coffee table and took it home with me.

This document turned out to be full of fascinating snippets. In one experiment, scientists decided to invert standard procedure and run HIV tests on people who were known to be HIV-negative but were sick with other diseases. Their blood was screened using the sophisticated Western blot method, and lo, the tests lit up. Among other things, I found out that 78 percent of hookworm-infested subjects were borderline positive. Malaria caused 81 percent of its victims to test indeterminate. Unspecified "bacterial infections" confused the test nine times out of ten.

This phenomenon—false reactions on the Western blot—is well known in the West, where a smallish (3 to 18) percentage of subjects test indeterminate, and some test falsely positive. The U.S. National Institute for Allergy and Infectious Diseases acknowledges that previous pregnancies are liable to confuse the outcome. In the early days of AIDS, researchers published similar findings in respect of more than fifty diseases, among them such everyday scourges as influenza, hepatitis, and measles and, in Africa, bilharzia, malaria, and yaws, which collectively afflict hundreds of millions. It is for this reason, among others, that the WHO now recommends that HIV testers drop the Western blot entirely. As Luc Noel explained it, second- and third-generation ELISAs use recombinant or synthetic HIV antigens, whereas the Western blot doesn't. It is these modern ELISAs that are presumed to be almost perfectly accurate.

There was a way of checking this. I looked up the results of the WHO's evaluation of two leading ELISA brands—Recombigen HIV-1/HIV-2, manufactured by Trinity Biotech, and Wellcozyme HIV Recombinant from Murex Biotech. Test-driven in the WHO's lab, the Wellcozyme test scored 99.1 percent, while the Trinity model achieved a perfect 100. In the field, in Africa, it was another story entirely. In the course of 1999, the Uganda Virus Research Institute screened thousands of blood samples with these two tests. Exactly 3,369 lit up at least one ELISA, but only 2,237 (66 percent) remained positive after confirmatory tests. In other words: 34 percent of Ugandans who tested positive on just one ELISA were not really carrying the virus. The outcome is even more intriguing if you consider the 88 who twice tested positive, but only weakly so. When their blood was subjected to Western blotting, still held to be the definitive test in America, only 11 to 13 percent turned out to be genuinely HIV-infected.

Whichever way you figure it, this falls short of perfection, which is why the UVRI does rigorous confirmatory testing. The same does not necessarily apply in the pregnancy clinic screenings on which Africa's AIDS estimates are based. Here, the WHO says it's okay to drop all confirmatory tests in high prevalence settings. I took this up with UNAIDS epidemiologist Neff Walker, who pointed out that most African countries had "quality assurance" programs to guard against foul-ups. "I feel," he said, "that if a government found any evidence of too many false positives in their testing, they would report it. Governments would like to find evidence of lower prevalence (as would we all) and since they have the data to easily check your hypothesis, they would do so and report it."

Would they? I'm not so sure. In fact, I think some AIDS researchers have developed an almost religious attachment to dogma about ever-rising HIV prevalence. Here in South Africa, for instance, the Health Ministry informs us that the results of its annual antenatal HIV surveys are adjusted "so as to ensure that predicted prevalence trends are not disrupted." What manner of science is this, where predictions are allowed to influence or even determine the outcome? Who does the adjusting? What were their findings before predictions intervened? I don't have answers, but I can tell you one thing: high AIDS numbers are not entirely undesirable in Africa, or anywhere else, for that matter. High numbers mean deepening crisis, and crisis generates funding. The results are manifest: the skies of Africa are full of safari scientists, flying in to oversee research projects or novel interventions and bringing with them huge inflows of cash.

On the ground, these dollars translate into patronage for politicians and good jobs for their struggling subjects. An AIDS counselor earns thirty times more than a schoolteacher in Uganda. In Tanzania, doctors can double their income just by saving the hard currency per diems they earn while attending international AIDS conferences. Here in South Africa, entrepreneurs are piling into the business at an astonishing rate, setting up orphanages and consultancies, selling herbal immune boosters and vitamin supplements, devising new insurance products, distributing condoms, staging benefits, forming theater troupes that take the AIDS prevention message into schools. My buddy Jeremy Nathan is coproducing a slate of forty TV documentaries about AIDS, all for foreign markets. My buddy Shan Holmes, who sells HIV test kits to African governments, describes her industry as "a wall-to-wall cocktail party." My buddy Dave Alcock escorted representatives of the Bill and Melissa Gates Foundation around AIDS hot spots in the Zulu homeland. "By the time we got there," says he, "the AIDS orgs already had so much money they couldn't absorb any more. They couldn't find anyone to donate to."

Such surfeit is the result of dumbfounding AIDS estimates based on the presumed infallibility of blood tests. The guys in Geneva maintain that if there's a problem it would surely have been reported, but by my reckoning it has—back in the mid-1990s, South African AIDS authorities reported false-positive rates ranging as high as 26 percent when using a single ELISA. French army scientists working in neighboring Mozambique have just published results that raise far more alarming questions about the single-ELISA protocol. The best of the tests they evaluated achieved an 80 percent accuracy rate. Another was about as reliable as tossing a coin, and a third produced false positives at the rate of seven in ten. What if they'd thrown a Western blot into the equation? And some confirmatory tests for good measure? In 1988, the U.S. Army ran a battery of seven confirmatory tests on recruits who'd lit up at least one ELISA. After each round, the number of positives dwindled, and in the end barely 16 percent were shown to be truly HIV-infected. In 1992, a similar exercise in Russia produced an even worse outcome: only one in a hundred suspected infections were genuine.

So what happens if you treat Africans as equals, and test them as rigorously as everyone else? I can't say. All I can tell you is that the fate of a continent depends on a clear answer, but there doesn't seem to be one.

And so we return to where we started, standing over a coffin under a bleak Soweto sky, making a clumsy speech about a sad and premature death. Adelaide Ntsele died of AIDS, but the word didn't appear on her death certificate. Here in Africa, the three little letters stigmatize, so doctors usually put down something gentler to spare the family further pain. In Adelaide's case, they wrote TB. But her sister Elizabeth had no need of such false consolation. She donned a red-ribbon baseball cap and appeared on national TV, telling the truth: "My sister had HIV/AIDS." As a nurse, Elizabeth had no qualms with the doctors' diagnosis, and she concurred with their decision to forgo surgery and let Adelaide die. "It was God's will," she says, and she was at peace with it. I was the one beset by harrowing doubts.

Did Adelaide really have AIDS? It certainly looked that way, but she also had TB, the second most frightening infectious disease in the world today, on the rise everywhere, even in rich countries, sometimes in a virulent drug-resistant form that kills half its victims, according to the CIA's recent report on infectious disease. Eight years ago, the WHO declared resurgent TB a "global emergency," and the contagion continues to spread, particularly in a cluster of southern African countries simultaneously stricken by the worst TB and HIV epidemics on the planet.

Here in South Africa, incidence of TB has quadrupled since 1980. Most victims are young adults in sexually active age brackets. They cough, hack, develop sores on the body, suffer from night sweats, grow emaciated, and, if not treated properly, are likely to die. In other words, the course of the disease is outwardly similar to AIDS. It takes a blood test to establish the underlying presence of an HIV infection, and no less a personage than Max Essex, president of the Harvard AIDS Institute, has imputed that the tests might not be entirely reliable.

Back in 1994, Professor Essex and fellow investigators observed a "very high" (63 percent) rate of ELISA false positives among lepers in Central Africa. Mystified, they probed deeper and pinpointed the cause—two crossreacting antigens, one of which, lipoarabinomannan or LAM, also occurs in the organism that causes TB. This prompted Essex and his collaborators to warn that ELISA results should be "interpreted with caution" in areas where HIV and TB were co-endemic. Indeed, they speculated that existing antibody tests "may not be sufficient for HIV diagnosis" in settings where TB and related diseases are commonplace.

After Adelaide's death, I wrote to Essex, asking if he was still of the opinion that ELISA results had to be "interpreted with caution" in a country like mine, where upwards of 60 percent of the population carries dormant TB infections. I didn't hear back, so I called Essex's office, left several messages, then wrote again. Eventually his assistant informed me that he was traveling and would not be available. I deduced that he was in Botswana, and called him there. Again, no response. Defeated on that front, I wrote letters to South Africa's Ministry of Health, and to seven scientists working in the arcane field of HIV/TB interactions. This is probably a stupid question, I said, but does this finding still stand? One researcher replied that he didn't know, and the rest failed to get back to me.

Some people tell me it's wrong even to pose such a question, especially at a moment when rich countries and corporations are mulling billion-dollar contributions to a global AIDS superfund. They have been brought to this point by a ceaseless barrage of stories and images of unbearable suffering in Africa, all buttressed by Geneva's death projections. Casting doubt on those estimates is tantamount to murder, or so said Ed Rybicki, a Cape Town microbiologist who caught sight of part of this article and found it appalling. "AIDS is real, and is killing Africans in very large numbers," he wrote to me. "Presenting arguments that purport to show otherwise in the popular press is simply going to compound the damage already done by Mbeki. And a lot more people may die who may not have to otherwise."

Rybicki is right. If I was poised to contribute billions to the campaign against AIDS in Africa, I would be shaken to hear that the statistics driving me toward such an epiphany of altruism might be shaky. Indeed, I would say stop right here, there will be no money until we know what the facts are. But what are the facts? American newspapers keep telling me that AIDS in Africa

is "worse than the Black Death," but I couldn't find rock-solid
evidence of this in any of the countries where I went looking.

In the end, only one thing seemed certain: the importance
of death data gathered by South Africa's government. When I
embarked on this story, as you may recall, no massive rise in registered deaths was discernible. A year later, I returned to my point
of departure to see if the discrepancy persisted. UNAIDS had yet to
update its figures, but a sister agency, the UN Population Fund,
projected around 400,000 AIDS deaths in the year 2000. How
many of these could be confirmed by death registration? I wrote
to the Department of Home Affairs, which manages the death
register, and asked for the latest numbers. In response came a set
of figures somewhat different from those initially provided—the
consequence, I am told, of late registrations trickling in from deep
rural areas. Here is the final analysis:

Deaths registered in 1996—363,238
Deaths registered in 2000—457,335

As you see, registered deaths have indeed risen rapidly. The
rise falls way short of the catastrophe predicted by the United
Nations, but there is definite movement in an ominous direction. What's more, deaths are concentrated among sexually active
young adults: females in their twenties and males aged thirty to
thirty-nine. What would account for this, if not AIDS?

But even this is not the end of the tale. In 1998, Nelson Mandela's government launched a campaign to improve death registration in villages and townships inhabited by black people whose
hardships and health problems had been largely ignored by the
apartheid regime. They introduced a new, user-friendly death
certificate, opened satellite government offices in remote areas,
and even introduced a subsidy for undertakers willing to register
the deaths of those they buried.

Last year, demographer Sulaiman Bah analyzed five years of
death data and found two factors at work. One is the presumed

impact of AIDS. The other is rising registration, particularly in rural areas where the government's campaign would have had greatest impact. In an attempt to untangle these influences, Bah stripped the statistics of every death that could possibly be attributed to HIV infection—every bronchitis death, every TB death, every death caused by pneumonia, infectious diarrhea, and all other AIDS-defining conditions. The pattern remained unchanged: deaths were still up across the board, and still concentrated most heavily in the same young-adult age groups. Bah's conclusion: increased reporting accounts for an unknown proportion of the apparent rise in mortality.

So that's the story: enigma upon enigma, riddle leading to riddle, and no reprieve from doubt. I have wasted a year of my time and thousands of your dollars, and all I can really tell you is this: ordinary Africans everywhere are convinced that a new scourge is moving among them, a mysterious disease whose symptoms are other diseases, now grown impervious to medication. I've grown skeptical of the AIDS industry, but I think these ordinary people should be helped if possible. But how? It'll cost a thousand dollars a year to put one African on AIDS drugs—a noble proposal, on its face, but ill-conceived if that one lucky person's neighbors are dying of starvation and lack of medicines that cost a few cents. So what's the right policy? The answer, as always, lies in Africa's AIDS estimates—16 million dead, last time I checked, and the toll rising daily. If these numbers are accurate, desperate measures are needed. But what if they aren't?

Feel free to publish this, but if it bored you to death, I'll understand.

Yours,
Malan

Postscript: Bill Tonelli was a genuinely nice guy, and I'd put him in a very awkward position. His boss, *Rolling Stone* founder and publisher Jann Wenner, discovered in his forties that he was gay, whereupon he left his wife and children and became, among other things, a star in New York's AIDS charity firmament. Bill and Jann never said so openly, but this report was not what they wanted. They wanted a piece that would illumine South Africa's AIDS tragedy and add to *Rolling Stone*'s luster as a magazine that stood for justice. They did not want a letter teeming with heresies.

The *Rolling Stone* dudes were good Americans whose commitment to free speech was religious. It was unthinkable for them to censor a writer whose opinions they disagreed with, so they said, Okay, we'll publish something, but first, answer this: who agrees with you? And I had to say, Nobody. The AIDS dissidents who'd captured Mbeki's ear wanted no truck with a writer too feebleminded to understand that the disease didn't exist at all. By the same token, the AIDS establishment was pathologically hostile to any suggestion that its claims regarding megadeath in Africa were exaggerated. I was on my own. I said, "Truth is not democratic. Facts are either wrong or right. As far as I'm concerned, the facts as stated in this letter embody the truth as I understand it."

Rolling Stone took this on the chin and did the honorable thing: they published the story, but only after every word had been challenged by the dogged Dave McNally and approved by *Rolling Stone*'s special consultant Dr. David Ho, a stellar AIDS researcher who'd recently been anointed *Time*'s "Man of the Year" for his work on protease inhibitors. The resulting article was dull and lifeless, so full of equivocations and digressions as to be barely readable. This isn't a criticism of *Rolling Stone*. It was courageous of them to publish anything at all. But the process was an ordeal that consumed months of my life and left me restless and dissatisfied.

I was also engaged in an extraordinarily intense conversation with an American named Rodney Richards. Rodney was a microbiologist who'd gone into AIDS research after obtaining his doctorate, becoming a member of the team that developed the first AIDS blood test authorized for use in the United States. Intrigued by the ambiguities attendant upon HIV diagnosis, he went on to develop a diagnostic machine he believed was infallible. Convinced that he'd made an historic breakthrough, he invited two notorious dissidents to work with him. One was Peter Duesberg, a brilliant cancer researcher who'd ruined his career by declaring that HIV science was invalid. The other was Kary Mullis, the Nobel Prize–winning researcher who said, "Anyone who believes HIV theory is so stupid they should be pitied."

Rodney thought Duesberg's and Mullis's endorsements would crown his discovery with irrefutable credibility, but he found, after six months in the laboratory, that he couldn't sustain his case. Crushed, Rodney resigned from his job and retired from AIDS research. I met him on the Internet, and he struck me as an interesting guy. He believed AIDS theory was profoundly mistaken, but he had the grace to acknowledge that he might be mistaken. I guess that's why he responded so strongly to the question I was posing: if AIDS doesn't exist, how come the death toll in South Africa is rising? I thought the evidence in this regard was pretty strong. Rodney couldn't accept that, but his lungs hungered for the oxygen of truth, so he and I threw ourselves into a year-long interrogation of African AIDS statistics.

I didn't write about this at the time, partly because I was intimidated by the consequences of getting it wrong, but mostly because my wife saw AIDS as a destructive addiction that was ruining our lives. She had a point. Rodney and I were spending almost every waking hour on our quest. There was no money coming in, and I was often absent and abstracted. Like all addicts, I started telling lies and fulfilling my dark cravings in secret. But she found me out in December 2003, when I wrote what follows, first for the muckraking Cape Town magazine *Noseweek*, and then for the *Spectator* in England.

AMONG THE AIDS FANATICS

It was the eve of AIDS Day here in Cape Town. Rock stars like Bono and Sir Bob Geldof were jetting in for a fund-raising concert with Nelson Mandela, and the airwaves were full of dark talk about megadeath and the armies of feral orphans who would surely ransack South Africa's cities in 2017 unless funds were made available to take care of them. My neighbor came up the garden path with a press cutting. "Read this," said Captain David Price, ex–Royal Air Force flyboy. "Bloody awful."

It was an article from the *Spectator* describing bizarre sex practices that allegedly contibute to the HI virus's rampage across the continent. "One in five of us here in Zambia is HIV positive," said the report. "In 1993 our neighbor Botswana had an estimated population of 1.4 million. Today that figure is under a million and heading downward. Doom merchants predict that Botswana may soon become the first nation in modern times to literally die out. This is AIDS in Africa."

Really? Botswana has just concluded a census that shows population growing at around 2.7 percent a year, in spite of what is usually described as the worst AIDS problem on the planet. Total population has risen to 1.7 million over the last decade. If anything, Botswana is experiencing a minor population explosion.

There is similar bad news for the doomsayers in Tanzania's new census, which shows population growing at 2.9 percent a year. Professional pessimists will be particularly discomforted by developments in the swamplands west of Lake Victoria, where HIV first emerged, and where the depopulated villages of popular mythology are supposedly located. Here, in Kagera district, population grew at 2.7 percent a year prior to 1988, only to accelerate to 3.1 percent even as the AIDS epidemic was supposedly peaking. Uganda's latest census tells a broadly similar story, as does South Africa's.

Some might think it good news that the impact of AIDS is less devastating than most laymen imagine, but they are wrong. In Africa, the only good news about AIDS is bad news, and anyone who tells you otherwise is branded a moral leper, bent on sewing confusion and derailing one hundred thousand worthy fund-raising drives. I know this because several years ago I acquired what was generally regarded as a leprous obsession with the dumbfounding AIDS numbers in my daily papers. They told me that AIDS had claimed 250,000 South African lives in 1999, and I kept saying, This can't possibly be true. What followed was very ugly—ruined dinner parties, broken friendships, ridicule from those who knew better, bitter fights with my wife. After a year or so, she put her foot down. Choose, she said. AIDS or me. So I dropped the subject, put my papers in the garage, and kept my mouth shut.

As I write, the madam is standing behind me with hands on hips, hugely irked by this reversion to bad habits. But looking around, it seems to me that AIDS fever is nearing the danger level, and that some calming thoughts are called for. Bear with me while I explain.

We all know, thanks to Twain, that statistics are often the lowest form of lie, but when it comes to HIV/AIDS, we suspend all skepticism. Why? AIDS is the most political disease ever. We have been fighting about it since the day it was identified. The key battleground is public perception, and the most deadly weapon is the estimate. When the virus first emerged, I was living in America, where HIV incidence was estimated to be doubling every year or so. Every time I turned on the

TV, Madonna popped up to warn me that "AIDS is an equal opportunity killer," poised to break out of the drug and gay subcultures and slaughter heterosexuals. In 1985, a science journal estimated that 1.7 million Americans were already infected, with "three to five million" soon likely to follow suit. Oprah Winfrey told the nation that by 1990 "one in five heterosexuals will be dead of AIDS."

We now know that these estimates were vastly and indeed deliberately exaggerated, but they achieved the desired end: AIDS was catapulted to the top of the West's spending agenda, whereupon the estimators turned their attention elsewhere. India's epidemic was likened to "a volcano waiting to explode." Africa faced "a tidal wave of death." By 1992 they were estimating that "AIDS could clear the whole planet."

Who were they, these estimators? For the most part, they worked in Geneva for WHO or UNAIDS, using a computer simulator called Epimodel. Every year, all over Africa, blood samples would be taken from a small sample of pregnant women and screened for signs of HIV infection. The results would be programmed into Epimodel, which transmuted them into estimates. If so many women were infected, it followed that a similar proportion of their husbands and lovers must be infected, too. These numbers would be extrapolated out into the general population, enabling the computer modelers to arrive at seemingly precise tallies of the doomed, the dying, and the orphans left behind.

Because Africa is disorganized and, in some parts, unknowable, we had little choice other than to accept these projections. ("We" always expect the worst of Africa, anyway.) Reporting on AIDS in Africa became a quest for anecdotes to support Geneva's estimates, and the estimates grew ever more terrible—9.6 million cumulative AIDS deaths by 1997, rising to 17 million three years later.

Or so we were told. When I visited the worst affected parts of Tanzania and Uganda in 2001, I was overwhelmed with stories about the disease locals called "Slims," but statistical corroboration was hard to come by. According to government census bureaux, death rates in these areas had been in decline since World War II. AIDS-era mortality studies yielded some of the lowest overall death rates ever measured in the region. Populations seemed to have exploded even as the epidemic was peaking.

Ask AIDS experts about this and they'll say, This is Africa, chaos reigns, the historic data are too uncertain to make valid comparisons. But these same experts will tell you that South Africa is vastly different —"The only country in sub-Saharan Africa where sufficient deaths are routinely registered to attempt to produce national estimates of mortality," says Professor Ian Timaeus of the London School of Hygiene and Tropical Medicine. According to Timaeus, upwards of 80 percent of deaths are registered here, which makes us unique: the only corner of Africa where it's possible to judge computer-generated AIDS estimates against objective reality.

In the year 2000, Timaeus joined a team of South African researchers bent on eliminating all doubts about the magnitude of the impact of AIDS on South African mortality. Sponsored by the Medical Research Council, the team's mission was to validate (for the first time ever) the output of AIDS computer models against real-life death registration in an African setting. Toward this end, the MRC team was granted privileged access to death reports as they streamed into Pretoria. The first results became available in 2001, and they ran thus: 339,000 adult deaths in 1998; 375,000 in 1999; and 410,000 in 2000.

This was grimly consistent with predictions of rising mortality, but the scale was problematic. Epimodel estimated 250,000 AIDS deaths in 1999, but there were only 375,000 adult deaths in total that year—far too few to accommodate the UN's claims on behalf of the HI virus. In short, Epimodel had failed its reality check. It was quietly shelved in favor of a more sophisticated local model, ASSA 600, which yielded a "more realistic" death toll from AIDS of 143,000 for calendar year 1999.

At this level, AIDS deaths were about 40 percent of the total—still a bit high, considering there were only 232,000 deaths left to distribute among all other causes. The MRC solved the problem by stating that deaths from ordinary disease had declined at the cumulatively massive rate of nearly 3 percent per annum since 1985. Where they got this from remains a mystery, but these researchers were experts, and their tinkering achieved the desired end: modeled AIDS deaths and real deaths were reconciled, the books balanced, the truth revealed.

The fruit of the MRC's groundbreaking labor was published in June 2001, and my hash appeared to have been settled. To be sure, I carped about curious adjustments and overall magnitude, but fell silent in the face of graphs showing massive changes in the *pattern* of death, with more and more people dying at sexually active ages. "How can you argue with this?" cried my wife, eyes flashing angrily. I couldn't. I put my AIDS papers in the garage and ate my hat.

But I couldn't help sneaking the odd look at science Web sites to see how the drama was developing. Toward the end of 2001, the vaunted ASSA 600 model was replaced by ASSA 2000, which produced estimates even lower than its predecessor: 92,000 AIDS deaths in the calendar year 1999. This was just more than a third of the original UN figure, but no matter, the boffins claimed ASSA 2000 was so accurate that further reference to real-life death reports "will be of limited usefulness." A bit eerie, I thought, being told that virtual reality was about to render the real thing superfluous, but if these experts said the new model was infallible, it was surely infallible.

Only it wasn't. Last December, ASSA 2000 was retired, too. A note on the MRC Web site explained that modeling was an inexact science, and that "the number of people dying of AIDS has only now started to increase." Furthermore, said the MRC, there was a new model in the works, one that would "probably" produce estimates "about ten percent lower" than those presently on the table. The exercise was not strictly valid, but I persuaded my scientist pal Rodney Richards to run the revised data on his own simulator and see what he came up with for 1999. The answer, very crudely, was an AIDS death toll somewhere around 60,000—a far cry indeed from the 250,000 initially put forth by UNAIDS.

The wife has just read this, and she is not impressed. "It's obscene," she says. "You're treating this as if it's just a computer game. People are dying out there."

Well, yes. I concede that. People are dying, but this doesn't spare us from the fact that AIDS in Africa is indeed something of a computer game. When you read that 29.4 million Africans are "living with HIV/ AIDS," it doesn't mean that millions of living people have been tested. It means modelers assume that 29.4 million Africans are linked via enormously complicated mathematical and sexual networks to one of the women who tested HIV-positive in one of those annual pregnancy clinic surveys. Modelers are the first to admit that this exercise is subject to uncertainties and large margins of error. Larger than expected, in some cases.

A year or so back, modelers produced estimates that portrayed South African universities as crucibles of rampant HIV infection, with one in four undergraduates doomed to die within ten years. Prevalence shifted according to racial composition and region, with kwaZulu-Natal institutions worst affected and Rand Afrikaans University (still 70 percent white) coming in at 9.5 percent. Real-life tests on a random sample of 1,188 RAU students rendered a startlingly different conclusion: on-campus prevalence was 1.1 percent, barely a ninth of the modeled figure. "Doubt is cast on present estimates," said the RAU report, "and further research is strongly advocated."

A similar anomaly emerged when South Africa's major banks ran HIV tests on 29,000 staff earlier this year. A modeling exercise put HIV prevalence as high as 12 percent; real-life tests produced a figure closer to 3 percent. Elsewhere, actuaries are scratching their heads over a puzzling lack of interest in programs set up by medical insurance companies to handle an anticipated flood of middle-class HIV cases. Old Mutual, the insurance giant, estimates that as many as 570,000 people are eligible, but only 22,500 have thus far signed up. In Grahamstown, district surgeon Dr. Stuart Dyer is contemplating an equally perplexing dearth of HIV cases in the local jail.

"Sexually transmitted diseases are common in the prison where I work," he wrote to the *British Medical Journal*, "and all prisoners who have any such disease are tested for HIV. Prisoners with any other illnesses that do not resolve rapidly (within one to two weeks) are also tested for HIV. As a result, a large number of HIV tests are done every week. This prison, which holds 550 inmates and is always full or overfull, has an HIV infection rate of 2 to 4 percent and has had only two deaths from AIDS in the seven years I've been working there." Dyer goes on to express a dim view of statistics that give the impression that "the whole of South Africa will be depopulated within twenty-four months," and concludes by stating, "HIV infection in SA prisons is currently 2.3 percent." According to the newspapers, it should be closer to sixty.

On their face, these developments suggest that miracles are happening in South Africa, unreported by anyone save *Noseweek*, a local monthly magazine. If the anomalies described above are typical, computer models are seriously overstating HIV prevalence. A similar picture emerges on the national level, where our estimated annual AIDS death toll has halved since we eased UNAIDS out of the picture, with further reductions likely when the new MRC model appears. Could the same thing be happening in the rest of Africa?

Most estimates for countries north of the Limpopo River are issued by UNAIDS, using methods similar to those discredited here in South Africa. According to Paul Bennell, a health policy analyst associated with Sussex University's Institute for Development Studies, there is an "extraordinary" lack of evidence from other sources. "Most countries do not even collect data on deaths," he writes. "There is virtually no population-based survey data in most high-prevalence countries."

Bennell was, however, able to gather information about Africa's schoolteachers, usually described as a high-risk HIV group on account of their steady income, which enables them to drink and party more than others. Last year, the World Bank claimed AIDS was killing Africa's teachers "faster then they can be replaced." The BBC reported that "one in seven" Malawian teachers would die in 2002 alone.

Bennell looked at the available evidence and found real-life teacher mortality to be "much lower than has been suggested." In Malawi, for instance, the all-causes death rate among schoolteachers was under 3 percent, not over 14. In Botswana, it was about three times lower than computer-generated estimates. In Zimbabwe, four times lower. Bennell believes that AIDS continues to present a serious threat to educators, but concludes that "overall impact will not be as catastrophic as suggested." What's more, teacher deaths appear to be declining in six of the eight countries he has studied closely. "This is quite unexpected," he remarks, "and suggests that, in terms of teacher deaths, the worst may be over."

In the past year or so, similar mutterings have been heard throughout southern Africa—the epidemic is leveling off or even declining in the worst-affected countries. UNAIDS has been at great pains to rebut such ideas, describing them as "dangerous myths," even though the data on UNAIDS's own Web site show they are nothing of the sort. "The epidemic is not growing in most countries," insists Bennell. "HIV prevalence is not increasing as is usually stated or implied."

Bennell raises an interesting point here. Why would UNAIDS and its massive alliance of pharmaceutical companies, NGOs, scientists, and charities insist the epidemic is worsening if it isn't? A possible explanation comes from New York physician Joe Sonnabend, one of the pioneers of AIDS research. Sonnabend was working in a Greenwich Village clap clinic when the syndrome first appeared and he went on to found the American Foundation for AIDS Research, only to quit in protest when colleagues started exaggerating the threat of a generalized pandemic with a view to increasing AIDS's visibility and adding urgency to their grant applications. The AIDS establishment, says Sonnabend, is extremely skilled at "the manipulation of fear for advancement in terms of money and power."

With such thoughts in the back of my mind, South Africa's AIDS Day "celebrations" cast me into a deeply leprous mood. Please don't get me wrong here. I believe AIDS is a real problem in Africa. Governments and sober medical professionals should be heeded when they express deep concerns about it. But there are breeds of AIDS activists and AIDS journalists who sound hysterical to me. On AIDS Day, they came forth like loonies drawn by a full moon, chanting that AIDS was getting worse and worse, "spinning out of control," crippling economies, causing famines, killing millions, contributing to the oppression of women, and "undermining democracy" by sapping the will of the poor to resist dictators.

To hear them talk, AIDS is the only problem in Africa, and the only solution is to continue the agitprop until free access to AIDS drugs is defined as a "basic human right" for everyone. They are saying, in effect, that because Mr. Mhlangu of rural Zambia has a disease they find more compelling than any other, someone must spend upwards of $300 a year to provide Mr. Mhlangu with life-extending AIDS medications—a noble idea, on its face, but completely absurd when you consider that Mr. Mhlangu's neighbors are likely to be dying in much larger numbers of diseases that could be cured for a few cents if medicines were only available. Around 350 million Africans—nearly half the population—get malaria every year, but malaria medication is not a basic human right. Two million get TB, but last time I checked, spending on AIDS research exceeded spending on TB by a crushing factor of ninety to one. As for pneumonia, cancer, dysentery, or diabetes, let them take aspirin or grub in the bush for medicinal herbs.

I think it is time to start questioning some of the claims made by the AIDS lobby. Their certainties are so fanatic, the powers they claim so far-reaching. All their authority derives from computer-generated estimates that they wield like weapons, overwhelming any resistance with dumbfounding atom bombs of hypothetical human misery. Give them an inch, and they will commandeer all resources to fight just one disease. Who knows, they may defeat AIDS, but what if we wake up five years hence to discover that the problem has been blown out of all proportion by unsound estimates, causing upwards of $20 billion to be wasted?

—*Spectator*, December 2003

Postscript: This article was an act of war against the AIDS establishment, and I was repaid in kind. Interested parties might wish to consult the Treatment Action Campaign's forty-page rebuttal, which still dominates the results when you Google my name, or the Pugwash Group's retaliatory carpet-bombing. On a more colloquial level, there was a piece in the *Washington Post* that described me as dirty, smelly, and half-deranged, and a profile in *Insig* magazine in which I was held out to be a harmless "court jester" whose "AIDS dissident clown" routine was causing great amusement in the corridors of South African universities. "We find Malan no threat," wrote Muff Andersson. "When a national fool emerges, rushing in and affronting the angels, we tend to look at the audience's sense of enjoyment. His approach is below the belt, comical, carnivalesque . . ." and so on.

The interesting thing about this global outpouring of ridicule and venom is that no one challenged the important facts in my article—all that stuff about UNAIDS's malfunctioning model, perplexing census outcomes, serial downward revisions of South Africa's AIDS estimates, and embarrassing shortfalls in African teacher mortality. The problem with these claims is that they were true, which is why the AIDS establishment and its media outriders had no choice other than to shout me down or dismiss me as a crackpot, an exercise to which I unwittingly lent myself by cracking jokes about the insane folly of spending years on a story nobody wanted to hear, and that nobody was paying me for. "Malan admits he needs therapy," said the *Washington Post*. Ah, well. If you live by the sword, you die by it, too.

But even as the AIDS bwanas and I exchanged insults, an American scientist was putting the final touches to a book that would settle the debate. Dr. James Chin was a former head of the United Nations' global HIV program. He was also the creator of Epimodel, the computer simulator used to produce the dumbfounding estimates I found so implausible. Turns out that Dr. Chin agreed with me, and was about to disavow his own creation. In his book *The AIDS Pandemic*—subtitled "The Collision of Epidemiology with Political Correctness"—Chin acknowledged that "the story of AIDS has been distorted by UNAIDS and AIDS activists in order to support the myth of the high potential risk of HIV epidemics spreading into the general population. Most policymakers have uncritically accepted UNAIDS's high prevalence estimates when in fact lower estimates are more accurate. Time, money, and resources are being wasted worldwide." Chin thought AIDS infections had been overestimated by around 30 percent. Other scientists put the overestimation as high as 50 percent.

At more or less the same time, American researchers working in Kenya published the results of a so-called population survey, which involved testing blood from a representative sample of the population.

Using the system designed by James Chin, UNAIDS had previously claimed 15 percent of Kenya's adults were HIV-infected. The new study, universally held to be more credible, suggested that the real HIV rate was 6.7 percent. The implications were staggering. Overnight, the estimated number of HIV-stricken Kenyans plummeted from "as many as four million" to "as few as one million."

After that, Kenya-style population studies were carried out elsewhere in Africa, with similar results. In Ethiopia, for instance, estimated HIV prevalence tumbled by 80 percent. In Burundi, 64 percent. In Mali, 57 percent. In Burkina Faso, 35 percent. In Zambia, 26 percent. Such results came as no great surprise in South Africa, where a population study carried out in 2002 by the Human Sciences Research Council revealed an HIV infection rate around 30 percent lower than UN estimates. This finding was initially trashed by the AIDS establishment and downplayed by the media, but the HSRC held its ground and was ultimately vindicated.

Interestingly, the 2002 HSRC study revealed shocking HIV rates among South Africa's racial minorities, with (for instance) 6 percent of white adults and 11 percent of white children allegedly infected. These implausible numbers raised questions about those supposedly infallible blood tests, so a follow-up survey in 2005 featured a battery of previously unheard-of confirmatory procedures. The outcome: HIV prevalence among whites fell to 0.6 percent, a tenfold drop. In the colored community, HIV prevalence plummeted from 6 to 1.9 percent. In the Western Cape, five out of six computer-modeled HIV infections vanished.

These outbreaks of good news were generally ignored by the South African media, but the cat was escaping the bag. The *Washington Post* decided to take a closer look at Rwanda, held in the 1980s to be "the fountain of death" from which AIDS flowed out into the rest of Africa. "AIDS deaths on the predicted scale never arrived here," the *Post* reported. The *Lancet* published an article charging that Uganda's advances in the war on HIV were a myth sustained by researchers eager to show at least one success for the billions spent on HIV prevention. The *British Medical Journal* reported that AIDS was receiving a vastly disproportionate share of health aid, and that "billions" had consequently been wasted. "AIDS has been treated like an economic sector rather than a disease," said Roger England, chairman of the UK's Health Systems Network.

And so the wheel began to turn. In 2001, when *Rolling Stone* asked, "Who agrees with you," I had to say nobody. By 2007, even UNAIDS had acknowledged that its estimates for Africa were flawed, and the painful process of correcting distorted spending priorities was under way. I will refrain from crowing, because AIDS is a serious problem in Africa. Almost every article I wrote on the subject acknowledged that point, if only in passing. My enemies and I differed largely on the question of degree.

In South Africa, we also disagreed on the question of timing. Back in 2000, at the height of the Mbeki AIDS furor, the U.S. Census Bureau stated that South Africa's AIDS problem was so severe that the population would start shrinking by 2003. When 2003 rolled around, however, our numbers were growing at a fairly health rate, and experts were beginning to acknowledge, sotto voce, that mistakes had been made. "The number of people dying of AIDS has only now started to increase," said a note on the Medical Research Council's Web site toward the end of 2003.

The MRC was right. Over the next four years, the death toll among people I knew personally began to increase. I remain skeptical of computer-generated estimates, but by 2007 the anecdotal evidence was overwhelming: the phantom catastrophe of 1999 had become real; considerable numbers of people were dying, and the legions who'd mocked and jeered Mbeki considered themselves vindicated.

This is profoundly unfair. Back in 1999, when Thabo Mbeki first rose in parliament to question the veracity of HIV science, UNAIDS was claiming that we were already living through an apocalypse, with AIDS killing a quarter million that year alone. This estimate was nonsense. Hindsight reveals that the real AIDS death toll in 1999 was closer to sixty thousand—fewer than a quarter of the number claimed by the AIDS establishment.

Put yourself in Mbeki's shoes. The highest scientific authorities on the planet were telling him that South Africa was passing through the worst catastrophe in its history, that AIDS had in a single year killed more South Africans than all the wars we ever fought among ourselves and against Britain and Germany. But when he looked around, there was a yodeling chasm between the UNAIDS's claims and the reality we were all then experiencing.

It's much to Mbeki's credit that he refused to crook the knee and praise the naked emperor's glorious raiments. It was not he who lost his head; it was the army of hysterics who believed every word uttered by the High Priests of HIV in Geneva. Mbeki was right to ask questions. His mistake was to accept the first answer given—AIDS could be a hoax—and proceed accordingly. Once he'd taken that position, he was too proud to back down, and a terrible price was exacted.

PART FOUR
TRUTH

A TRUTH OF SORTS

In the time of the Truth and Reconciliation Commission (1996–1998), every newspaper I read left me feeling as if someone were prodding at my anus with a broomstick, with a view to punishing me for being white, Afrikaans, and male. The only way to escape such indignities was to join the fawning ingrates who pretended that imperialism, colonialism, and apartheid were someone else's doing, but I was incapable. I thought my ancestors had done many stupid and vicious things since landing here in 1688. I even accepted the fashionable doctrine of collective guilt, but I wanted the charges formulated with some degree of precision, and I wanted the chance to defend myself. It seemed to me that whites who didn't take this line were forfeiting any claim to honor and, worse yet, putting themselves in a position from which they'd never recover politically. So I sharpened my pen and set forth to assail the commission's easy truths and glib pieties.

Truth Commissioner Mary Burton was upset. She wiped a stray lock of hair off her forehead and said, "The number of people who can say, 'I didn't know,' is too great to bear."

It was the final hour of the TRC's hearings on the role of the media under apartheid, and Mrs. Burton was nearing the end of her tether. The former Black Sash chairwoman had been sitting there for days, listening to grim testimony about the rape of truth during the apartheid

167

era. Ex–security policeman Craig Williamson had provided an analysis of the apartheid state's propaganda master plan. Two newsroom spies had been unmasked. Colonel Vic McPherson, former head of apartheid's Stratcom mind-control machine, had talked about his network of newsroom sources and informers.

Several black editors recalled the days of segregated canteens, distorted news values, and sinister injunctions from white editors to "tone it down" or be fired. Rashid Seria told of black journalists "shot, harrassed, and tortured." Don Mattera talked about "a holocaust of truth and of black lives." Jon Qwelane accused the mainstream press of "having a hand, directly or indirectly, in the murder of tens of thousands of black people." Max du Preez fleshed out the contention with a list of stories broken by *Vrye Weekblad* but ignored by the collaborationist bosses of the commercial media, who could, he charged, have stopped the killing and torture if they'd stood up for justice.

All that remained was for a Boer to step forth and heap the ashes of remorse on his head, lamenting his ignorance and castigating those responsible for it. "I did not know," said Professor Arnold de Beer of Potchefstroom University. "I remained silent when I should have protested. I was an accessory whose inaction allowed the shadow of apartheid to spread across the nation."

This, it seemed, was what the commissioners had been hoping to hear. "One can only hope there are more people like you," said TRC investigations chief Dumisa Ntsebeza, clearly taken by the spectacle of a Boer on his knees. Mrs. Burton made her remark about the unbearable extent of apartheid-induced ignorance, and that was more or less that. The commissioners thanked the witnesses and retired to write their report, which will be based, one fears, on the premise that most South African journalists were tools of apartheid, witting or otherwise, and collectively complicit in the suppression of truth on a massive scale—"denial of the human right to know," as Jon Qwelane phrased it.

South Africa, as the cliché has it, is a land of contradictions, a place where mutually annihilating truths can be simultaneously valid. It is true, for instance, that we once had—at least on paper—one of the world's harshest regimes of press censorship, and that many people remain justifiably upset about it. It is also true that the English press was timid and centrist, that the South African Broadcasting Corporation was a state propaganda tool, and that the Afrikaans papers were so many Boer *Pravda*s, slavishly loyal to the government of the day. But whether this adds up to the crime against humanity alleged before the TRC is open to debate.

In fact, I would argue that Jon Qwelane has it upside down: far from being suppressed, the grim facts of apartheid were exaggerated by decades of ceaseless anti-Pretoria propaganda. Indeed, bad press was the primary cause of the National Party's downfall, at least insofar as it triggered a wave of revulsion in the West that, in turn, led to sanctions and a massive inflow of apartheid-fighting dollars to bankroll the trade unions, churches, and NGOs that ultimately brought the tyrants to their knees.

Much of the credit goes to the foreign media, of course, but the staid old aunties of the English press did their bit, too, patiently chipping away at the story for decades. The precise details might have remained obscure, but readers of the *Star* and its sister papers were left in little doubt that the police were vicious, the cabinet full of brutes and liars, and dark deeds afoot in secret police cells. In apartheid South Africa, the violence of "the system" was almost always systematic— every bullet had to be accounted for, and every corpse subjected to a postmortem, followed by an inquest at which the police would put forth fatuous explanations that were duly ridiculed in editorials, lampooned in cartoons, raised in parliament by Helen Suzman, picked up by the foreign press for worldwide amplification, and ultimately synthesized into novels and plays and Hollywood epics of *A Dry White Season* variety. In the end, there were even pop songs about apartheid on the world's hit parades. Only the willfully self-blinded could have failed to notice, and they have no one but themselves to blame.

As for Colonel McPherson and his Stratcom cronies, they were anything but the diabolical propaganda masterminds of popular imaginings. On the contrary: they were losers, and pathetically incompetent to boot. By the time their war ended, Pretoria had the most widely vilified and discredited government on the planet. Nothing it said was ever believed, even when it was telling the truth. Afrikaners had sunk so low in the world's estimation that even respectable media organs like *Newsweek* had taken to opining that liberal clergyman Beyers Naudé was the only Boer worth saving. The rest of us were racists, fascists, genocidal maniacs. Comparisons between Nazi Germany and apartheid were taken seriously everywhere.

And still are, for that matter. Consider the results of a small and entirely unscientific poll conducted among my friends and acquaintances, to each of whom the following question was put: how many political detainees died in the dungeons of the secret police during four decades of apartheid terror? "Around four hundred," said Steve Sidley, a Johannesburg computer analyst. "One thousand," said journalist Philippa Garson. "Fifteen thousand?" guessed Morgan Entrekin, a New York publisher. "Oh, about four hundred thousand," said Susan Minot, an American novelist en route to Lesotho.

The correct figure, according to Archbishop Tutu's Truth Commission, is seventy-two—an average of just under two a year between 1948 and 1990. That's seventy-two too many, and a brutal way to make a point, but still, the question stands: from whence came such skewed apprehensions? From the media, of course—a fact at serious odds with heated charges of truth suppression made before the TRC.

How does one reconcile these contradictions? Perhaps the easiest way is to acknowledge that the flow of news about apartheid was controlled by two forms of censorship. One was imposed by Pretoria in its ham-fisted and generally unsuccessful attempts to shield misdeeds from public view. The other was an invisible force that acted on the hearts and minds of apartheid's journalistic enemies. Looking back, it's sometimes hard to say which was the more powerful of the two.

In 1989, an academic quarterly commissioned me to do a study of the U.S. media's coverage of South Africa, and lest it seems that what I am about to say applies only to gormless Yankees, please bear in mind that the Americans' local operation had a rather South African complexion when you looked at it closely. The mighty TV networks hired scores of South African researchers, fixers, and cameramen. Allister

Sparks (now head of SABC TV news) was writing for the *Washington Post*. The *New York Times*'s correspondent was John Battersby, now editor of the *Sunday Independent*. Phillip van Niekerk, now editor of the *Weekly Mail & Guardian*, was working for the *Boston Globe*. Apartheid was an extremely hot story at the time, with the bitingly articulate and enormously telegenic Winnie Mandela always at center stage.

The American media's love affair with Winnie began in earnest toward the end of 1985, when she moved back to Soweto in defiance of her banning order. In the ensuing year, she made seventy appearances on network television and merited twenty-two stories in the hugely influential *New York Times*, more than most heads of state. Scores of flattering magazine profiles were written, and HBO produced a teleplay. She was nominated for a Nobel Peace Prize and showered with honorary degrees. She was one of the most famous women in the world, the brave and selfless Mother of the Nation.

She was also in deepening trouble in Soweto, where her thuggish palace guards were committing dark deeds the American press refused to look at, even when they were aired in court in broad daylight. Circa 1986, Winnie's henchmen were accused of hunting down and executing two Soweto men who'd defeated them in a shebeen fistfight. No stories appeared in America's papers of record. A few months later, they were accused of etching struggle slogans into the flesh of suspected informers during a torture session at the Mandela home. Again, no stories. On July 28, 1988, they dragged a schoolgirl off the street and raped her, providing journalists with a very big story indeed: a mob burned Winnie's house down in retaliation.

A funny thing happened, though: no one reported it that way. Local papers noted the event, but their stories were extraordinarily elliptical—the consequence, Jon Qwelane once told me, of terror: the *Star*'s bosses feared for their delivery fleet, and black reporters feared the necklace, a uniquely South African means of getting rid of "enemies of the people," who were frequently adorned with old car tires, doused with gasoline, and burned alive. The *Washington Post* attributed the attack to faceless "vandals," while CBS spoke of an amorphous "black gang." Nobody said anything about rape and retaliation. As for

NBC, it sidestepped the truth entirely and presented the incident as yet another apartheid atrocity in a report so detailed that it took up more than half the prime-time newscast. Trevor Tutu, son of the famous archbishop, made much of the fire brigade's tardy arrival. The revolutionary cleric Allan Boesak said he knew for a fact that "the system" was to blame. In the end, NBC's man on the spot knelt solemnly at Winnie's feet and invited her to comment on her suffering at the hands of Boer racists.

And this, I'm afraid, was par for the course for the American media. In fact, it was par for almost everyone else, too; Winnie enjoyed almost total immunity from criticism until January 1989, when her own comrades denounced her misdeeds and sanctioned the publication of negative stories. Prior to that point, Afrikaans newspapers were clueless, the state broadcaster asleep on its feet. The English press looked the other way, and foreigners buried their heads in the sand lest they damage a myth of their own creation. Only two reporters broke the taboo, and the consequences were unsettling. Peter Godwin of the London *Sunday Times* received death threats after reporting that Winnie was becoming an embarrassment to her cause. Nomavenda Mathiane, who provided *Frontline* with an eyewitness account of a kangaroo court at which Winnie presided, wound up trapped in a Braamfontein bank while Mrs. Mandela's bodyguards bayed for her blood on the pavement outside.

It seems odd that we didn't hear a bit more of this at the TRC's hearings, especially from black journalists like Jon Qwelane, Aggrey Klaaste, and Thami Mazwai, who cut their teeth in the struggle years and are now household names in the South African media. To a man, they were once supporters of the Black Consciousness movement Azapo, and they paid a price for it in 1986, when the ANC's young lions set out to obliterate Azapo's township structures. Around seventy people died in that war, the precise nature of which black reporters were too scared to explain for fear of incurring the murderous wrath of "a certain movement," a phrase that became an accepted usage in the *Sowetan* for a while. Azapo members would die at the hands of "supporters of a certain movement." Azapo leaders would beg "a certain movement" to control its unruly youth. American newspaper readers were spared such painful circumlocutions, because American newspapers didn't cover the ANC-Azapo feud at all.

Asked about such lapses, American hacks made lame excuses about "confusion" and the "complexity" of South African politics, but the truth is simpler: they didn't want to spoil the plot. Apartheid South Africa was supposed to be the one place on the planet where everything was simple, the one hard rock in a global swamp of relativistic equivocation. There were no communists in the American portrayal, no revolutionaries who believed it was acceptable to break eggs in order to achieve the desired Sovietist omelette. The ANC was almost always portrayed as an army of hymn-singing moderates in the sentimental American civil rights tradition. Anyone who disagreed too strongly was racist or reactionary, if not an apartheid spy. Under the circumstances, the stories most likely to be ignored or suppressed were those that reflected poorly on the forces of liberation.

Consider the case of five ragged young ANC deserters who showed up in Kenya in May 1990, having walked hundreds of miles in search of food, shelter, and a sympathetic ear for a story no one wanted to hear. They were about to be thrown out of Nairobi's press center when Julian Ozanne, a young freelancer who grew up in southern Africa, recognized their accents and invited them to come home with him. Forty-eight hours later, Ozanne filed a story so explosive that the London-based *Sunday Correspondent* declined to run it before checking with their man in South Africa—Shaun Johnson, now editorial director of the Independent Newspapers group.

Back came a seventeen-point memo tearing the article to shreds. The tone of Johnson's missive, says Ozanne, was one of amused contempt: "Your stringer in Nairobi is clearly a naive young chap who has no understanding of South Africa," and so on. "His argument was, 'I'm an expert on the ANC. I know these guys. The allegations in this story are rubbish.'" The *Sunday Correspondent* went back to Ozanne, who filed thirty-five pages of supporting material. The issue hung in the balance for days before the paper decided to override Johnson's objections and run the story. "Shaun was furious," says Ozanne. "He said, 'We're going to be laughed out of South Africa for this. I'm not going to be your correspondent anymore.'"

And the nature of the story Johnson didn't want printed? It was the first account of life inside ANC detention camps, where guerrillas who'd fallen afoul of the movement's arbitrary and paranoid security system were locked up in coffinlike cages, whipped, tortured, and sometimes executed. The revelations were a mortification for Nelson Mandela, who was about to embark on his first post-release tour of Europe, and also, presumably, for Johnson himself, because his faith in the ANC was palpably sincere and deep-seated.

And this did not necessarily mark him a maverick in the English newspaper culture of the time. On the contrary, his faith was shared by many of his colleagues and even his bosses, who rewarded his generally pro-ANC stance with plenty of space and rapid promotions, which would tend to prove a second point: claims of martyrdom to the contrary, condemning apartheid was the smart option for South African hacks. If you were good at it, you were promoted and praised. If you were particularly good, you might get elevated to the ranks of international TV network fixer or foreign correspondent, in which case the hard currency rewards were intoxicating. The downside risk was so small as to be barely measurable—unless you were working for one of the alternative newspapers, in which case the security police were liable to keep an eye on you, or for the armed underground, in which case you might land in real trouble.

How many of us were playing that game? It's impossible to say, but one couldn't help wondering as former *Star* reporter Craig Kotze struggled to explain his motives for joining the security police as an undercover agent. "Everybody was forced to choose sides," he said, and having had his fill of "arbitrary revolutionary violence," Kotze chose the side of the police, the government, and law and order. His link with the state was supposed to be secret, but Kotze wore his heart on his sleeve and the truth was widely suspected. As a result, Kotze claims he was subjected to "high levels of psychological intimidation" and the occasional anonymous death threat.

His TRC audience rolled its eyes and tittered, but this had the ring of truth to me. South African journalism became a bitterly contested site of struggle in apartheid's declining years. The newsroom in which I worked in the 1970s featured a copy editor widely (and correctly, as it turns out) suspected to be a Stratcom agent. John Horak was an isolated and despised figure. We'd snub him in the corridors and get up and leave if he joined our table in the staff canteen.

We didn't threaten to kill him, but as the struggle intensified, attitudes hardened. Of the dozen or so friends I made in those years, two or three evolved into volunteers for the ANC, using their pens as weapons against apartheid and occasionally hiding guns or fugitives in their homes. Another three became full-time secret agents, using journalism as a cover for spying. One worked for Stasi, the notorious East German secret police. Another ran a small press agency in a neighboring state while smuggling Soviet arms on the side. Howard Barrell (whose name I use because he has already come clean) joined the ANC's intelligence service in the early 1980s and used his position as a reporter to further the movement's propaganda objectives.

If I knew three, how many reporters were secretly working for the ANC and its allies? Certainly more than Stratcom, which had only two full-time agents in place in the late 1980s, according to TRC testimony. And did ANC agents serve the truth any more than Craig Kotze or John Horak? Only if you accept that all propaganda is truth told from a certain point of view, with embarrassing contradictions excised.

Mary Burton believes there was too little truth in our coverage of apartheid. I believe there was too little in our coverage of those fighting to bring it down. The truth probably lies somewhere between.

—*Frontiers of Freedom*, volume 15, 1998

THE QUEEN

I *met Winnie Mandela once. It was a rainy night in the early 1990s, and I'd been dragged to a primary school concert by a friend. At the time, Sacred Heart convent was the school of choice for the ANC's senior leaders, and several of the tiny ballerinas twirling around on stage had last names like Sisulu or Mandela. I was standing outside the hall, smoking, when Comrade Winnie turned up to fetch a granddaughter. We fell into conversation, and I wound up bewitched, for lack of a better term. Winnie was beautiful and charming. Her dark eyes danced, and her laughter was infectious. As for hauteur, there was no sign of it. On the contrary, she seemed to derive genuine pleasure from this chance encounter with a grubby white stranger. What can I say? Winnie was a star. When the concert ended and she drove away, the light in that foyer seemed to fade to gray.*

This will sound trite, but I found it hard to reconcile the woman I met that night with the monster I'd been reading about for years. I searched her eyes for signs of evil, but none were apparent. I found myself wondering (for the thousandth time) whether the charges brought against her were really the fruit of secret police dirty tricks and black propaganda campaigns, as she'd always claimed. As the years wore on, that seemed less and less likely, but the enchantment lingered. When her case came up before the Truth Commission, I persuaded London's Independent on Sunday *to let me cover it.*

176

"This is witchcraft," said Governor Mntonga, the house painter from Malawi. It was a hot Wednesday in Johannesburg and we should have been working but the Winnie Mandela hearings were live on TV so we'd been glued to the set all morning. Winnie's former henchman-in-chief, Jerry Richardson, was on the witness stand, looking debonair in his dark suit and flashy gold rings, regaling the nation with tales of torture and murder. And then, around noon, the lights went out in the hall where the hearing was under way. I could have sworn it was just a power failure, but Governor thought otherwise. It was, he said, an indication that Winnie's powerful magic was finally kicking in.

Unlikely, I thought, but it was certainly a turning point. The hearings had been under way for eight days and had hitherto been a nightmare for Mrs. Madikizela-Mandela. The erstwhile "Mother of the Nation" and present-day candidate for the deputy presidency of the ruling African National Congress had been called before the Truth and Reconciliation Commission to discuss the reign of terror perpetrated by the Mandela United Football Club, a loose aggregation of homeless teenagers, guerrillas, and struggle fanatics who took up residence in her backyard in 1986, dubbed the "Year of People's War" by ANC commissars.

Bearing nicknames such as Ninja, Killer, Scorpion and Slash, the youngsters' true function was less to play soccer than to assist Mrs. Mandela's drive to render Soweto ungovernable, a noble enterprise that ultimately degenerated into a confused mess of kangaroo courts, gang-style feuds between rival factions, and cannibalistic witch hunts for sellouts and spies. As many as sixteen people died at the hands of the Mandela footballers, according to press reports, and several team members—including Jerry Richardson—had landed in prison on charges ranging from armed robbery to murder.

Mrs. Mandela's role in all this was under consideration. Several witnesses announced that they were tired of lying to protect her and would now tell the truth, which appeared to be hair-raising. Mrs. Mandela, it was claimed, had often presided at meetings of the club's "disciplinary committee," where offenders were sentenced to torture or beatings in which she and her daughter Zinzi allegedly participated with relish. A convicted assassin swore that Winnie had offered him R20,000 to knock off a potentially troublesome doctor. Three mothers claimed she'd had their children abducted or murdered. Five eyewitnesses—including Katiza Cebekhulu, who had been hurled into a dungeon in Zambia so that he couldn't testify at Winnie's criminal trial—alleged that Winnie had led the assault on Stompie Seipei, the child activist famously butchered by Winnie's sidekicks in January 1989.

The climax came on day eight, when Jerry Richardson admitted that it was he who had committed the foul deed and three additional murders besides, all at the behest of the woman he called Mommy. "I killed Stompie on the instruction of Mrs. Mandela," he cried, pointing across the hall. "She does not even visit us in prison! She used us!" Until that moment, the noose appeared to be tightening around Winnie's neck, but then the power failed and events began to turn in her favor.

Hitherto quite jocular and cocky, Richardson suddenly seemed unnerved. "I get scared when the lights go out," he said, peering around apprehensively. They came back on moments later but Richardson never quite regained his poise. Within minutes, he'd been forced to acknowledge that he was a police informer, an admission that destroyed his credibility with black South Africans. Soon after, he began to ramble incoherently, answering in non sequiturs. At one point, he delved into his briefcase and insisted that the commission study photographs of people who seemed to have no relevance whatsoever to the proceedings. By day's end, Richardson had become a jabbering ruin, incapable of answering any questions at all. Things were looking up for Mrs. Madikizela-Mandela.

Next morning, she showed up in a pair of rhinestone-encrusted spectacles that gave her face a strangely reptilian aspect. She looked like a turtle: heavy, slow-moving, totally nerveless and inscrutable behind her tinted lenses. Her counterattack was based on the hallucinatory premise that the Mandela United Football Club had ceased to exist at the time of its reign of terror. Her husband had ordered her to disband it in April 1987, and she had obeyed. How then could she be held to account for alleged club misdeeds that had taken place months or years later?

Lawyers pointed out that she had been filmed as late as February 1989, surrounded by youths in full Mandela United regalia. Winnie conceded that she hadn't the heart to take fancy tracksuits away from poverty-stricken working-class lads. Otherwise, the point stood: there was no such thing as a football club after April 1987, and as for the murderous "disciplinary committee" over which she had allegedly presided, this was the first she'd heard of it. For the rest, her accusers were variously lunatic, deluded, mistaken, deranged, drunk, senile, pawns of the secret police, or victims of police brutality forced to make accusations against her under torture. Anyone who disagreed too strongly was regally censured: "I will not tolerate you speaking to me like that! I will not!"

There was something hypnotic about these blunt denials and their steady repetition. Winnie didn't counter accusations; she annihilated them with refutations so sweeping that her questioners were left gaping, as if socked in the stomach. She said she had never even met several of her alleged victims, or else barely remembered them. She had no idea why the ANC's internal wing had found it necessary, in 1988, to set up a crisis committee to curb her behavior. She had no recollection of this committee begging her to release Stompie and his three fellow captives, because they had never been captives in the first place, or if they had been, it was none of her doing, because she could not—"for God's sake"—be held responsible for the actions of all the waifs and runaways who had taken shelter on her premises.

Yes, there had been a "perception" that some of them were running amok, but it had been vastly exaggerated by the apartheid state's disinformation machine and her enemies in "the cabal," a grouping within the ANC that was supposedly out to get her. Toward the end, commissioner Yasmin Sooka put it to her that she was forcing listeners toward a rather improbable conclusion: "If we believe your evidence, everyone else is lying." Winnie smiled. "Yes," she said. "It's true."

Appearances to the contrary, Ms. Sooka could not have been surprised, because all this was a replay of a closed-door hearing five weeks earlier, where Winnie had countered all charges with similar blanket denials. Why was the Truth Commission allowing her to get away with it? In cases involving white policemen, the commission has shown no lenience. Indeed, all its breakthroughs have been the consequence of months of investigation by TRC staff who smashed alibis and sought out new evidence, forcing the guilty to seek amnesty rather than face criminal charges and possible life imprisonment.

No similar efforts seemed to have been made in Winnie's case. The various Ninjas and Killers who once lived in her garden remained names on yellowing police statements. No new evidence was brought forth to break your-word-versus-mine deadlocks of many years' standing. Indications that Winnie had perjured herself in her 1991 Stompie trial were allowed to go unpunished, and alarming allegations of witness intimidation went largely unexamined.

Consider the case of Mike Seakamela, whose testimony might have wiped the smirk off Mrs. Madikizela-Mandela's face if he'd showed up to testify as scheduled. Once a driver in Winnie's employ, Seakamela is possibly the only source capable of verifying a story provided to the TRC by Nicodemus Sono. A plump office worker in his early fifties, Nicodemus once had a son named Lolo and a nephew named Tebogo, the latter of whom left the country to undergo military training. When Tebogo returned to Soweto in 1988, carrying a bag of hand grenades and an AK-47 assault rifle, sixteen-year-old Lolo became his courier, scuttling back and forth between Tebogo and Winnie Mandela, a fellow operative in the ANC's underground army.

On November 9, 1988, Tebogo was betrayed, and he and a comrade died in a fusillade of police bullets. It emerged this week that the real traitor was Winnie's confidant Jerry Richardson, but at the time, Lolo Sono was the prime suspect. He and a friend were allegedly picked up and subjected to a savage interrogation by Winnie's football team. Later that night, a powder-blue microbus turned up outside the Sono home. Nicodemus Sono was called outside. He saw his son sitting in the back of the vehicle, bloodied and shivering. He begged Winnie to let the boy go, but she refused. "The movement will decide what to do with this dog," she said as the microbus pulled away. It was the last anyone saw of Lolo Sono.

His father has been telling this story for years, and Winnie has always dismissed it as a fantasy, occasionally imputing that the boy had actually fallen afoul of the security police and been blown up along the border. The only man capable of breaking the deadlock was Mike Seakamela, who was in the blue microbus on the night of Lolo's disappearance and who provided critical corroboration of the father's evidence. Mike made a statement to the police in 1988, but they failed to act on it. He repeated his contention in 1995, but the second statement also vanished, along with the original case file. He informed the Truth Commission that he was willing to testify this week, but when the day came he failed to show. Lawyers said he'd received a visit from Winnie and gone into hiding. Winnie denied this, along with everything else, and there the matter ended.

In the hearing's closing moments, Archbishop Tutu was reduced to begging for a display of remorse from the obdurate figure on the witness stand. "You are an icon," he told Winnie, "a stalwart of the liberation struggle. You have no idea how your greatness will be enhanced if you said, 'Sorry, things went horribly, horribly wrong.' Please," he concluded, almost sobbing. "I beg you. I beg you. I beg you."

Winnie shot a glance at her lawyer, who nodded. Then she turned back to Tutu, smiled condescendingly, and tossed him a crumb or two. "It's true that things went horribly wrong," she said, pausing before adding a critical rider: ". . . when we were away. For that I am deeply sorry." She appended a murmur of compassion for the bereaved next of kin, and that was the end of that. The hearing was over, and Winnie had somehow emerged largely unscathed. Pundits were left scratching their heads. Governor Mntonga said, Told you so.

—*Independent on Sunday* (London), December 1997

Postscript: A week or two later, in Mafikeng, Winnie was persuaded to abandon her run for the ANC's deputy presidency. But she remained a parliamentary backbencher, constantly fulminating against the Great

Compromise engineered by her former husband, and exhorting the masses to push for true revolution. These positions earned her a following that seemed totally impervious to ongoing scandals. In 2002, parliament complained that Winnie was refusing to account for outrageous expense claims. In 2003, she was found guilty of fraudulently abstracting money from the ANC Women's League's funeral fund and sentenced to five years' imprisonment, reduced to a fine on appeal. None of this dented her popularity. When she stood for election to the ANC's national executive in 2007, she came first, an outcome that confirmed her standing: Winnie Mandela was, and remained, the queen.

Novelist Achmat Dangor once wrote a short story about a Winnie-like figure who rises from her bed on the night of "the old president's" death, declaring, "The time has come." She rouses the masses, marches on the capital, and puts half the cabinet before a firing squad, along with an innocent bystander whose squint strikes her as an evil omen. Elsewhere in the world, this would be magic realism. In South Africa, it was social comment of an oddly ominous variety.

A QUESTION OF SPIN

An early version of this piece appeared in Frontiers of Freedom, *the quarterly journal of South Africa's venerable Institute of Race Relations. I wanted to call it "South Africa's Reichstag Fire," but staff at the institute felt this was needlessly provocative. They were probably right, but there were some uncomfortable parallels between that event and the Boipatong massacre.*

This is a story about South Africa's Truth and Reconciliation Commission, but it properly begins in August 1992, when I authored a shallow and facetious article in *Esquire* magazine about the infamous Boipatong massacre. Anyone who lived through Boipatong and its aftermath will recall that it seemed a watershed, an event on the scale of the Sharpeville shootings of 1961 or the Soweto uprising of 1976. Nelson Mandela said, "South Africa will never be the same again," and I believed him. It thus seemed terribly important to establish what really happened in that tiny Vaal Triangle township in forty-five fateful minutes on the night of June 17. I set forth to find out but failed, and then resorted to the classic expedient of the slack reporter, the story of how I tried to get the story. It was not my finest hour.

So I acquired the habit of clipping newspapers in the hope that the truth might one day emerge. Six years passed. Four public inquiries were held. I wound up with a crate of documents that traveled with me from city to city. Friends left the room when I began talking about its contents, which were arcane beyond comprehension. By October 1998, I seemed to be the only person interested, judging by the silence that greeted the TRC's Boipatong findings. There were no news stories on the subject, probably because the TRC had simply confirmed a narrative that most South Africans already took for granted. But was it true?

It will take many thousands of words to answer that question, and you will almost certainly suffer boredom en route. All I can promise is that by the end, you will be better positioned to assess the manner in which the TRC worked, the nature of its biases, and the gravity of a finding that will be with us, as Archbishop Desmond Tutu put it, "for generations."

Why should anyone care?

Most accounts of South Africa's perilous transition hold that the Boipatong massacre caused a breakdown of peace talks between Nelson Mandela's African National Congress and the government of President F. W. de Klerk, a development that almost plunged the country into war. This is untrue. The talks actually died a month earlier, on May 15, 1992, as the result of a deadlock engineered by the ANC's chief negotiator, Cyril Ramaphosa. Several insider accounts published after the event confirm that Ramaphosa had lost patience with government demands for a mechanism that would make it almost impossible for the ANC to change constitutional principles once they'd been agreed to at the negotiating table. Rather than compromise on this issue, Ramaphosa argued that the ANC should simply drive De Klerk's government out of power with "rolling mass action"—a coordinated wave of strikes, street protests, and factory occupations. Moderates cautioned that Ramaphosa was playing "an intensely dangerous game," but they were overruled; on May 15, Ramaphosa presented De Klerk's team with an ultimatum he knew would be refused, and the peace talks deadlocked.

In ensuing weeks, it became clear that South Africa was heading toward an apocalyptic showdown in which the central issue would be political violence, which was then claiming around sixty lives a week. The ANC and its allies blamed all such violence on a nebulous "Third Force" of tribal conservatives, secretly armed and controlled by De Klerk's generals. De Klerk countered that the real cause was a ruthless power struggle between the ANC and its chief rival, the Zulu nationalist movement Inkatha.

De Klerk also warned that a return to mass action would inevitably worsen the mayhem. The ANC laughed this off, claiming that its coming campaign would be nonviolent, but residents of Boipatong may have formed a different impression. In early June 1992, a commissar of the ANC's underground army appeared on the front page of their local newspaper, vowing to "arm thousands" and turn the area into a "liberated zone." Communist Party boss Chris Hani made a speech in nearby Sebokeng, warning militants that they were "facing a war situation." Meanwhile, Mandela was touring Europe, drumming up support for the ANC's forthcoming push for power. At several stops, he likened F. W. de Klerk's regime to Hitler's. This was war talk. Stomachs began to knot everywhere.

The mass action campaign began quietly on June 16, when a mere ten thousand supporters turned out to see Mandela open a memorial in Soweto. (Some reports put the figure as low as two thousand.) Barely five thousand attended a similar launch event in Cape Town. This fell woefully short of the million-strong demonstrations envisaged by ANC radicals. A spark was clearly necessary to rekindle flagging anti-apartheid passions and one came on the night of June 17, when an army of five hundred men fell on the ANC stronghold of Boipatong, perpetrating a ghastly slaughter of innocents. Women were raped, babies were axed, countless houses were ransacked, and forty-five people were murdered. Scores more were injured, causing the death toll to rise, ultimately, to forty-nine.

At first glance, the atrocity appeared to be the work of Inkatha members wreaking vengeance on a community perceived to support the ANC. As such, it was of little use to ANC spin doctors. If whites and police were implicated, on the other hand, they had something to work with. ANC leaders therefore insisted that Boipatong was no ordinary outbreak of "black on black violence," preferring to depict it as a "carefully planned and executed strategic operation," with white police and soldiers providing logistic support to the Zulu attackers and mysterious white gunmen taking part in the killing. In other words, a Third Force operation, organized by F. W. de Klerk and his apartheid state.

Before Boipatong, F. W. de Klerk's stature was surging, especially in the international arena. After the massacre, he was just another racist, presiding over a security force of "beasts." Ignoring the fact that his own negotiators had already forced a stalemate, Nelson Mandela announced that he was pulling out of peace talks. "I can no longer explain why we keep on talking to men who are conducting a war against us," he said. His underlings moved to sabotage South Africa's planned readmission to the Olympic Games. In Europe and the United States, reliable old warhorses of the anti-apartheid movement lumbered back onto the battlefield, demanding a return to sanctions and international isolation. Coretta Scott King voiced "outrage." Church of England Archbishop Trevor Huddleston said, "We in the West have forgotten how to hate." There was a huge outcry at the United Nations, which devoted a special sitting to Boipatong. On the ground, violence intensified, and South Africa began to slide into the abyss.

By September, De Klerk and his negotiators were so exhausted that they caved in, making far-reaching concessions to get the peace talks going again. Beyond that point, the ANC began to dictate the pace of change, and wound up a year later with a constitution so weak in terms of minority protections that the comrades (in U.S. journalist Patti Waldmeir's account) walked away laughing, claiming that the Boers had given the farm away.

It could thus be argued, for better or worse, that Boipatong determined the shape of the society we live in today. That's why we should care. In particular, we should care about the widely held perception that De Klerk's security forces planned and executed a murderous rampage designed to block progress toward democracy. We will now consider the case for and against.

A grand conspiracy arises

Located some forty miles south of Johannesburg, Boipatong is a place of tiny face-brick houses loomed over by the smokestacks of a giant steelworks. It is a small township, isolated from others, and surrounded by factories that provide jobs that tend to be well paid in South African terms. Until June 17, 1992, Boipatong was considered a fairly desirable place to live. Then night fell, and something terrible happened.

Just before 9 p.m., a motorist called police, saying he'd seen an ominous mass of men crossing a road and disappearing into a stretch of dark industrial wasteland on Boipatong's western outskirts. Shortly thereafter, police were inundated by calls from Boipatong residents who claimed to be under attack by "Zulus" based in KwaMadala, a disused migrant labor barracks over the road.

The first reporters to arrive on the scene the following morning were greeted by an extraordinary sight: a Zulu *impi* advancing on Boipatong in front of hundreds of witnesses, and nothing to stop them but a thin line of nervous policemen. Boipatong's ANC comrades had regrouped during the night and were threatening to launch a retaliatory strike against KwaMadala. The Inkatha-supporting Zulus sallied forth to meet them, armed to the teeth with sticks and spears and drenched with battle medicine, apparently determined to fight a second round in broad daylight, in front of the world's TV cameras. These men were part of a covert conspiracy? At first glance, it seemed unlikely, but ANC propagandists rose to the challenge.

The first claims of police complicity were made around 11 a.m. that day by ANC spokesman Ronnie Mamoepa. At the time, nobody had a clear idea of what had happened in Boipatong the previous night. Mamoepa was so ignorant of the facts that he put the death toll at five, but no matter, it was time to join battle. "The attackers were brought into the township in police Casspirs," Mamoepa stated. (The Casspir is an armored personnel carrier.) The police, he continued, had ignored warnings that Boipatong was about to be ransacked. Indeed, they had prepared the ground for the invaders by chasing ANC self-defense units off the streets with "tear gas and live ammunition" before the attack commenced.

"Shortly thereafter," Mamoepa said, "police were seen escorting groups of armed men into the township. The armed men attacked the township with an assortment of weapons, including firearms. In those homes where the attackers could not gain entry, police used Casspirs to break down walls and enable the attackers to assault residents and to loot their furniture and other valuables." In some cases, he concluded, the attackers were seen loading loot onto police or army vehicles.

In the next twenty-four hours, this theme was embellished and hugely amplified by the press, aided by violence monitors from ANC-aligned NGOs like the Human Rights Commission and Peace Action. These "peace activists" took reporters and diplomats around Boipatong and introduced them to eyewitnesses who backed the ANC's claims. Trusted journalists were granted special access to "hundreds" of witness statements said to contain damning evidence about the presence of whites among the attackers. Some were said to be uniformed policemen. Others were described as wearing military-style camouflage gear. There were reports of white men in blackface, in balaclavas, even a white man armed with a spear. By week's end, Boipatong was as famous in its way as Buchenwald or Mai Lai, and observers had little reason to doubt where the blame lay. "I hold De Klerk personally responsible," said Cyril Ramaphosa. The entire planet seemed to add, Amen.

The grand conspiracy shows cracks

Let us step now into the mind of President F. W. de Klerk, who woke up on the morning of June 18 to find himself stigmatized as the "satanic" butcher of Boipatong. Powerless to halt the propaganda juggernaut, he did the next best thing—he picked up the telephone and bawled at his subordinates. As soon as the news broke, awed Vaal Triangle detectives began to receive calls from the president's office. Two days later, De Klerk stormed into their offices in person. "He wanted results," said an officer who was present. "He wanted action."

Police responded by drafting two hundred detectives into the investigation, but even so, it would be months before the first charges were laid. Meanwhile, De Klerk was still twisting in the wind. Desperate to defend himself, he asked Judge Richard Goldstone to draw international figures into his investigation of the killings. Mr. P. N. Bhagwati, former chief justice of India, agreed to act as an observer. The British government dispatched a team of detectives led by Dr. P. A. Waddington, an eminent criminologist.

Commissioned in crisis and concluded in haste, the Waddington Report was cursory, but nevertheless illuminating. Waddington established that the police were indeed in Boipatong during the massacre. In fact, there was a police station inside the township, staffed by lowly black municipal police who did nothing to stop the violence. The same was true of the handful of white soldiers and policemen who congregated at a petrol station across the road while the killings were under way. On its face, this seems shameful, but these were ordinary policemen; they believed it would be suicidal to enter the battle zone in unarmored vehicles, and besides, their cars and vans wouldn't have made it anyway, because the streets of Boipatong had been trenched and barricaded by ANC comrades. So they lurked on the outskirts, raising the alarm on their radios.

The first armored vehicles arrived at about 10:20 pm, manned by conscripts from a military base. At this point, the attackers were retreating across a dark stretch of industrial wasteland, blowing whistles and firing the occasional gunshot. Minutes later, they surged across a main road, passing within fifty meters of one of the army vehicles. The soldiers could have machine-gunned them at this point, but no one knew exactly who they were or what they'd just done. The Zulus were heading back to KwaMadala hostel, a disused labor barracks that served as refuge and stronghold for some twelve hundred Inkatha members. The soldiers followed and parked outside to await further orders.

Waddington's assessment of all this was scathing. The response of the security forces he said, was "woefully inadequate," poorly coordinated, and badly planned, indicative of a disturbing indifference to black lives. On the other hand, he concluded that there was no reliable evidence of police complicity. In fact, he found that several of the ANC's propaganda charges were baseless. Boipatong's streetlights had not been switched off, as alleged, and charges regarding ignored warnings were far-fetched. True, Methodist activist Paul Verryn told police that "something is going to happen," but the given location was Sebokeng, ten kilometers away.

A few weeks later—on July 6, 1992—the Goldstone Commission began its Boipatong hearings. The ANC produced a dozen or so witnesses who told sensational yarns of police complicity, but in other respects the evidence was a setback for conspiracy theorists. Allegations of houses rammed by rampaging armored cars were reduced to a single fence accidentally knocked down by a reversing Casspir. A critical ANC witness, special constable Ntsietsi Xhaba, who made world headlines in the days after the massacre with a detailed and apparently damning account of gunmen climbing in and out of police vehicles, was taken back to Boipatong on a nocturnal inspection in loco. The outcome was embarrasing, with even ANC lawyers conceding that Xhaba could not possibly have seen what he claimed to have seen. The Goldstone hearings continued until November, when they were suspended so as not to prejudice the forthcoming trial.

By then, some three hundred suspects had been arrested, all residents of KwaMadala hostel and members of the Zulu Inkatha movement. If these men were allies of the police, as claimed by the ANC, their treatment during interrogation was inexplicable. Many were beaten. Some were subjected to electric shock. Particularly hard cases were allegedly buried alive. According to a police source, scores of confessions were obtained in this manner.

In the darkest days of apartheid, this would have presented few problems, but the political climate was changing and prosecutors felt that confessions extracted under torture were vulnerable to challenge. They thus chose to build their case on the testimony of four accomplices—hostel dwellers who had taken part in the rampage but who turned state's evidence in return for immunity. On the basis of their testimony, murder charges were brought against seventy-four KwaMadala inmates, who went on trial before Judge J. M. C. Smit in May 1993.

The trial was a marathon affair, lasting nearly a year and producing a record running to 3,879 pages. The state maintained that the killers had acted alone, while the Inkatha defense took a line that surely amused the gods of irony: "My clients are innocent," said Advocate Vic Botha. The true culprits, or so he claimed, were the police, soldiers, and mysterious Third Force elements featured in the ANC's press releases.

Given Botha's stance, the court was obliged to devote months to a forensic examination of alleged security force involvement. Indeed, the entire trial came to turn on this issue, with the judge ultimately concluding that ANC-aligned witnesses were lying. To understand how this happened, two critical factors must be kept in mind. First, the massacre took place in a concentrated time span—about forty-five minutes, rather than the five hours initially postulated by the ANC. And secondly, it took place in a tiny township, barely a thousand meters from end to end.

At the start of their case, prosecutors set up a map and traced the route followed by the attackers. Almost every house along this Via Dolorosa had its windows shattered. Those that lacked sturdy defenses were invaded and ransacked, their inhabitants shot, hacked, or speared. Every survivor had a story to tell, and the state called 120 of them. "Not one," said Judge Smit, "observed police support for the attackers." As for dissenters called by the defense, they were bracketed by neighbors who discounted their stories.

Consider, for instance, the testimony of Abednego Mabuza, whose Goldstone appearance caused a sensation. He was drinking with a friend on the night of the massacre. Just after ten, he left his house to walk the friend home. Outside, they found a small boy named Sibusiso, running from some unspeakable terror. Mabuza took the child by the hand and led him toward his granny's house, which lay diagonally over the road. He heard a noise and saw men approaching. They were wearing headbands and waving sticks and spears. He ducked into Sibsusiso's grandmother's garden and watched in disbelief as a Casspir glided by at walking pace, escorting a host of Zulu warriors who were attacking innocents as they passed down the street.

It was a compelling story, but it failed to survive closer scrutiny. Under cross-examination, Mabuza acknowledged that if his version was correct, "everyone on Hlubi Street would have seen or heard the Casspir." But the lost boy's grandmother, Mrs. Msibi, looked outside as her windows shattered and saw only Zulus. The same was true of Mr. Siyane, who lived a few doors down, and Mrs. Manyika across the way. In all, eight witnesses from that block told the same story. The only person who supported Mabuza's version was Mr. Hlubi at Number 745, but he was flatly contradicted by his neighbor Mr. Ramothladi, who neither saw nor heard anything of the sort. On the balance of probabilities, the judge concluded that Mabuza was mistaken or lying.

Why would he do such a thing? At the outset, Mabuza described himself as an ANC member. When his partisanship came under scrutiny, he retracted the statement, insisting he was neutral. He was, however, unable to explain a second set of claims clearly intended to cast the police in the worst possible light. The first police to arrive on the scene, he charged, just took some pictures and drove away, leaving the injured to bleed to death. This contention was obliterated by fellow residents who testified that ambulances were summoned immediately, and that most of the injured had been removed by the time a forensic investigator began photographing the crime scene.

Finally, the court demanded an explanation for Mabuza's behavior at 10:25 pm, when a Casspir piloted by a certain Sergeant Schlebush rolled into Boipatong to investigate reports of a shooting in progress. A man ran into his path, waving his arms and shouting for help. The man was Abednego Mabuza. He leaped into the armored vehicle and guided Schlebush to houses where people had been killed or wounded. The court wanted to know why he did such a thing if police were murdering his neighbors. Confronted with this contradiction, Mabuza lapsed into sullen silence and refused to say anything at all.

In the end, Judge Smit found seventeen of the accused guilty as charged, but dismissed allegations of police complicity as baseless. The left will say that Smit is an old-regime conservative, and that the case before him was prepared by a police force with a long history of cover-up and chicanery. This may be true, but it is not entirely relevant. In believing Smit, you were not necessarily believing the police. You were believing figures like Elias Nyokong, a young ANC comrade who shadowed the *impi* for several hundred meters and insisted that he saw no whites or armored vehicles. Or ANC civic leader Ismael Mahasela, who acknowledged that even he had been unable to find anyone who had actually *seen* police among the attackers. Such accounts were entirely congruent with the stories told by accomplices and victims. In the end, they carried the day.

Did the ANC manipulate the evidence?

This was certainly Judge Smit's conclusion. Here is how he reached it.

In the hours after the massacre, ANC comrades and street committee members went around Boipatong instructing residents not to speak to police or outsiders. If they wished to make a statement, they were to report to the school, where they could make a statement to "the ANC." At the school, they met white people who were attached to either the Human Rights Commission or Peace Action, violence monitoring groups with strong pro-ANC sympathies. Statements taken under these circumstances were gathered at the law firm of Nicholls, Cambanis and Sudano, a law firm that acted for the ANC and its allies. These statements were made available to sympathetic reporters but withheld from police, who were then accused of failing to investigate the incendiary charges they contained. Police attempts to hold an identification lineup had to be abandoned because victims were scared they'd be punished for cooperating with the state.

In the end, as we have seen, detectives made a case against the Boipatong killers by other means. Some victims had no idea that they'd succeeded in this until they saw news reports about the trial, whereupon a group of them showed up in Judge Smit's courtroom, demanding that their stories be heard. When Smit asked why they had not come forward earlier, they said "the ANC" had told them not to. Indeed, Mrs. Alice Nonjoli told the court she knew of someone who had been murdered for disobeying this edict. Eyebrows were raised, but the trial proceeded.

Eight months later, the defense began to present its case, which was based, as noted, on the notion that white security forces were to blame. To prove this, Advocate Botha subpoenaed eleven ANC-aligned witnesses who had previously offered firsthand accounts of police complicity to the Goldstone Commission and the anti-apartheid press. These witnesses were horrified to discover, upon arrival, that they had been called to testify on behalf of their Inkatha enemies. "We're only allowed to talk to the ANC," they said. Asked what they meant by "the ANC," many spoke of a white woman they knew only as Caroline—properly, Caroline Nicholls, of the law firm Nicholls, Cambanis and Sudano.

A former student activist, Nicholls was a central figure in the ANC's long-standing campaign to have KwaMadala hostel shut down. In fairness, many of the points she raised were valid. The hostel had indeed become an Inkatha military barracks from which attacks were launched on surrounding communities. It had also become an operating base for criminals who liked the fact that it was a no-go zone for police and anticrime vigilantes.

On the other hand, Nicholls's representations entirely ignored the fact that KwaMadala hostel was at the vortex of a conflict in which her ANC clients were anything but innocent victims. Almost everyone inside the fortified hostel had an atrocity story to tell, usually about being singled out for attack on account of suspected Inkatha sympathies. Some were Zulu migrant workers, driven out of a hostel in Sebokeng during a bloody ANC putsch two years earlier. Others were apolitical township people whose adherence to Zulu custom brought lynch mobs to their doors. These refugees had reason to hate the ANC and seek vengeance. It wasn't just that they'd lost their homes and, in many cases, loved ones. Conditions in KwaMadala were unbearable.

They couldn't buy food because it was too dangerous to venture outside. Their wounds went untreated because the nearest hospital lay in an ANC-controlled area. Even going to work was dangerous. In the week prior to the June 17 killings, three stray Zulus were allegedly picked off and murdered in the hostel's vicinity.

Be this as it may, Nicholls regarded the hostel dwellers as the fount of all evil in the area. She agitated against KwaMadala for almost two years, and when the massacre took place, she was one of the first outsiders on the scene. As Abednego Mabuza told it, ANC comrades came looking for anyone who could implicate the police. When he offered his services, he was taken to "Caroline," who debriefed him and prepared him for his appearance before the Goldstone Commission. She was similarly involved with Eugenius Mnqithi, whose surprise appearance was the sensation of the trial.

Mnqithi was a teenager from Small Farms, about five kilometers from Boipatong. About a week before the massacre, a young woman was murdered on her way home from a drinking party at his parents' house. Mnqithi claimed innocence, but ANC-aligned vigilantes necklaced a friend of his and then torched his parents' home. Young Eugenius fled for his life. Like many before him, he knocked on the gates at KwaMadala, begging for protection. He was admitted after undertaking to join the war on Inkatha's side. A few nights later a siren sounded and all males were summoned to the hostel stadium. The Zulus were on the warpath, and Mnqithi was dragooned into participating in the June 17 attack.

The following morning, young Eugenius awoke to find KwaMadala surrounded by hundreds of policemen and soldiers, and realized he'd leaped from the frying pan into the fire. He escaped and returned to Small Farms, where his reappearance aroused furious suspicions. Saved from hanging by a street committee, he was handed over to intelligence operatives from the ANC's Shell House headquarters. They arranged a safe place for him to stay and introduced him to Caroline, who debriefed him. His eyewitness account was considered so important that "Mr. Chaskalson"—presumably Arthur Chaskalson, the famed struggle lawyer and now chairman of the Constitutional Court—was called in to hear it, too. Mnqithi swore that he signed a statement, but this document was never seen again.

Why did the ANC fail to disclose Mnqithi's evidence? A possible reason emerged a year later, when prosecutors got wind of the fact that the ANC was in touch with a key witness. At the time, their own key witnesses—the four accomplices—were being battered by insinuations that police had bribed them to lie. Prosecutors needed independent corroboration of their evidence, and they suspected Mnqithi could provide it. Caroline Nicholls agreed to bring him in rather than face a messy subpoena battle.

And so, on August 11, 1993, the ANC's inside source took the witness stand and identified the perpetrators of the Boipatong massacre: the Inkatha warriors in the dock. That is the man whose Zulu poems whipped the warriors into battle frenzy, he said. That is the man who administered battle medicine, and that is the *induna* who distributed AK-47s. Mnqithi insisted that no whites were involved, and that no police were present. He said the only armored vehicles he saw that night were the two army Buffels that showed up as the *impi* was withdrawing toward the hostel, blood-spattered and laden with loot—in Mnqithi's case, a beer crate full of LP records. His story meshed with a huge mass of corroborating evidence.

Smit concluded that ANC partisans had kept Mnqithi out of the public eye "because he didn't support their case." In his judgment, he expressed "shock" at the manner in which "certain people and organizations" had interfered in the investigation. The ANC issued no rebuttal and the Boipatong drama appeared to have ended—at least with regard to charges of overt police and white complicity.

Which is not to say that a deeper conspiratorial nexus had been ruled out entirely. It had always seemed possible, or even likely, that shadowy figures from apartheid's secret services had covert links with Inkatha fighters. In 1995, the *Weekly Mail* alleged that the massacre had been carried out by ex–special forces operatives now working as security guards for South Africa's telecommunications service. A frisson of excitement swept the left, but the story collapsed under scrutiny.

A year later, the *Observer* of London claimed that Colonel Eugene de Kock's Vlakplaas counterinsurgency unit was responsible for the June 17 killings. "Police set up the Boipatong massacre that nearly derailed South Africa's peace talks," said the headline. The report went on to claim that the killings were "planned and executed" by De Kock and his "paid Inkatha collaborators."

But this, too, turned out to be wrong. Found guilty of running a "horrible network" of assassins and dirty tricksters and sentenced to life in prison, Colonel de Kock turned against his former political masters and blew the whistle on all manner of apartheid crimes. Boipatong was not one of them. "I was convinced that South Africa was on the verge of civil war," de Kock told his biographer, Jeremy Gordin. Realizing that whites were "too spoiled to fight," he decided to break with De Klerk's pro-peace faction and join Inkatha. Over an eighteen-month period in the early 1990s, he supplied Inkatha with such weapons as he could lay his hands on. He acknowledged that some of his guns may have wound up in KwaMadala hostel, but as for planning and executing the atrocity with "paid Inkatha collaborators," it was nonsense.

And so by the end of 1997 the Boipatong controversy seemed to be fading into history. The last piece of the puzzle fell into place when the seventeen convicted killers applied to the Truth Commission for amnesty. They admitted their role in the massacre, portraying themselves as foot soldiers in a war not of their own choosing. Some said the attack was sanctioned by senior Inkatha leaders. The rest claimed it was their own idea. But on one score they were unanimous: the fleets of Casspirs and hosts of white gunmen who appeared on the world's front pages in June 1992 were figments of someone's imagination.

Enter the Truth Commission

In terms of its founding legislation, South Africa's Truth and Reconciliation Commission was supposed to be an independent body led by "impartial and respected" figures who would probe the nation's war wounds in an evenhanded manner. Up close, it had a different complexion. In the estimation of National Party MP Jacko Maree, all but one of the sixteen commissioners were ANC supporters or sympathizers. White liberals who'd opposed both apartheid and the Communist-led ANC were excluded, Inkatha likewise. The sole Afrikaner conservative resigned in midstream, declaring he could no longer stomach his fellow commissioners' bias.

Beyond that, says Maree, the TRC's workings were heavily influenced by its staff of several hundred researchers, investigators, and logisticians, "almost all of whom had the same political profile" as their bosses. The researcher tasked to write up the commission's Boipatong finding, for instance, was Vanessa Barolsky, an ANC-aligned "peace activist" in the early 1990s. She reported to Charles Villa-Vicencio, an ANC-aligned liberation theologist, who, in turn, reported to TRC chief executive Biki Minyuku, a career ANC apparatchik.

Such a cabal was unlikely to produce anything that embarrassed the ANC, but even so, nothing prepared me for the conclusions presented in volume three of the commission's massive final report: "The Commission finds that KwaMadala hostel residents, together with the police, planned and carried out [the massacre]. The Commission finds that the police colluded with the attackers and dropped them off (in the township). The commission finds that white men with blackened faces participated . . ." And so on. The grand conspiracy of June 1992 had been resurrected in its most hallucinatory form. As far as I could tell, the TRC hadn't even bothered to read the trial record or the Goldstone papers, let alone refute their contents.

Consider, for instance, the matter of police radio tapes, which the TRC baldly states were "erased" as part of a cover-up. There was global media pandemonium when these charges were first brought up before Judge Goldstone. And the tumult redoubled when a report drafted by British intelligence confirmed that the tapes had been "hurriedly erased" with "masking sound." At the trial, there were hundreds of pages of testimony on this issue and the final outcome was humiliation for both conspiracy theorists and UK spymasters.

Skeptics are invited to consult the record for themselves but, briefly, this is what it states: three months before the massacre, a machine designed to record radio traffic was installed at a riot police base near Boipatong. It looked like an ordinary double-deck cassette recorder but it was actually a marvel of high technology and digital sequencing, designed to record on four tracks simultaneously at one-sixth speed. If the vaunted computer experts of British intelligence were baffled by its workings, what hope had Constable Ilse O'Reilly, who had no training and barely glanced at the manual? She proceeded as if she were taping songs off the radio, flipping the tapes whenever one side was full. As a result, most of the recordings she made were gibberish. "*Dit klink Russies*," as one witness memorably stated—it sounds Russian. It was a blunder, not a cover-up.

One's judgment might be tempered if TRC investigators had revisited these matters and come up with new evidence, but this was not the case. Jan-Ake Kjellberg, a Swedish policeman seconded to the TRC to beef up its investigative capability, had seen the TRC's Boipatong file and said it was empty save for some stray documents pertaining to the provenance of two AK-47s that might at some point have been in KwaMadala's armory. Otherwise, there'd been no investigation at all. The Swede seemed as perplexed by the TRC's finding as I was. "Based on what, I wonder?"

A phrase in the TRC's finding had a familiar ring, so I delved into my files and found the source: an article in the left-leaning *Weekly Mail*, authored by one of the sympathetic reporters granted access to Caroline Nicholls's witness statements in the days after the massacre. Paul Stober's report had the grace to note that claims made in those statements appeared to be contradictory, but the author of the TRC report had no such compunctions: after borrowing a sentence or two from Stober's article, she lifted great chunks verbatim from a post-massacre "repression report" issued by the Human Rights Commission, a pressure group so close to the ANC that most trial witnesses couldn't distinguish between them. These propaganda claims had been fed to the Truth Commission and adopted, without further inquiry, as legal fact.

For the KwaMadala prisoners, the implications were Orwellian. They were entitled to be pardoned only if they told the truth, but "the truth" had already been decided by the body that held their fate in its hands: they had acted in concert with the police and mysterious white gunmen. But they swore they hadn't. At their amnesty hearing, every one of the convicted killers said the massacre was "a Zulu thing," driven by their desire to avenge themselves on their ANC-aligned tormentors. Advocate Danny Berger, appearing for the Boipatong victims, strove valiantly to break them, but three weeks into the hearings, he'd made no headway at all. To a man, the Zulus insisted there were no white police or soldiers present, and no armored vehicles. By August 9, Berger appeared to be on the verge of losing his case.

The following morning, however, he produced a document that purported to shed sensational new light on the killings. This, according to Berger, was an affidavit sworn in June 1996 by one Andries Matanzima Nosenga, a sad, feral creature from the Sebokeng underworld. Orphaned at an early age, Nosenga drifted into political activities in his teens. At some point in the early 1990s, he and his ANC comrades burned down a service station owned by a prominent black businessman. The businessman demanded retribution, and Nosenga found himself on the run from his own side. Like many before him, he landed at KwaMadala, begging for refuge. Hostel dwellers took him for an ANC spy, and he was beaten up and confined. A month or so later, he popped up at an Inkatha rally in the Zulu capital Ulundi, where he was paraded on stage as an enemy who had decided to confess and recant.

Nosenga's conversion appeared to be genuine, because he was subsequently convicted and imprisoned for murdering a youth on Inkatha's behalf. After the establishment of the TRC, he filed two amnesty applications, asking to be pardoned for the crime for which he'd been jailed. Boipatong was not mentioned.

According to Berger, however, Nosenga had filed a third amnesty application that had somehow been mislaid by the TRC. In this unsigned document, Nosenga confessed to a leading role in the Boipatong massacre, claiming he'd marched into the township carrying an AK-47 and personally killed "eight or nine people." Moreover, he was willing to name the white policemen who had provided guns as well as "four to six" armored vehicles to carry the Inkatha forces into battle.

Here, at last, was the proof for which the anti-apartheid movement had so long yearned. Reporters scrambled for telephones. Nosenga's bombshell allegations made front-page news throughout the country.

Others were less impressed. Amnesty judge Sandile Ngcobo was so skeptical about the last-minute introduction of "lost" evidence that he took the unusual step of cautioning ANC lawyers to watch their ethics. I dug through the records at Groenpunt prison, establishing that Nosenga was being held elsewhere on the day TRC officials claimed to have deposed him there. I also spoke to Constable Ignatius Ferreira, the detective who'd put Nosenga behind bars on a murder charge. He described Nosenga as a weirdo who'd walked into Sebokeng police station on February 14, 1993, begging to be arrested.

As Ferreira recalls it, Nosenga presented himself as a KwaMadala resident who knew several notorious Inkatha gunslingers and was willing to spill the beans about killings they'd committed together. Ferreira put him in a car and drove him around Sebokeng, but Nosenga was so vague as to time and place that Ferreira and his colleagues concluded he was lying, if not deranged. They tried to chase Nosenga out of the police station, but he refused to leave. So they gave him another chance, showing him a file of photographs of murder victims in which he came across a face he recognized. This is Sipho, he said. This is one of the people we killed.

Sipho was an ANC comrade who met his death in a drive-by shooting. Nosenga was able to take detectives to the scene of the crime and provide an account that agreed with those of eyewitnesses. Ferreira arranged for him to make a formal confession, and Nosenga was convicted on the basis of his own testimony. But Ferreira had nagging doubts. Sipho and Nosenga were of a similar age and had grown up in the same neighborhood. Ferreira couldn't rule out the possibility that Nosenga had learned the details of Sipho's demise by other means, and confessed to a murder he hadn't committed.

Why would anyone do such a thing? Ferreira said he'd heard that Nosenga was involved in a car-theft racket based in KwaMadala and that its ringleaders suspected him of informing against them. Remaining in the hostel under such circumstances would have been extremely dangerous, and returning to Sebokeng could also have been fatal. For a man in such a position, a stint in prison might have seemed attractive.

When Nosenga took the stand to testify about Boipatong, it was immediately clear that something was wrong. He failed to recognize his own signature on certain documents. He claimed to have relatives in Boipatong whom he'd visited on innumerable occasions but couldn't remember their names. When the bombshell affidavit was read back to him, he repudiated part of its contents, saying it contained things he would not have said. Furthermore, he said he'd never seen the document before, and had no idea where it came from. "Lots of people came to see me in prison," he said, mentioning the names of Caroline Nicholls and Mongezi from the ANC, among others.

Under cross-examination, Nosenga's problems deepened. Shown a map of Boipatong, he misidentified the route followed by the attackers. He said the Casspirs that allegedly ferried the Zulu warriors into battle were parked near a four-lane highway, where scores of previous witnesses would have seen them. He said the armored vehicles drove the combatants a hundred meters before dropping them off again, an action that did not seem entirely logical. Nosenga claimed he then walked into the nearest house and started shooting with an AK-47. Asked to point out approximately where this happened, he indicated a section of Boipatong where no houses were attacked at all. Deepening his own grave, he insisted that all six houses he'd attacked were on that same street. Finally, he swore he'd shot all his victims at close range with his AK-47, but no corpses bore corresponding entry or exit wounds.

Beyond a certain point, Nosenga's demolition was almost too painful to watch. As Judge Ngcobo later put it, "Mr. Nosenga was an appalling witness, to say the least." Ngcobo went on to list a host of contradictions and improbabilities in Nosenga's testimony and concluded that "We have no hesitation in rejecting his evidence as untruthful."

Oddly, ANC partisans seem to have reached a similar conclusion years earlier. After interviewing Nosenga in prison in February 1996, they forwarded his Boipatong allegations to the attorney general, who concluded after a cursory investigation that Nosenga was unreliable.

This decision was accepted without protest, and no more was heard about Nosenga until it became clear that the amnesty hearings were not going the ANC's way. At this point, the "lost" affidavit appeared as if from nowhere, unsigned and allegedly taken in a prison where Nosenga wasn't. I tried to discuss this with Nosenga but my attempts were blocked by the mysterious men in dark glasses who escorted him to the hearings. The issue remains unsolved.

So what really happened at Boipatong?

As we have seen, Boipatong altered the trajectory of South African history, and the Truth Commission had already published a finding: the massacre was planned and executed by De Klerk's government. To challenge that finding was to challenge a critical fragment of the ANC's political mythology, and I doubted Judge Sandile Ngcobo and his three amnesty committee colleagues were so brave. I was wrong.

Ngcobo's verdict opened with an evenhanded description of the state of war that existed between Inkatha and the ANC in the early 1990s. Both movements had established strongholds and no-go areas where political opposition was not tolerated, he said, and both had inflicted severe casualties on the other. "A cycle of attack and counterattack ensued," he continued, "with each side avenging the killing of its members." In this regard, he accepted the evidence of Zulu hostel dwellers who said the massacre arose from their desire to retaliate for their sufferings at the hands of the ANC, even if that entailed murdering innocent women and children. The applicants had furthermore told the truth about their crimes, he concluded, and were thus entitled to amnesty. In other words, Ngcobo found that there was simply no convincing evidence of overt white or police participation.

What then of the ANC-aligned witnesses whose claims to the contrary made Boipatong world famous? "It is common cause that shortly after the attack there was chaos and confusion in the township," Ngcobo said, with throngs of residents moving about the streets in search of missing relatives even as police armored cars arrived to investigate.

"It is against this background that the evidence relating to the presence of police vehicles during the attack must be evaluated." Ngcobo went on to analyze how easy it would have been for witnesses to misinterpret what they saw in the aftermath.

It doesn't follow that Ngcobo's judgment exonerated apartheid's police. He found it extraordinary that an army of nearly five hundred men had managed to cross a main road, ransack Boipatong, and return to KwaMadala before police intervened. "The timing of the attack and lack of detection is indeed a cause for concern," he wrote. "This strongly suggests that the attackers had information on the movements of police patrols. We need not speculate on how such information could have been obtained. Suffice to say that there is no credible evidence to suggest a conspiracy between the leaders of the attack and the police in this regard. All that is there is a suspicion."

The verdict was released on November 24, 2000. After eight years, four exhaustive inquiries, and stupefying legal expenses, the Boipatong affair had finally ended.

Moral of the story

This has been a cold-blooded exercise, given that most of those who died in Boipatong were defenseless noncombatants whose only crime was to live in an area perceived to be controlled by the ANC. If I have caused offense, I regret it. But the ANC's propaganda campaign was based on the equally offensive assumption that the death of forty-nine black people was of no consequence unless it could be shown that their blood was on white hands. ANC charges in this regard served their immediate purpose, inspiring a global firestorm of outrage, a significant weakening of President F. W. de Klerk's position, and a last flickering of militancy on the part of the international anti-apartheid movement.

Unfortunately, the ANC's charges were untrue, but nobody wanted to hear that, so the gradual destruction of its case was entirely ignored by the media. As far as I know, no newspaper reported Judge Smit's remarks about the ANC's manipulation of witnesses. Flimsy claims implicating Eugene de Kock made international headlines, but no one said anything about their ultimate dismissal. Andries Nosenga's sensational yarn was a major news story in South Africa, but his subsequent annihilation under cross-examination was not reported by anyone. As for Judge Ngcobo's final verdict, the only newspaper in the world that covered it was *Die Burger,* Cape Town's Afrikaans daily. For the rest, it threatened one of the myths we've chosen to live by, so it was ignored entirely.

—*Frontiers of Freedom,* volume 20, 1999

PART FIVE
LIGHT

THE APOCALYPSE THAT WASN'T

When the tenth anniversary of democracy rolled around and we weren't all dead yet, I decided it was time to apologize to my fellow South Africans for my lack of faith in our great nation-building enterprise. The results were not quite what I'd anticipated.

As the story passes into legend, it serves to remember the abyss into which South Africans were staring ten years ago today. De Klerk and Mandela were engaged in a vicious squabble over their shared Nobel Peace Prize. A sinister alliance of white right-wingers and Bantustan dictators was plotting to subvert the army and stage a coup. Mandela's people were smuggling arms to counter that threat. Buthelezi's people had set up secret military training camps. Political intolerance was absolute. January 1994 was the bloodiest month on record. I knew what was coming on election day. As it neared, I bought a flak jacket, drew up a will, and went off to cover the coming apocalypse in KwaZulu, at least half-expecting to die.

Only I didn't. Nor did anyone else. Since the details are familiar, let's just say there was a miraculous reprieve, and by April 27 I was back in Johannesburg, putting my cross on South Africa's first democratic ballot. Outside, the streets were empty and a reverent silence lay on the city. Somewhere in the bush to the north, a white-robed prophet had been praying for days on a mountaintop for salvation, and lo, here it was.

I was suddenly so tired I could barely stand. I staggered home and lay on a couch for days, drifting in and out of sleep while pundits bickered on TV and the counting degenerated into an amicable chaos. In this dreamlike state, I saw many amazing things, but none quite as telling as the parable of the lost Afrikaners who sold their worldly goods and took their guns, Bibles, and families to a gathering point on election eve. When the sun rose on April 27, 1994, every man was at his post, waiting for the blacks to attack. Nothing happened, so they set off in convoy, searching for the war their leaders had prophesied. By the time the camera found them, they'd been wandering for days, children crying, wives sweaty and ill-tempered, husbands with four-day beards and the dazed, haunted look of men who were beginning to realize they'd made terrible fools of themselves.

No, I'm not mocking them. I was in much the same position, hoist by my own dark prognostications. As I saw it, it was futile to talk of a peace in South Africa. There was too much history, too much pain and anger. "Civil war is inevitable," I declared. I wound up shamed and chagrined, with great coagulations of egg on my face.

Unwilling to accept such humiliation, I set out to discredit the outcome. The peace is illusory, I sneered; anarchy is still coming. Look at crime! Rape! Guns and mayhem! Decaying cities! Abandoned factories! Incompetence and corruption everywhere! When our new black rulers dismissed such criticism as racist, I said, fine, if that's the price one pays for speaking truth, I will consider myself honored and continue. Hospitals that don't work anymore! Surly nurses! Drunken teachers! A civil service where the phones just ring!

All this was true, but my complaints were pointless. There came a day when I realized that history had marched on and left me high and dry, a middle-aged white male fulminating to no effect to a tiny audience of like-minded bad losers. Anything I said was irrelevant, and I had become ridiculous. This realization drove me first to the bottle and paralyzing depression, and then to some dimly remembered texts from the hippie era.

Buddhist texts, if you must know. "Be here now," said Baba Ram Dass. I interpreted this to mean, be in Parkview, Johannesburg, in this vegetable garden, with these dogs, fixing this old house, consorting with these old friends, smoking the herb on a sacramental basis and generally attempting to add to the sum of light rather than stink everything up with septic negativism. I stopped reading newspapers and started talking nonsense. If it is true, I said, that materialism coarsens the spirit and that life itself is something of an illusion, it is surely a blessing to live in a country where you are constantly being relieved of your possessions and risking having your head blown off en route to the shops.

My wife rolled her eyes. We were newly married at that point, and my rehabilitation was greatly assisted by the fact that she was a foreigner who saw everything with fresh eyes. Being American, she placed much store in hygienic bathrooms and bright shopping malls, and Johannesburg had these, along with skyscrapers, freeways, and high technology. But it also had noisy bars where fifty African languages were spoken, and nightclubs that played Congolese *kwassa-kwassa* all night. Jo'burg was the envy of all Africa, a magnet for dreamers and success-mongers from as far afield as the Nile. On a good night in Yeoville you'd see more beautiful black people than in all the *Shaft* movies put together, and hear more shooting, too.

I loved it, but the Contessa (for this is her nickname) had reservations about the guns and violence, so we'd leave the city whenever we could. For a foreigner, everything out there was a revelation. Wild animals. Deserts. Beaches. Mountains so remote it took days to walk out of them. Landscapes so vast they took your breath away, skies so big they defied belief, cathedrals of cloud towering over yellow plains, and so on. I'd grown blind to these splendors, but whenever she gasped, I looked again and gasped, too. I fell in love with the country all over again, eventually softening to such a degree that I agreed to move to the Cape.

You must understand that Jo'burgers regard moving to Cape Town as an admission of defeat. We think of it as a fool's paradise where trendies sip white wine on seaview terraces, congratulating each other for finding the last corner of Africa that is immune to chaos and madness. Naturally, it was this very aspect that the Contessa found seductive. "It's like Europe or America," she said. "Only better."

This is true. Cape Town is impossibly beautiful, improbably clean, and overrun in summer by crews shooting international TV commercials. Parts of downtown resemble London. The Atlantic seaboard is easily mistaken for the French Riviera. Out in the wine lands, the oak groves and pastures are somehow Dutch in their gentleness, and the arid west coast easily doubles for Spain. As for the better suburbs, frame your shot to exclude smoke from the shacks where poor blacks stay, and you're in an upper-middle-class anywhere: Connecticut, Marin County, Surrey, or Neuilly.

Who wants to live in an upper-middle-class anywhere? Not I. I wanted to buy a log cabin out in the wilderness near Cape Point, where we could live a simple life of spartan purity among trees tormented into strange shapes by howling gales. Unfortunately, the Contessa had other ideas, and we wound up with a sensible house in St. James, where the imperialist Cecil Rhodes had his holiday pad. From our porch we can see sixty miles, Cape Point this way, Groot Drakenstein the other, and before us a giant horseshoe of blue water rimmed by purple mountains.

There is an impossibly quaint fishing harbor below us, full of wooden boats and grizzled old salts of the sort beloved by watercolorists. There is also a row of quaint antique shops and galleries, interspersed with trendy boîtes where the cappuccino is served by beautiful girls with rings in their lips and eyebrows. It is a place well suited to the quasi-Buddhist lifestyle. Every dawn brings an awesome sight—a storm, clouds streaming over mountain crags—that reminds me of my insignificance in the overall scheme of things. Every day I can go fishing, if the spirit moves. On dark stormy nights, I repair to a waterside bar called Polana and wait for high tide, when giant seas heave up in floodlights and come racing toward the picture windows in a great tumult of spume.

Live in Cape Town long enough and you lose interest in the outside world. Visitors from more exciting cities start yawning at your dinner table, but I no longer care. They have no possible conception of the unbearable bliss of fine summer days when the sea is warm and the figs are ripe and you start the morning with a dive into a cool green rock pool, followed perhaps by coffee in one of those impossibly quaint cafés and a spot of light typing, if I can manage to ignore the drama outside my window—tides rising, whales blowing, birds diving, the boats coming back to the harbor below. The Contessa and I often walk down to meet them, and come home with a fat Cape salmon or snoek. Come sundown, we set the fish to grill on an open fire, uncork a bottle of wine, and, yes, congratulate ourselves for living in the last corner of Africa that is immune to chaos and madness.

In season, tour buses park on the road above our house, disgorging foreigners who gape at the view, dumbfounded, and then turn their binoculars on us, clearly wondering what entitles us to live in this paradise. I often ask myself the same question, and the answer is *nothing*. My life is absurd in every aspect. The first Malan arrived in Cape Town in 1688 and owned slaves. His sons trekked into the interior and dispossessed the Khoisan. Their sons moved even deeper into Africa and, by 1840, Malans were spreading like a plague, eating up landscapes, mowing down game, subjugating everyone they came across. My sort wound up owning almost everything and it was nice while it lasted, but by rights we should have been wiped out in the great war of 1994, or at least dispossessed. Instead, here we are, citizens of a stable democracy with an independent judiciary and a constitution that is a beacon unto nations. To be sure, there are problems, but it is not the ending I imagined.

All I can say as the tenth anniversary nears is that the Bible was right about a thing or two. It is infinitely worse to receive than to give, especially if one is arrogant and the gift is forgiveness. The gift of 1994 was so huge that I choked on it and couldn't say thank you. But I am not too proud to say it now.

—Sunday Telegraph, January 2004

Postscript: President Thabo Mbeki quoted this article at considerable length in his 2004 "state of the nation" address, a development that provoked rabies in certain circles. The central accusation was that Mbeki had chosen to elevate me above your average hack as a reward for my writings about AIDS, which were said to have "provided oxygen" for the president's own views on the subject. Pundits like Professor Anton Harber resurrected all the heresies I'd uttered about the Boipatong massacre, the Truth Commission, and the AIDS establishment, concluding that I was a "carbuncular" person whose writings were poisonous. The reaction from right-wing friends was equally unfriendly; they thought my brain had rotted in the Cape's sea air. Myself, I think the piece was just a somewhat belated display of good manners.

THE PEOPLE'S REPUBLIC
OF YEOVILLE

Once upon a time in Africa, there was a Camelot where people said what they felt and did as they pleased in defiance of their hard-hearted rulers. It was a place where forbidden love flourished, where every conceivable rule was broken, and for a brief shining hour, ten years ago, it was the capital of South Africa.

So, then—welcome to Yeoville, founded in 1890 on a rocky ridge just north of the world's richest gold reef. "Magnificent views," said the developer. "Healthy air." He was a Scotsman named Thomas Yeo Sherwell, and he was hoping to attract the rich. He never quite managed that but he did get the infant Johannesburg's middle classes and, after the turn of the century, the Jews, who came mostly from the Baltic states and gave Yeoville an intellectual and cultural ambience considerably out of the colonial ordinary. Some Jews went on to become capitalists but others were Bolsheviks who immediately set about organizing revolution, first and rather embarrassingly under the slogan "Workers Unite for a White South Africa" but, after 1927, on behalf of "the natives."

The presence in Yeoville of this small band of rebels attracted kindred spirits in the form of bohemians (most famously, Herman Charles

Bosman), jazz musicians, and dope fiends, all of whom lived furtively until 1978 or so, when a gay nightclub called Casablanca opened on Yeoville's main road. In the larger scheme this was a nothing event, but it was one of the first signs that the ruling Calvinists were losing their grip, especially when Casablanca was joined by Rumours, a jazz bar that daringly featured black musicians. When Rumours got away with it, similar joints sprang up nearby, and by 1986 Rockey Street was the hippest place in South Africa—racially integrated in proportions comfortable to whites, lined with fashionable nightspots, and overrun by trendies.

Everyone lived in Yeoville. Okay, everyone who was anyone in the alternative society that styled itself the vanguard of political and social change. The pop star Johnny Clegg learned to play Zulu guitar on Yeoville rooftops. Barney Simon lay in his bed on Muller Street, dreaming up stories that became world-famous Market Theatre plays. All the seminal anti-apartheid movies were cobbled together in Yeoville. The suburb even had its own Beat poet, Sinclair Beiles, a witty old madman who'd knocked around with William S. Burroughs in Paris. On any given night, Yeoville's entertainment zone was awash with famous actors, human rights lawyers, Marxist academics, gay activists, and radical feminists whose unshaven legs were known locally as "Yeoville stockings."

Reshada Crouse did not wear Yeoville stockings, but then she was always contrary. Immortally beautiful and talented, she was smitten at an early age by the paintings of grand masters and decided, after art school in Cape Town and London, to become a portraitist "in the tradition of Goya, Caravaggio, and Michelangelo."

In South Africa, in the 1980s, such an ambition was almost insanely inappropriate. Taking their cues from the greats overseas, the local art police had declared Eurocentrism a dirty word and figurative painting largely passé. Artists were expected to become "cultural workers" celebrating the struggle of the masses against racial capitalism. To stand up in such a revolutionary climate and declare yourself a painter in the grand tradition of Dead White Men was a provocation that invited savage retaliation. "Highly skilled, highly horrible," said one leftist critic of Reshada's early work. "Absolutely masterly," said another, "but I am reminded of political works done under Hitler."

One night, at a party, a dogfight broke out on the dance floor. I pulled the slavering beasts apart and got bitten for my trouble, whereupon Reshada offered to take me for a tetanus shot. En route to the hospital, she told me about her war with the art police and I immediately clocked her as an ally in the struggle against suffocating political rectitude. I moved into her spare room a while later, and we became a team of sorts, roaming from bar to bar in Yeoville's combat zone, picking arguments with art critics and other forms of leftists. The critics were amateurs, but there were real revolutionaries in Yeoville, real guerrillas and trade union organizers plus any number of left-wing journalists who were always game to drink and debate.

By the end of the 1980s, even the hippies and junkies were politicized, and Yeoville was a liberated zone of sorts. Bars stayed open till dawn, defying the liquor laws. Rastas sold dope on the street almost openly. It was almost like Amsterdam in Africa, and it got even better after February 1990, when Mandela was released from prison and the exiles came home from Russia or military camps in Africa. Yeoville was cheap and ideologically congenial, and almost the entire executive corps of the African National Congress settled there. Wally Serote was the movement's cultural commissar, Pallo Jordan its leading intellectual. Also present were future cabinet ministers Geraldine Fraser, Jabu Moleketi, and Derek Hanekom, plus future Constitutional Court judge Albie Sachs. Communist Party boss Joe Slovo grew up on Rockey Street and returned to live a few hundred yards away.

Living amid such a dense concentration of revolutionaries was fascinating. Every stroll on the streets yielded snippets of intelligence; one night in the right bar, and you'd have the lowdown on almost everything. In the nerve-wracked run-up to our 1994 election, Yeoville insiders started telling me to ignore what I read in the newspapers. A deal has been struck in high places, they said; the revolution has been postponed indefinitely. I found this hard to believe. At the time, right-wing Boers and Bantustan dictators were plotting to stage a military coup and annihilate the ANC, which was itself embroiled in a bloody

217

fratricidal war against Inkatha and infested with wild-eyed insurrectionists still bent on F. W. de Klerk's violent overthrow. One morning, we were woken by war cries. A Zulu *impi* was marching down Cavendish Street, brandishing spears and clubs and looking to bash in the heads of Mandela loyalists. I took this as a sign that the violence was becoming uncontrollable and would soon engulf all of us. "Civil war is inevitable," I wrote. "We are walking the plank."

What can I say? I was wrong. Seven weeks later, Reshada and I strolled through the cathedral calm of a bright autumn morning and cast our ballots in South Africa's first democratic election. Given my erroneous predictions, it was not my proudest moment, but once I'd wiped the egg off my face I had to concede that what was embarrassing for me promised to be good for others.

Here's the thing, though: at that moment, Yeoville was the epicenter of everything. Six residents of the suburb and its immediate surrounds were about to be drafted into Mandela's first cabinet. Another forty or so became national or regional Members of Parliament, and hundreds, perhaps thousands, were headed for big jobs in the civil service.

It's hard to convey how odd this was. The Yeoville power zone was so small you could walk across it in twenty minutes, its 35,000 people a drop in the ocean of the nation's 40 million. It was as if a single extended family had taken control of the country, and great things seemed to lie in store for Yeoville residents. In my mind's eye, I saw the suburb becoming a bright shining showpiece of the Rainbow Nation, with fine schools and clinics, an efficient police station, and plaques on buildings saying, "Childhood home of Joe Slovo," or, "Here lived Barbara Hogan, first white woman jailed for taking up arms against apartheid."

Three years later, Yeoville was a hellhole. Read on.

"Let's cartwheel, everybody!" shouted the polished swell with the upper-caste British accent, draining his wineglass and calling for more. It was May 1994, and Reshada and I were in the throes of a party that started on election day and continued without letting up for weeks on end. This one took place in a Moorish courtyard, under a big tree, and the polished dark-skinned personage turned out to be Trevor Tutu, wayward son of the famous archbishop.

Like most males, Trevor was smitten by Reshada, the Aryan siren, and became a regular at our semidaily "tea parties," which started around sunset and continued indefinitely. Another courtier was Samuel Johnson, an amiable giant who'd come out from Britain to fight apartheid, only to find himself fighting off white girls who saw him as something of a dream date—big, black, and very threatening with his Mohawk and biker leathers, but a gentle poet once you got to know him.

Sam liked to shoot pool. I dimly remember doing a lot of that in the postelection period, and also hanging out at the Blue Parrot, a Yeoville bar patronized by the local black nobility and touring celebrities—Mick Jagger, Wesley Snipes, Morgan Freeman, even Hillary Clinton. I think I met Peter Gabriel there one night, but my brain was so addled by booze and euphoria that I wouldn't swear to it. There was a lot of irrational crying in that period, especially on the day of Mandela's inauguration, itself cause for further bouts of indiscriminate celebration.

But all good things end eventually, and there came a day when I woke up sober and noticed that something odd was going on in Yeoville. It suddenly seemed more crowded. Traders were setting up fruit and vegetable stands on any sidewalk they pleased, or knocking holes in garden walls so that they could sell cheap phone calls to passersby. One day, pirates tapped into Reshada's telephone connection and she couldn't make any calls for two days on account of voices speaking in tongues on her line. Shortly thereafter, Telkom presented her with a bill for R8,000 to cover hundreds of calls to Ethiopia, Zimbabwe, and Nigeria. Foreigners were pouring into Yeoville from all over Africa, lured by the promise of jobs, money, and, in the case of our tiny neighborhood, cheap accommodation.

Unfortunately, cheap accommodation often consisted of a single room divided by curtains so that eight or ten people could share it. Looking back, Yeoville patriot Maurice Smithers identifies this as the root cause of the suburb's troubles. As apartheid crumbled in the 1980s, laws enforcing residential segregation were ignored and Yeoville became in official parlance a "gray area" where racial mixing was tolerated. This caused a huge upsurge in demand for accommodation, which, in turn, enabled greedy landlords to double or triple their rents. The newcomers, being poor, could only pay by stuffing subtenants into every nook and cranny. Overcrowding was illegal, but the municipality—staffed mostly by whites in the predemocracy period—lost interest in enforcing its own bylaws.

After 1994, border controls collapsed almost entirely, and Yeoville's decline gained pace, spurred by epidemics of apathy in the liquor licensing department, among health inspectors, and, especially, among the police, who seemed to be losing the battle against crime. Until 1993 or thereabouts, it was safe to walk around Yeoville at night. By 1995, doing so was almost suicidal. One by one, the trendy bars and restaurants on Rockey Street called it a day, only to be replaced by dank, unlicensed drinking holes whose clientele were young, aggressive, and almost entirely male. Reshada and I started staying home at night, flinching at the sound of gunfire and distant screams. And when we ventured out in the morning, we'd inevitably see a removal van drawing up somewhere along Becker Street.

One day they were there, and the next—poof!—they'd vanished. I refer here to the white leftists and art police with whom Reshada and I once sparred so pleasantly. It's a bit unfair to blame the politicians among them for leaving, because parliament was located in Cape Town, but the broad mass of anti-apartheid activists, academics, and journalists had no such excuse. They'd spent years jeering at anyone who resisted racial integration but as soon as it came to Yeoville, they packed their belongings and fled en masse, trailing feeble justifications. "Couldn't work because of the noise," they said. Or, "Our friends wouldn't let their children come to play with ours anymore."

I seldom lost an opportunity to tilt an eyebrow and remark on the hypocrisy on display here. On the other hand, I was growing uneasy myself. Two visitors to Reshada's house had their cars stolen. Then Reshada's car was stolen, too, and mine had its windows smashed. I would lie in bed at night, listening to distant gun battles and wondering how big my own balls were. One day, I found my laptop gone, nicked through an open window. I bought a replacement, but within a week it was stolen, too, so I said, that's it, I'm out of here. I invited Reshada to come with me, painting a picture of a rambling commune in some safe, leafy suburb where we could continue to host tea parties behind high walls and an electric fence. But she was made of sterner stuff. I went; she stayed.

And so it came to pass that by 1999, my circle of Yeoville friends had dwindled from hundreds to half a dozen, all of whom were struggling. David Heitner sunk his life savings into an advanced edit suite with a plush private cinema attached, only to find that customers were too scared to come to him. Adriaan Turgel was robbed so often that he turned into a vigilante of sorts. Tony Richard, a legal aid lawyer, was woken one morning by shouting and pounding on his garden gate. He went out to find an angry mob standing guard over a naked, terrified wretch who'd been caught breaking into cars. "You're a lawyer," they said, "you pass sentence." Sensing that the crowd was in a murderous mood, Tony presented the captive with a choice: private punishment or the police station. He sobbed, "Police station! Police station!" and his life was saved.

Still, it was one incident too many, and Tony decided it was time to go. But he'd left it too late. All over Yeoville, houses and flats were on sale, but the area had been unofficially redlined by banks, and there were no buyers at any price. Tony gave his house to a friend and walked away.

Which left Reshada the last white person on her street, bar two or three, and harrowingly vulnerable, or so it seemed to me—no gun, no perimeter wall, not even a gate to keep her and her two children safe from the forces of darkness. Visiting her became a nerve-wracking ordeal. I'd drive with knotted guts and white knuckles, chain-smoking, eyes peeled for hijackers. Every time I opened a newspaper, I half-expected to read that she'd been murdered.

Why did she stay? It would have been easier to understand if she'd been a self-flagellating white leftist, but that wasn't the case. She wasn't really poor, either. She was just difficult, in life as in her beautiful but unfashionable paintings. "I'll do what I want to do when I want to do it," she said. She wouldn't even admit to being afraid.

And so, as Yeoville disintegrated and white capital fled, Reshada started investing in its restoration. Her house was a grand old Victorian, with generous rooms and high ceilings, but the roof leaked, the wiring was wonky, and hot water came from an old coal stove. Reshada rolled up her sleeves and set to work, assisted by an unskilled laborer named Innocent. She fixed the wiring, nearly electrocuting herself in the process. Innocent took some interior walls down. The donkey stove gave way to a rooftop solar geyser, and then came a semiformal English garden in the backyard, strewn with sculptures and overhung with wisteria. "It's not a house," she explained, "it's a love affair." I said, "Yes, Reshada, but it's in Yeoville." She shrugged and said, "I'm not willing to leave just for the sake of having white neighbors."

So then—meet her neighbors. Owen Phiri is a boilermaker who immigrated to South Africa from Malawi in the seventies, seeking escape from "low living standards." He was a sweet, soft-spoken man, very concerned about crime and very protective toward Reshada. One night, he found eight sinister shadows clustered around her car, tampering with the ignition. "Go away," he said. They whispered, "What's wrong with you? She's white." Owen shouted, "Go away or I'll shoot," and they went.

On the other side is Aletta Khubeka who was born in a mud hut on a Free State farm and spent most of her life on her knees as some white madam's maid. Now she and her janitor husband were the burstingly proud owners of a three-bedroom home with a tiled bathroom and a kitchen so clean that every surface could be eaten off of. They were also burstingly proud of their son Sibusiso, aged fifteen, a promising squash player who attended King Edward VII, the school that produced artist William Kentridge plus any number of industrialists and South African cricket captains. "It's nice here," Aletta told me, in a sitting room lined with pictures of the Zulu prophet Shembe, her spiritual leader.

And finally there was Teresa, who knocked on Reshada's door wearing a frilly hat and an apricot suit, "looking like something from

Gone with the Wind." Teresa wanted a room. Reshada couldn't help her, but she came back twice, and was eventually invited in for a cup of tea. She turned out to be a Kenyan who had worked in a bank and been married to a judge who decided, at the age of forty-something, to exercise the African patriarch's right to a second wife. Mortally offended, Teresa walked out and made her way to South Africa, penniless. Sensing a kindred spirit, Reshada offered her a backyard shack. Teresa stayed for four years, doing Reshada's washing in lieu of rent and furiously striving for success on the side.

Teresa tried selling cosmetics. She did a computer course, but couldn't get a job because she lacked working papers. Eventually, it dawned on her that Yeoville was full of Kenyans aching for chapatis cooked Nairobi-style, so she established a cottage industry, and next thing, she was an independent businesswoman with a flat of her own and several assistants. "I don't want to sound like a liberal," Reshada said, "but these people have humbled me. They're so decent and hardworking, so determined."

A while back, a Buddhist dropped in for tea while I was visiting. Patrick Booth was one of those delightful creatures you keep meeting in the new South Africa—a colored boy from a small country town, largely self-educated and ravishingly charming. In 1999, he moved to the big city, becoming Reshada's protégé and house guest. She introduced him to people who were involved in New Age pursuits, and next thing, Patrick was out in the formerly white suburbs, laying his mystic healing hands on the stressed bodies of politicians and executives in an exclusive health retreat. He lived in Illovo, as I recollect, close to the designer boutiques of Sandton and the dreamy greensward of Wanderers cricket ground. From this lofty perch, he looked back on Yeoville with something approaching disdain.

"Yeoville is sick," he informed us, sitting in the lotus position in Reshada's studio, swathed in robes. "It's not evolving in a way most people perceive as positive or in keeping with the changes taking place in South Africa." Reshada's nostrils flared, a sure sign of coming trouble. "Excuse *me*," she said, reeling off a string of small acts of kindness she'd recently experienced. One day, for instance, her car broke down some distance from her home. A group of young black males approached, but instead of robbing her they offered to help and proceeded to push her home. Next morning, a backyard mechanic made a house call, crawled under the car with a gun on his hip, reconnected some wires, and waved away Reshada's offers of payment.

"Something good happens almost every day," she said. "It's like living in an African village. People look after each other. Children play in the street. I bet you don't even know your neighbors' names!"

The Buddhist rolled his eyes. In truth, he and I thought Reshada had long since gone off her rocker, throwing good money after bad in a hopeless slum. The mansion over the road had become a seedy boarding house, crammed full of Nigerians and Congolese who valued the thick steel burglar bars installed by some previous owner. Those bars kept thieves at bay, but they were also the death of twelve people who couldn't get out when the house caught fire. A nearby block of flats was tragic in a more ordinary way, abandoned by its landlord and infested now with blank-eyed glue heads and crack addicts who shat in the stairwells and burned trash in art deco fireplaces around which I once sat drinking with tormented white revolutionaries, back in the time when playing proletarian was a game. The reality years later was unbearable. And that is why I don't live there anymore.

Since liberation, South Africa has become a country where those who claim to speak for the black poor usually live at the farthest possible remove from them. As far as I know, Winnie Mandela is the only ANC politician who still lives full-time in a township. Her ex-husband has settled among the capitalist robber barons of Houghton. Tokyo Sexwale, the erstwhile revolutionary turned billionaire, lives in Houghton, too, and State President Thabo Mbeki is renovating a property nearby. These and other black nobles are seldom seen in township shebeens. On Friday nights, they gather at a Rosebank bar called Katzy's, where a whiskey costs R30 and the parking lot is crammed with high-end BMWs and Mercedes-Benzes.

Lurking on the fringes of the Katzy's set, you often hear older black cats talking fondly of Yeoville in the old days, but their children are scathing. "Yeoville?" said a bright young thing, her face disfigured by a sneer. "Yech. I could never live there." Such opinions are seized on with glee by whites who fled the area. They say, "Hey, it's not a race thing. My black friends also regard Yeoville as a no-go area."

Well, yes: for people like us. People with at least a bit of money. Given half a chance, we'll try to convince you that ours is the real South Africa, but I'm not sure we should be listened to. South Africa remains a country where most people are poor and desperate, and Yeoville has always been a weather vane that points where the whole is going. It was one of the first places where you saw racially mixed couples, one of the first white areas to turn gray, and then one of the first gray areas to topple into what struck me as a typically African state of dysfunctionality. On the eve of democracy's tenth birthday, I returned to Yeoville to divine what next.

Much was as I remembered it—streets clogged with fuming taxis, live chickens for sale on the pavements, formerly illustrious nightspots boarded up or reduced to smoke-blackened holes out of which emerged blasts of the urban dance music known as *kwaito*. But here and there, piglets were taking wing. After years of agitation, Jo'burg's municipality was pulling its socks up. The streets were swept fairly regularly. Council workers were fixing broken streetlights. The worst slum buildings were slated for demolition, and nocturnal gun battles had become vanishingly rare. Banks had reversed their no-loans policy, which led, just the other day, to a truly confounding development: Yeoville property prices pulled out of their decade-long nosedive. In Johannesburg, this was greeted with headlines.

All this coincided with the triumphant conclusion of Reshada's renovations, which included, by the time she was done, a rose garden on the front lawn, an imposing palisade fence, and lights to play on the house's ice-white facade. It looked astonishing after dark, a gleaming shrine to some European concept of art and beauty, looming over a street thronged with African prophets, Rastafarians, Senegalese traders in flowing robes, and street people in rags and tatters.

Word of this oddity reached certain arbiters of style, and Reshada's house became the subject of a spread in the opulent pages of *House & Garden*, under a headline reading, "Artist in Residence." The rich

and famous were rendered green with envy, especially by passages re-
counting the achievements of Reshada's children. Raised in a slum,
they were paragons of art, music, and intelligent conversation. One
obtained an MBA from Wharton, the world's premier business school,
the other won a scholarship to Princeton. Reshada looked upon what
she had done and pronounced herself satisfied.

"I just hope it doesn't get boring now," she said. "I'd hate to have
to move away."

—*Sunday Telegraph*, April 2004

Postscript: Years later, I took Sir V. S. Naipaul on what purported to be
a tour of Johannesburg's underbelly. I had primed the great novelist
with stories about Yeoville's glory days and its subsequent degenera-
tion into squalor, but when we got there humiliation awaited. The government had recently spent R70 million on a World Cup–related urban
upgrade. Yeoville looked neat, orderly, stable, and even prosperous. I
suspect the grand old man thought I was a complete bullshitter.

PART SIX
DARKNESS

HOUSE FOR SALE
IN DOOMED COUNTRY

Nothing lasts in the deepest south. Moments of optimism give way to seasons of despair, or, in my case, to long periods of amused skepticism about almost everything, including myself. Americans seldom get my jokes, but I found a home of sorts at a grand old British institution called the Spectator, *founded in the 1840s and still dedicated to a drily cynical form of High Toryism. In my imagination, the* Spectator *was a place of dark wood panels where hock-swilling Old Etonians sat around in leather armchairs, chortling about the glories of empire and the vicissitudes of Her Majesty's subject nations. We never met in person, but the magazine's esteemed editors were often willing to print chatty dispatches from a former colony.*

Nine months ago, South Africa seemed to be muddling through in a happy-go-lucky fashion. The economy was growing, albeit slowly. Trains ran, if not exactly on time. If you called the police, they eventually came. We thought our table was fairly solid, and that we would sit at it indefinitely, quaffing that old Rainbow Nation ambrosia. Now, almost overnight, we have come to the dismaying realization that much around us is rotten. Nearly half our provinces and municipalities are said to be on the verge of collapse. A murderous succession dispute has broken out in the ruling African National Congress. Our auditor-general reportedly has sleepless nights on account of the billions that cannot be properly accounted for. Whites have been moaning about such things for years, but you know you're in serious trouble when President Thabo Mbeki admits the "naked truth" that his government has been infiltrated by chancers seeking to enrich themselves and "plunder the people's resources."

I knew in my bones that it would come to this, but somewhere along the line I got tired of stinking up my surroundings with predictions of doom, so I shut up and went with the flow. Ergo, I cannot say, told you so. But I have a pretty good idea why things went wrong, and it all began with transformation, a euphemism for ridding the civil service of whites, especially white males. Under apartheid, those chaps ran everything. Clearly, this had to change, but white males carried the institutional memory in their brains, and blacks who replaced them tended to flounder. This led to what we call "capacity problems," a euphemism for blacks who couldn't or wouldn't carry out the jobs for which they were paid. Capacity problems in turn led to crises in electricity supply, refuse removal, road maintenance, health care, law enforcement, and so on. Again, white malcontents have complained about such things for years, but you know you're in trouble when an eminent black journalist like Justice Malala dismisses the Mbeki administration as an "outrage," characterized by "a shocking lack of leadership" on the part of a cabinet riddled with "incompetent, inept, and arrogant" buffoons.

In short, we're in crisis. Everyone acknowledges it but somehow we never see firm corrective action. Previously we were told it was awkward for a black liberation movement to purge black appointees, even if they were useless. This year, a new excuse emerged.

Back in April, around the time of the ominous table-leg incident, the actress Janet Suzman and I dined with a bossy American woman who bit my head off when I opined that our recently deposed deputy president, Jacob Zuma, would one day step into Nelson Mandela's shoes. For a foreign feminist, it was unthinkable that a man with four years of schooling and rape and corruption charges pending should become president of anything. My explanations to the contrary were dismissed as racist rubbish, but let me air them anyway.

Zuma is a Zulu, and when he became a target for criminal investigation, many fellow tribesmen suspected he was being stitched up by President Mbeki, who was reputedly keen to eliminate him as a potential successor. Conspiracists noted that Mbeki was a Xhosa, and that various members of what we call the "Xhosa nostra" had become billionaires as a result of their political connections, whereas Zuma's allegedly improper payments were limited to a trifling £100,000. They found it even more fishy that the sad and desperate young woman who invited herself to spend a night in Zuma's home, only to accuse him of rape in the aftermath, was acquainted with Minister of Intelligence Ronnie Kasrils, a KGB-trained master of the dark arts of espionage, presumably including honey traps.

Zulus are a warlike bunch, as we know, and the Zuma affair got their blood up. Thousands turned out to cheer their homeboy at his rape trial, and to denounce his accuser as a harlot bribed to bear false witness. Zuma's acquittal sparked riotous celebrations, and when his corruption trial started, the crowds were even larger. T-shirts reading "100% Zulu Boy" were still evident, but now there were red flags, too, because radicals had started rallying to the Zuma cause. First to join were the young lions of the ANC Youth League. They were followed by the Young Communists, then by large sectors of the trade union movement and the Communist Party proper. All that remained was for Winnie Mandela to take sides, and lo: when the judge dismissed Zuma's corruption charges in late September, she materialized among the jubilant masses, praising the Lord for answering her prayers.

These developments dumbfounded naive left-liberals, who had repeatedly assured us that Zuma was politically dead. Feminists recalled how a dalliance with Ms. Lewinski almost destroyed Bill Clinton. AIDS activists were scandalized by Zuma's failure to use a condom during the rape-case escapade, even though the woman involved was HIV-infected. Moralists contended that even though criminal charges had proved unsustainable, there were enough facts on the table to show

231

that Zuma was sorely lacking in probity. For such people, it was un-hinging to see Zuma become the leading contender for South Africa's presidency, greeted at every turn by adoring supporters who informed reporters that the Ten Commandments were an alien invention that didn't apply to African males. Their campaign song was even more un-nerving: "Bring me my machine gun." A Serbian journalist presently resident here took one look at this and wrote a piece headlined "Time to Panic?"

Hmm. My friend Steve, a capitalist who golfs with the black elite, says this is nonsense. "Zuma is charming," he says. "Things will settle down. We can do business with him." Maybe so, but the next general election is three years away, and meanwhile, government is incapable of acting against the borers in our woodwork.

Let's look at law enforcement, one smallish aspect of the growing problem. After years of slow decline, crime surged earlier this year, with insurance companies reporting a 20 percent rise in claims. Some blamed a strike by security guards, who took to looting shops they had previously guarded, and throwing scabs off trains. Others pointed the finger at feral refugees from Zimbabwe. "Capacity problems" in the police were certainly a factor, too. In the midst of all this, a convoy of expensive cars carrying senior ANC dignitaries rolled up at a prison outside Cape Town. Uniformed warders swarmed out of the gates, and the gathering turned into a revolutionary song and dance extravaganza in honor of Tony Yengeni, a popular ex-MP about to start serving four years for fraud.

Is this not bizarre? A politician accepts a discounted Mercedes from an arms contractor, lies about it and gets nailed—and several of the ruling party's most prominent leaders hail him as a hero, a stagger-ing insult to their own criminal justice apparatus. In her eagerness to charm the rabble, National Assembly Speaker Baleka Mbete went so far as to claim that Yengeni had never committed fraud, even though he pled guilty to it. The main opposition party, the Democratic Alli-ance, termed her behavior "disgraceful," but there was no retribution.

Why? Because a crackdown by Mbeki might cause figures like Mbete to defect to Zuma, who is not particularly punctilious about whom he accepts as allies. Don Mkhwanazi, for instance, got into hot water after hiring a "well-known crook" to assist him in his duties as boss of the Central Energy Fund. Mkhwanazi claimed racists were defaming him, but fell silent when it emerged that his bent chum (who earned £300,000 a year) was channeling money into a bank account that paid Mkhwanazi's mortgage in a posh Jo'burg suburb. Mkhwanazi resigned in disgrace. Today he is a trustee of Zuma's unofficial presidential election campaign.

My pal Steve says one shouldn't take such things too seriously, noting that respectable people have also cast their lot in with Zuma. Maybe so, but Zuma's core supporters are scary. The other day, they put on a spectacular display at a conclave of Cosatu, the mighty Congress of South African Trade Unions. Whenever an incumbent cabinet member appeared, delegates surged to their feet, waving red flags and chanting, "Tell us, what has Zuma done?" One minister was jeered off the podium. The deputy state president was "humiliated and degraded" by hecklers, who went on to sing, "It is better for us to take over this country, we will go with the Communists." President Mbeki wisely kept his distance, but they had a song for him, too: "We will kill this big ugly dog for Zuma."

Alas, poor Thabo. I'm no great fan of our remote and autocratic president, but the charges emanating from the red brigade—"betraying the poor" and "tolerating inequality"—are asinine. A former Communist, Mbeki saw the light in the late 1980s and cajoled his comrades into a historic compromise with capitalism. His saturnine manipulations of business and labor led to a massively increased tax harvest, which, in turn, financed the creation of a welfare state, with 11 million poor now receiving subsistence grants of one sort or another. This is amazing. A welfare state in Africa!

Unfortunately, such goodies are the fruits of gradualism, and I can't see us staying the course. Jacob Zuma wants the big job, so he promised to resurrect the ANC's revolutionary tradition, and the movement's most dedicated activists immediately rallied to his standard. As I see it, the only way for Mbeki loyalists to block him is by promising even more loot to the masses, and once they do that, Zuma will surely move even further leftward. Nobody (save opposition leader Tony Leon, who is white and therefore irrelevant) is going to stand up and say, "Sorry, folks, this isn't the answer, we have to work harder, exercise self-discipline, and bring white technocrats back into government so as to make things work again."

And besides: if by some miracle Mr. Leon started swaying the electorate, would our rulers put up with it? The ANC dominates almost everything else, but it has never won an election here in Cape Town. This enrages the city's black power faction, which has prevailed upon the ANC to oust Democratic Alliance mayor Helen Zille and impose a multiparty government. The stated reason for this initiative is that Zille's coalition is weak and unstable. Maybe so, but we all know it's really a power grab, inspired at least in part by fears that Africa's last white- and Creole-controlled city will continue to prosper while all else hurtles into a black hole of dysfunctionality. What can we do? Some in the ruling party have a peculiar view of democracy. They see it as a system designed to put themselves in power. If voters fail to understand this, their mistakes must be corrected by fiat.

No, there won't be civil war. Whites are finished. According to a recent study, one in six of us has left since the ANC took over, and those who remain know their place. For apartheid-era police minister Adriaan Vlok, this turned out to be on his knees, washing the feet of those he sinned against during the struggle. Truly! He carried a briefcase and a basin into various government buildings and performed acts of abject contrition in public. No doubt Mr. Vlok's bones were warning him to repent before the end came.

Ah, well. Let's look on the bright side. Osama bin Laden has no beef with us, we are not sinking into a Mesopotamian quagmire, and the weather is wonderful in summer. Anyone want a house here?

—*Spectator*, October 2006

UGLY SCENES
IN BOER PROVENCE

On the day that Robert Mugabe's genocidal regime acceded to the chair of the UN's Commission on Sustainable Development, I found myself in the lovely Cape village of Franschhoek, once a Boer farming town but now more French and precious than Provence itself. Even as bitter debate broke out in the distant UN, I was checking into a luxurious hostelry and trimming my nostril hairs in preparation for meeting such luminaries as Liz Calder, publisher of the Harry Potter books, and Siri Hustvedt, a glamorous blonde novelist. We had come to participate in the inaugural Franschhoek Literary Festival, but my thoughts were in New York with UK Environment Minister Ian Pearson, who was attempting to convince African diplomats that one could not appoint a malignant regime like Zimbabwe's to the chair of anything, let alone a committee on development. The Africans did not take this kindly. "It's an insult to our intelligence," said Boniface Chidyausiku, Zimbabwe's UN ambassador. Most African delegates agreed, and Pearson went down in flames, victim of what the press called an "overwhelming" snub to the West.

I first saw Robert Mugabe in the flesh at a UN Earth Summit in Johannesburg in 2002. His appearance on the podium was preceded by U.S. Defense Secretary Colin Powell, who was booed and jeered, and by British Prime Minister Tony Blair, who met with similar indignities. Mugabe, on the other hand, was greeted by a tumultuous standing ovation. It was shocking to see diplomats according such an honor to a malevolent little shit whose genocidal proclivities were already apparent, but I wrote it off as a passing fad. At the time, black power fanatics were still pumped up over Mugabe's seizure of white-owned farmland, and one assumed their enthusiasm would wear off once the consequences of Comrade Bob's folly manifested themselves.

Not so. By 2004, Zimbabwe's economy was in freefall and his subjects were growing hungry, but Mugabe was more popular than ever in the black diaspora. He received standing ovations in many African capitals. At President Thabo Mbeki's 2004 swearing-in ceremony he had an entire stadium on its feet. By then, it was clear that Mugabe's "fast-track land reform program" had reversed his popularity at home, forcing him to resort to bludgeoning opponents and rigging elections in order to stay in power. His black supporters didn't care at all. Mugabe was giving the whites hell. Mugabe was therefore a hero. "Mugabe is speaking for black people worldwide," wrote Johannesburg commentator Harry Mashabela.

One assumes this accounts for the Mbeki administration's reluctance to criticize Mugabe in public. We were told that the situation in Zimbabwe was very delicate, and that "quiet diplomacy" offered the best shot at staving off anarchy. For a while this seemed plausible, but in time it became clear that quiet diplomacy was mostly a cover for covert support. Western moves to expel Mugabe from the Commonwealth were initially blocked by Thabo Mbeki. He also blocked attempts to place Mugabe's atrocities on the agenda at the UN Security Council and the UN Human Rights Committee. These developments allowed Comrade Bob's popularity in the black diaspora to swell to rock star proportions. Last year, the cocky little psychopath informed an audience of African-American New Yorkers that his rule had created "an unprecedented era of peace and tranquillity" back home. They gave him a standing ovation.

One understands the wounds of history, but even so, I thought there would come a day when Mugabe's fans realized their hero's behavior was restoring the reputation of Ian Smith, widely reviled for predicting that Rhodesia would be buggered if blacks took over. Well, they took over, and Smith stands vindicated. Today's Zimbabwe is a very sad place. Eight out of ten citizens are jobless, and those who have work are screwed, too, because inflation is 2,200 percent and they can't afford food. Hospitals and schools are collapsing, factories closing. R. W. Johnson of the *Sunday Times* recently interviewed a game ranger who said Zimbabwe's hyena were developing a taste for human flesh, the result of scavenging on corpses "cast into collective pits like cattle." Johnson concluded that Mugabe's misrule had resulted in as many as two million deaths and that "the number is now heading into regions previously explored only by Stalin, Mao, and Adolf Eichmann."

It was against this backdrop that the UN's Commission on Sustainable Development met to elect a new leader on May 11. The chair of this body rotates between regions; this year, it fell to Africa to make an appointment, and African countries seemed bent on installing Mugabe's man. At first, Western diplomats thought this was some sort of joke, but as the day passed, it emerged that Africans were indeed of the opinion that a body dedicated to fostering development could credibly be chaired by a murderous regime that had reduced a once-thriving nation to absolute penury. The reaction of Western diplomats and journalists was disbelief. "This is beyond parody," said an Australian newspaper columnist. "Preposterous," said the human rights lobby Freedom House. But Africans wangled support from Latin America and their motion was carried.

News of their triumph cast me into abject gloom, and I made it my business to stink up Franschhoek's rarefied air with predictions of impending trouble here in South Africa. This was not what civilized whites wanted to hear on a lovely autumn day, what with the economy growing at 5 percent and surprising numbers capable of forking out £50 a plate to dine with visiting writers. One such dinner took place on an achingly lovely wine estate that calls itself Haute Cabrière, if you don't mind. I was seated alongside Bevil Rudd, grandson of Cecil Rhodes's right-hand man and close to the widow of late *Observer* publisher David Astor. Mrs. Astor was eager to tell of the *Observer*'s role in the downfall of apartheid (the Astors were good chums with Mandela and hired Anthony Sampson and Colin Legum to agitate against the dreadful Boers). Bevil Rudd was a genial old eccentric with a mad scientist hairdo, keen to describe his friendship with the African writer Can Themba.

Opposite us, a spiky-haired codger was rattling on in a dismissive way about skeptics who doubt the sustainability of the South Africa miracle. "This is a wonderful country," said Ken Owen, esteemed former editor of South Africa's dominant Sunday paper. "I just get richer and richer. Read this week's *Economist*! Our economy is roaring ahead at four times the rate of New Zealand's," and so on. With several glasses of wine under my belt, I was emboldened to say, "Pardon me, but your optimism seems unfounded." My fellow diners looked mystified, so I explained what had just happened in New York. "You'd have to be blind to misread the writing on the wall here," I concluded.

The grand personages looked as if a bad smell had reached their noses. Owen said he'd been reading my scribblings in these very pages and hadn't liked them at all. "I thought you were just playing up to the Brits for the money," he said, "but you actually believe this stuff!" Then he explained to the gathering that ANC policy toward Mugabe was entirely rational and designed to prevent Zimbabwe imploding. "Ah, come on," I said. "Zimbabwe imploded years ago." Jonathan Shapiro, aka the eminent leftish cartoonist Zapiro, intervened at this point, because things were getting nasty. He was willing to allow that the ANC was guilty of double standards when it came to human rights, but I wasn't having any of that. I said, "Screw double standards. Mugabe's country is ruined and his people are starving, but he smashed the white farmers, so blacks—our government included—support him regardless. These people hate us," I concluded. Whereupon Owen lost it entirely. "You're pathetic," he shouted. "Pathetic!"

I was heavily outnumbered, so I sallied forth into the night at that point, only to hear that I'd been trashed in absentia at a parallel literary dinner on the far side of town. There the antagonist was eminent leftish journalist Max du Preez, who told the gathering he'd been pleased to see the back of J. M. Coetzee, our greatest novelist, now consumed by pessimism and residing in Australia. Max opined that the dreadful Malan should leave, too. He said he was even willing to pay my ticket.

Ah well, *c'est la vie*, as they say in Franschhoek. I'd picked the wrong time and place to don sackcloth and utter prophesies of doom, and it's just as well I left before they heard what else I had to say about liberals and their craven appeasing of the Mugabe beast.

It seems to me that last week's events in New York render a terrible verdict on well-intentioned do-gooders and the climate of impunity they create for African dictators. These thugs know there is no downside; their own subjects are helpless, and their supporters in the black diaspora don't seem to care what happens so long as the great dictator strikes a heroic anti-imperialist pose. As for Western and UN charities, they will happily take any insults dished out to them and come to feed the hungry anyway, thereby sparing dictators the consequences of their criminality.

There can be little doubt that this was an essential part of Mugabe's calculation. I mean, the man has something like eight university degrees. It cannot possibly have escaped his notice that overnight elimination of white commercial farmers would precipitate a food crisis. But why worry? He knew that the UN and allied charities would step in to feed the starving. Indeed, he was so confident of their generosity that he did not scruple to use donated food as a political weapon, rewarding his loyalists with free grub and punishing rebellious villages by withholding same while loudly proclaiming that food shortages were caused by drought rather than his own deranged policies.

This year, the rains truly failed and millions now face starvation. The response of Mugabe's government was dumbfounding: it announced that it would revoke the licenses of aid organizations unless they "stick to their core business" and otherwise behave themselves. "Government will not accept food offers from anyone for political purposes," said Information Minister Sikhanyiso Ndlovu. Furthermore, offers of help will be accepted only if they are "not attached with innuendos of failure." The reason for this, explained Comrade Ndlovu, is that "Zimbabwe deserves the same dignity as any other country."

I read this and think—pardon the language, but I think—"Fuck you!" This parasite doesn't even have the manners to say please or thank you. But this is beyond etiquette. In the absence of food aid, a ruler who behaves like Mugabe would long since have been torn limb from limb by his starving subjects. One recalls the demise of Louis XVI, of Mussolini and Ceauşescu. Is it not time to abandon Mugabe to a similar fate?

Liberals will think this unfair to innocent people, and they are right: hundreds of thousands might die if the food convoys do not start rolling into Zimbabwe soon. On the other hand, as R. W. Johnson reminds us, armies of the innocent have already perished at Mugabe's hand, but he continues to thrive. His party recently announced that his reign has been extended to at least 2010. He presumes to dictate terms to charities. Fellow African leaders continue to adulate him and insult the West by appointing his despicable government to positions of honor, and whenever he appears in public outside the country deluded blacks accord him a standing ovation. There is only one way to end this farce: cut off the aid and let Mugabe face the consequences.

The trick would be to tie food aid to acceptance of some very modest preconditions. Let's say: an end to torture, respect for the rule of law, and no political interference in the distribution of donated food. In other words, conditions so reasonable that even Mugabe's most ardent fans cannot dispute their justness. If he rejects them, the fans will be left in no doubt as to his moral repugnance, and his long-suffering subjects will know exactly who to blame for their hunger pangs.

—Spectator, May 2007

Postscript: It is ironic to note that Zimbabwe's 2,200 percent inflation rate seemed shocking in May 2007. Within a year, it had soared to 160,000 percent and starving Zimbabwe exiles were swapping billion-dollar Zimbabwe banknotes for a crust of bread on the streets of Jo'burg. South Africans don't have to travel to witness Zimbabwe's tragedy. We just walk out of our doors. Every third person on the streets of my suburb is a Zimbabwean, driven here by desperation.

There was a time when I thought such direct experience of Zimbabwe's misery would steer South Africa in a different direction. I am not so sure anymore. The ANC's last congress passed a resolution calling for closer ties with Mugabe, and its youth wing upholds his ruined country as a model for the next stage of our own "revolution."

NEMESIS

I'd like to dedicate this story to Branko Brkic, a Yugoslav who arrived in Johannesburg in 1991, on the run from Slobodan Milšoević's murderous regime and speaking not a word of English. Like Joseph Conrad, Branko came to love our language, and, especially, to love American magazines that devoted great swathes of space to the genre some call literary nonfiction. In about 2005, he was possessed by a very strange idea: why not create a magazine of this kind of writing in Johannesburg? I warned that his seed would perish on arid ground, but Branko was a braver man than I, and for three glorious years South Africa had a monthly that strove, in its way, to be The New Yorker *of Africa. It was called* Maverick.

Is it chaos theory that holds that a butterfly flaps its wings in Tasmania, causing an enormously complex chain reaction that eventually results in a devastating hurricane on the far side of the planet? This story opens with just such an event. It takes place outside international arrivals at Johannesburg International Airport on a hot morning in March 2000. A South African Airways flight has just arrived from Germany. Passengers are edging out into the sun. Among them is a forty-five-year-old businessman in a black suit, carrying two suitcases. He puts them down and lights a cigarette. He spots his driver approaching and steps off the curb to wave him down.

Just then, a loiterer dashes forward, grabs one of the unattended cases, and runs. The man in the black suit looks an easy victim, balding and a bit soft in the middle. He isn't. He runs the felon down and drops him with a rugby tackle. An accomplice leaps into the fray, but by now the driver is out of the car and coming toward them, so the second hoodlum flees, leaving his buddy and the black suit wrestling on the pavement. Black suit sees security guards across the road and shouts for help, but they ignore him. At this, black suit loses his temper. He gives the struggling felon "a few taps" and warns that if he doesn't come quietly, he'll get hurt for real. Then he hauls the felon to his feet, twists his arm behind his back, and frog-marches him toward justice. The driver picks up the suitcases and follows. Onlookers shrug, go on their way.

The butterfly has flapped its wings. Eight years hence, this minor event will result in a scandal that reveals the outlines of a plan to subvert South Africa's justice system, inflicts mortal damage on State President Thabo Mbeki, and leads, ultimately, to the downfall of Jackie Selebi, chief of South Africa's national police force and president of Interpol as well. It's a story that reveals more than you want to know about South Africa's dark side, and it all began, improbably, with a bungled petty crime at the airport.

The improbable Mr. O'Sullivan

Paul O'Sullivan is a cautious man. You send an e-mail inviting him to dinner at a Rosebank steak house. He fires back a response saying, Sorry, I'm out of the country, try another date. Seconds later, he phones to say this is just a ruse; he can come, but suspects that sinister forces are intercepting his e-mail and wants to be sure they don't show up for dinner, too. O'Sullivan has many enemies, and he's reluctant to say too much about his survival strategies. "If I tell you what precautions I take," he says, sliding into a booth and ordering a Guinness, "I'm telling you how to defeat me."

In his fifties, O'Sullivan has the fleshy face of a prosperous banker. The blond hair is thinning, jowls forming. His skin is almost translucently pale, and his eyes a wary, washed-out blue-gray. Tonight he's wearing a bomber jacket and jeans, and there's a bulge on his hip that looks like a handgun. In this guise, he resembles a veteran detective sergeant in some 1980s British TV crime series, but appearances can be deceptive. Four days hence he'll be wearing a suit and tie, playing the polished toff at a chamber of commerce gathering. A week after that, drinking beer and chowing tripe in Soweto with black empowerment luminaries. The next afternoon, sunning himself at a Houghton poolside in the company of a hauntingly beautiful Russian who turns out to be his third wife, Irina, aged thirty-two.

O'Sullivan says he's Irish, but his accent shifts chameleonlike from British midlands to hard-core Johannesburg southern suburbs and even Afrikaans. He says he visited South Africa in the 1980s but was never comfortable because of apartheid. When Mandela was freed in 1990, however, "I came screaming down here with the wife and kids."

He was an electrical engineer by profession, but he'd made some sound investments and when he liquidated everything in the UK he was worth a shade over a million pounds; nice money when converted to rands at the preferential rate offered to immigrants. He bought a faux Cape Dutch mansion in Bedfordview and dabbled in property development before taking a job with Highmoon Properties. His starting salary was R100,000 per annum, but O'Sullivan was a driven man; by the end of the decade, he'd held senior executive positions in a string of firms like Chubb or Sage Properties, and his salary had risen tenfold.

That's the mundane part of his extraordinary CV. O'Sullivan describes himself as the son of a postwar colonial police officer who taught him to pull his weight and do his duty. So he'd pull weight at the office, and then pull a second shift as a volunteer for worthy causes. He was a director of the Johannesburg Tourist Board, chairman of the inner-city Community Policing Forum, director of the Tourism Business Council. According to the CV, he was the man who persuaded sponsors to install closed-circuit cameras throughout Johannesburg's crime-blighted downtown. The man who felt it was an insult for the city's main police station to be named after apartheid premier John Vorster and organized for it to be renamed Johannesburg Central. The man who raised R16 million to build a museum at the spot where schoolboy Hector Pieterson died in the opening minutes of the 1976 Soweto uprising.

O'Sullivan thought of South Africa as "paradise on earth." He loved the sun, the company of Africans, even loved crime, if only in the sense that it provided opportunities for high adventure. He joined the police reserve in 1992, and spent thirty hours a week pulling his weight there, too. He lectured at the police college, assisted in the prosecution of white-collar swindlers, and patrolled the streets as a beat cop. One night, on the East Rand, he and his partners stopped a car that had just been reported hijacked. O'Sullivan took three bullets in the ensuing shoot-out but lived to tell the tale. One of the bad guys didn't.

Three bullets would dampen most people's enthusiasm, but not O'Sullivan's. He's still inclined to get a faraway look in his eyes and say corny things like, "My old man taught me that if a country is worth living in, it's worth fighting for." Or, "I firmly believe that the world's next great civilization will rise right here in South Africa."

In pursuit of this vision, O'Sullivan flies to a tourism conference in Berlin in March 2000, representing the Soweto Tourism Development Association. He spends three days handing out glossy brochures and assuring apprehensive Europeans that no harm will befall them if they visit South Africa. Then he steps off the plane back home, and someone steals his suitcase. This does not amuse him, and there is worse to come.

"What happened," he says, "is that we arrive in the charge office and the sergeant behind the desk says, 'Ah, thanks, man, we'll take care of it from here.'" Being a part-time cop, O'Sullivan knows the sergeant can't do anything without a statement, so he insists on making one. Then he insists on being given a case number, or at least a cell register number. The sergeant says he can't help. By now, O'Sullivan's bones are telling him that this policeman is planning to cut a deal with the suspect as soon as his back is turned, so he whips out his camera, pops a flash in the sergeant's face, and says, "Right. If you don't phone me in twenty-four hours with a case number, I'm going to make sure you get fired or locked up or both."

After that, the law takes its course and the thief goes to prison, but the experience sets O'Sullivan thinking that someone ought to do something about the gauntlet tourists have to run after their jets touch down. Their baggage is sometimes rifled or stolen. In the concourse, they're besieged by dodgy taxi drivers. Petty thieves and armed robbers lurk outside, and from what he's seen, policing is pretty slack. So he arranges a reservist transfer to the airport's border police unit, and a year or so later accepts an offer to become group executive for security at the Airports Company of South Africa (Acsa), the partly state-owned group that manages the country's ten largest airfields. It's the perfect job for a man of his skills and inclination. He dusts off his hands and says, "Right, let's get stuck in."

Nature of the beast

"All international airports," says criminologist Mark Gurkel, "are sites of struggle between justice and criminality." Johannesburg International (as it was in 2001) holds its head high in this regard. In the course of the 1990s, South Africa became one of the planet's great marijuana-exporting nations, as well as a major transshipment point for Europe-bound cocaine.

An unknown proportion of this contraband is passing through JIA, which is also a hot spot for human traffickers who fly Third Worlders into Johannesburg, kit them out with fake identity documents, and ship them on to the UK, where a South African passport allows visa-free entry.[2] Policing this zoo requires the services of 1,200 people per shift: customs officers to inspect cargo; clerks to check passports; cops and intelligence specialists to watch out for smugglers, terrorists, or wanted criminals; and security guards to patrol the perimeters. In theory, it's the most tightly policed forty square kilometers in the country. In theory.

---

2. The British government withdrew this privilege in 2009, citing rampant corruption in the bureaucracy that issues South African passports and ID documents.

Five days after O'Sullivan starts his new job in July 2001, a truck rolls up to a perimeter gate that is supposed to be locked at all times. It isn't. There are supposed to be two guards on duty, but there's only one. He's supposed to be armed, but he isn't. Gunmen overpower him and proceed to the precious goods cargo terminal, where a Swissair plane is unloading a $16 million consignment of cash and diamonds. The gunmen help themselves and leave without being detected. This fiasco sets the tone. There will be five similar robberies before the year is out.

"Security was useless," says O'Sullivan. He catches guards sleeping on the job or accepting bribes to escort illegal immigrants around passport control; customs agents being paid to overlook containers full of counterfeit goods; cops who would, for a fee, smuggle a suitcase full of hot cash or contraband through security and hand it back to you in the departure lounge. According to O'Sullivan, you'd see airport workers lining up outside exchange bureaus after every shift change, waiting to convert their foreign currency bribes into rands. His boss, Acsa chairman Mashudu Ramano, shares his concerns, describing airport crime as "unbearable" and backing the Irishman's efforts to fight it.

O'Sullivan has no authority over policemen or customs agents, but he and Ramano can crack the whip over the Airports Company's private security contractors. The largest of these is Khuselani Security, the outfit whose supine guard let the Swissair robbers through the gates in the first week of O'Sullivan's tenure.

After that, the Irishman keeps an eye on Khuselani's operations and discovers dismaying shortcomings. Guards absent from their posts. Guards so ill-trained they barely understand their standing orders. In some instances there are guards who don't exist at all: the Airports Company is being billed for their services but when O'Sullivan makes surprise checks in the dead of night there's no one there. He starts documenting these lapses. Each time one occurs, he sends a letter to Khuselani's owners. By October 5, 2001, O'Sullivan has sent twenty-three such warnings and he's ready to take it to the next level: a legal letter informing Khuselani's owners that he's converting their contract from a yearly to a monthly basis and giving them thirty days to shape up or ship out.

A few days later, a giant Mercedes-Benz ML glides into Acsa's parking lot. It's a so-called Yengeni Benz, one of the seventy-odd luxury cars offered at steep discounts to figures positioned to ease approval of South Africa's purchase of some very expensive German warships. Out of it steps your proverbial fat cat—a giant Zulu, weighing at least 150 kilograms. He introduces himself to O'Sullivan as Noel Ngwenya, and says, "I understand you want to alter my contract." O'Sullivan assents. The visitor seems amused. He says, "You don't know who you're dealing with." Paul O'Sullivan has arrived at the base of a steep learning curve.

The battle of Johannesburg Airport

Professor Noel Ngwenya is a comet who blazed brightly for a year or two before vanishing into the obscurity from whence he came. Some say he once taught at Rand Afrikaans University, but that could not be confirmed. He apparently spent time in Canada and when he returned to South Africa was given a seat in the senate of a technology university in Durban. In the late 1990s, he comes into focus as an executive at arms manufacturer Denel's Isando facility. While there he comes to realize that vast opportunities are opening up in the security field: every national key point requires protection, and the ANC government is determined to swing the business to black-owned entities.

So Ngwenya quits Denel and becomes chief executive of a company called Khuselani Security, which, in 2000, bids for a giant contract put out by the state-owned Airports Company. The incumbent is Fidelity, an old-guard firm that stands little chance against a bright and shiny "black empowerment" outfit whose shareholders include Noel's brother Jerome, an eminent lawyer, and Vuyo Ndzeku, described by the *Mail & Guardian* as a man who could "open doors" and "take you to minister level, to premier level" in the ANC government.

Khuselani has little experience in the security field and only sixty employees, whereas the airports contract calls for 3,700, but these are minor problems. The political climate favors Khuselani, and it winds up winning a contract potentially worth R280 million over the next five years. Noel Ngwenya celebrates by throwing a victory bash at which the guest of honor is his friend Jacob Sello Selebi, the recently appointed national commissioner of police.

After taking his cut, Ngwenya discovers that he's underbid on the contract and there's too little money left to do the job properly. He pressures rank and file guards to accept minimum wage and newcomers are given little or no training. "If they were short staffed," says O'Sullivan, "they'd just go out into the street and hire anyone who fit the uniform." Some of the guards thus dragooned are good men, but others are bent or incompetent, and their managers are useless, in O'Sullivan's estimation. This leads, as we have seen, to an avalanche of complaints about Khuselani's performance and ultimately to a visit from the corpulent Ngwenya, who smiles and says, "You don't know who you're dealing with."

O'Sullivan registers the implied threat but it doesn't faze him, not even when two eminent empowerment wheeler-dealers come to warn him to tread carefully. Lungi Sisulu is a son of the illustrious Walter, who spent twenty-six years on Robben Island with Nelson Mandela. Sisulu tells O'Sullivan that Khuselani Security is actually his baby; he founded the firm and laid the groundwork for the Acsa bid before moving to New York, where his wife had been appointed South Africa's consul general. On his return, he says, he discovered Ngwenya had cut him out entirely.

His companion, the aforementioned Vuyo Ndzeku, says he was similarly treated and then thrown into prison—on the personal orders of Jackie Selebi, no less—when he threatened to cause a fuss. This strikes O'Sullivan as wildly implausible. The commissioner of police misusing his position to settle a business dispute? He offers Ndzeku a cup of tea, but secretly dismisses him as a nutter.

The very next morning, O'Sullivan receives a phone call saying Commissioner Selebi wants to see him. Selebi is an avuncular ANC veteran who served as South Africa's ambassador to the United Nations before being deployed to the police force. Friends describe him as a charming bon vivant and raconteur. Underlings dread his temper.

O'Sullivan is impressed by his uniform, a gold-braid-encrusted affair that steals the show in the VIP lounge where their meeting takes place. Selebi tells O'Sullivan that he's unhappy to hear that Acsa is at odds with his friend Noel Ngwenya. According to O'Sullivan, he bashes his fist on the table and says, "If you cancel that contract I'll have to take over security at the airport." This is reinforced the following morning by a call from Selebi's deputy Andre Pruis, who says, "The commissioner doesn't want you to make any changes to the existing contract."

O'Sullivan declines to follow these orders, pointing out that the police have no right to intervene in a dispute between Acsa and one of its contractors. In subsequent court papers, the police will claim that they were acting pursuant to a cabinet-level reevaluation of airport security in the wake of the September 11 terrorist attacks. O'Sullivan counters that if this is indeed the case the order should have come from Transport Minister Dullah Omar, under whose control the Airports Company falls. He asks the cops to make their case in writing, but nothing materializes, so O'Sullivan, with the backing of his board, proceeds with his plan to oust Khuselani.

On October 29, Ngwenya is formally notified that Acsa intends to revoke his contract on grounds of nonperformance. In response comes a letter accusing O'Sullivan of "violating the direct instructions of the National Commissioner of Police." The Airports Company's lawyers respond by again raising the issue of legal authority: on what grounds do the police presume to issue orders to Acsa? Nothing more is heard on this score, and the game moves in a new direction.

Mashudu Ramano is a financier who rose to prominence in the early 1990s as general secretary of the National African Federated Chamber of Commerce, or Nafcoc, a racially exclusive black business lobby. After the fall of apartheid, he rocketed to the top of the corporate world, becoming head of Nafcoc's investment arm, chairman of African Harvest, and, in August 2000, chairman of Acsa. On November 21, 2001, this corporate star sits down in front of a tape recorder to dictate an extraordinary story.

"The name is Mashudu Ramano," he begins. "Over the past four months, I have had a security problem." It all began, he says, when a disgruntled former employee warned him that "the ANC is doing an investigation of Mashudu" and that "he knew people who would put bullets in my head." Such talk initially struck Ramano as absurd, but as the Khuselani dispute intensified, he began to wonder. Strange things were happening around him. Spurious salesmen made calls to his home, asking questions about his family. Armed men came piling over his garden wall one night and traded shots with his security guards, an event that left Ramano so shaken he moved into a hotel and took the precaution of making this recording.

"Sometime during October," he continues, "we changed the contract of Khuselani Security, headed by a gentleman named Noel Ngwenya, who apparently has certain relationships with certain politicians. When we canceled the contract Noel appealed for help to the commissioner of police." Ramano notes that Selebi has approached employees with a view to getting the Khuselani decision reversed, but refuses to meet Ramano himself on the grounds that "he has instituted an investigation into my affairs and within two weeks he would have a report exposing whatever their findings are going to be." Ramano observes that these threats are "almost identical" to earlier warnings and concludes, "Perhaps there is a link between the security problems I am experiencing and the events that are now beginning to unfold."

He leaves the tape with his secretary, who is instructed to release it should any harm befall him. Five days later, policemen rock up at Ramano's hotel and haul him off to Pretoria, claiming they have discovered he is an illegal alien living in South Africa on forged identity documents. This is bizarre, given that Ramano was born and raised in Soweto, but it doesn't stop police spin doctors from leaking the story to the media. The same spin doctors launch a simultaneous strike against O'Sullivan, using credit card records and bank statements allegedly stolen from his office. These are handed to an investigative reporter at the *Mail & Guardian*, along with a briefing to the effect that they contain proof of corruption.

A reporter by the name of Evidence wa ka Ngobeni is particularly interested in a R400,000 deposit into O'Sullivan's bank account. O'Sullivan says he'd sold a tranche of shares on the stock market, but

Ngobeni seems to have been told the money is a bribe from the security company angling to replace Khuselani. Ngobeni is also interested in a credit card transaction involving the purchase of a voice-stress lie detector from the U.S. Federal Bureau of Investigation. "You impersonated a law enforcement officer here," he says. "You claimed you were with the border police."

"But I *am* with the border police," protests O'Sullivan. He pulls out his badge. "Detective Sergeant O'Sullivan, reservist attached to the border police." O'Sullivan's explanations notwithstanding, the *Mail & Guardian* publishes a story noting that Ramano and his security chief are facing investigation. If this is intended to intimidate them, it fails: the Acsa boys stand firm and, at midnight on November 30, Khuselani's contract is canceled. This is a crippling blow to Ngwenya and his allies, who go to court to have the revocation overturned.

A week later, a red Volkswagen with tinted windows falls in behind O'Sullivan as he leaves the office. As the VW draws abreast, he says, its passenger window slides down and he sees a man in a balaclava raising a gun to take aim at him. The Irishman does a hand-brake turn and screams off in the opposite direction. He's initially willing to regard this as just another Jo'burg hijacking attempt, but a month later there's another incident, in which shots are fired. There is no evidence to link either of these attacks to Khuselani, but this doesn't stop O'Sullivan from feeling someone has declared war on him, and retaliating in kind.

His chosen weapon is a tip-off to tax authorities, who are told that Khuselani is evading taxes. A raid on Khuselani's office reveals evidence of tax fraud that will eventually land Ngwenya in jail. Meanwhile, Ngwenya has the satisfaction of seeing O'Sullivan booted out of the police reserve, a move that drastically limits his ability to maneuver.

By now, O'Sullivan claims to have established that someone inside Acsa is reporting his every move to Ngwenya, so he starts investigating fellow executives for fraud and conflicts of interest, creating an atmosphere so toxic that only one end is conceivable: in January 2003 O'Sullivan is fired. In Acsa's view, the Irishman is the architect of his own misfortune. The company's lawyers say his behavior became "rude and aggressive," and that he spurned attempts at mediation.

They see this as an "incompatibility dismissal." O'Sullivan counters that his anticorruption activities continued until the day he was fired, "and if there was an incompatibility issue, this was its root cause."

In the aftermath, the Irishman files a wrongful dismissal suit, portraying himself as the victim of a conspiracy orchestrated from deep behind the scenes by police chief Selebi. But his case is crippled by reliance on conjecture. O'Sullivan can show that Selebi and Noel Ngwenya had a relationship, and that Selebi attempted to intervene on his friend's behalf when the Irishman moved to cancel Ngwenya's contract. But he cannot prove this had anything to do with his ultimate dismissal. The Public Protector ignores his appeals for an investigation, the police's Independent Complaints Directorate likewise. In April 2004, he convinces a judge to order the ICD to look into his complaint, but the outcome is a disaster for him: the Scotland Yard detective who conducts the inquiry concludes that O'Sullivan is unable to sustain his charges against Selebi, who has by now risen to global prominence as president of Interpol.

By January 2005, O'Sullivan is on the streets, all orthodox avenues of redress exhausted and his chances of landing another senior executive position fatally damaged. "And that," he says, "is when the war began."

O'Sullivan in the underworld

We are now entering murky territory where hard men carry guns and kill those who threaten their secrets. O'Sullivan is our guide in this netherworld, and when he talks about it, his narratives are so riddled with half-truths, ellipses, and evasions that they read like a cut-up William Burroughs novel. O'Sullivan says this is as it must be: "It's called securing your sources, your assets. If you don't protect them, they get terrified and refuse to testify. Or die." Almost all his sources are therefore nameless, and state law officers, who feature heavily in what follows, are under strict orders not to talk to the press. So then: should we trust our guide?

This turns out to be an interesting question. Over the years, O'Sullivan has acquired a chorus of supporters who see him as a self-sacrificing altruist who simply cannot be stopped once he gets his teeth into an investigation. "He'll work his butt off just for the honor of it," says Lungi Sisulu. "A man of the highest integrity," says former Chamber of Commerce and Industry president Patrick Corbin. Corporate lawyer Ronnie Napier got to know O'Sullivan while they were jointly investigating a giant fraud case in the nineties. "Paul's a serious operative with a focused and all-consuming passion for justice," he says. "God knows when he sleeps. This is a very unusual human being."

In the middle ground, battered by gales of disinformation, stands a small group of investigative reporters who have known O'Sullivan for years and rate him a reliable source. And in the opposite corner we find the police, who say the Irishman is a liar, a wife beater, a foreign secret agent, mentally unstable, an arms dealer, and a sexual predator besides.

As for *Maverick*, we yawed between these extremes on a daily basis, our confusion exacerbated by O'Sullivan's reluctance to disclose all the cards he was holding and offer details that could be independently verified. At times, we were ready to write him off as a fantasist, but we were always checked by the one unassailable fact on view here: the Irishman got it right. For years, he stood alone in a storm of derision, saying, "The police chief is a crook." Nobody believed him, so he squandered millions of his own money on the quest for proof, and lo, he now stands vindicated. The tale of how he did it reads like a spy novel, and may in parts be one. But it certainly merits hearing.

Some time in early 2005, we are told, O'Sullivan established an operations room in his Bedfordview home. He says the walls were covered with organograms showing the overlapping structures of half a dozen Johannesburg crime syndicates, with dotted lines linking crime bosses to shadowy intermediaries who were, in turn, linked in unknown ways to police headquarters in Pretoria. There were also aerial photographs (he's a pilot) of places of interest. A farmhouse where drugs were stashed. A security company's sprawling operations base. A holiday complex on the Indian Ocean where Selebi and his family once spent a holiday. The shelves in this room were laden with lever-arch files containing reports and statements, all meticulously typed by his own hands. All told, he estimates there were around 2,000 names in those files. The names were on his computer, too, in a law enforcement software program designed to find connections that elude human analysis. O'Sullivan also had recording devices, eavesdropping gear, and guns, because he was playing a dangerous game.

If you'd been standing outside a certain strip joint in Rivonia on certain nights in early 2005, you would have seen O'Sullivan rolling up in his Audi roadster, wearing his standard jeans and bomber jacket with a pistol bulging beneath. O'Sullivan has been hanging out here, trying to get a handle on who comes in, what they talk about. He's particularly interested in the bouncers, steroid-crazed gorillas with shaved heads who do dirty work on the side, like smashing up nightclubs that decline to hire the protection services of an outfit called CNSG—the Central National Security Group.

CNSG is one of several giant private security outfits that rose to power in the chaotic aftermath of apartheid's downfall, providing investigative and protective services to corporations that could no longer rely on the police. CNSG's owner, Clinton Nassif, grew up in a tough white working-class neighborhood called Mayfair and knows his way around racecourses, bookies, used car lots, and pawnshop fencing operations. These days, he appears to be a respectable businessman but O'Sullivan doesn't buy it. He believes Nassif is involved in all sorts of rackets, and that he has police protection.

Exactly how this works O'Sullivan has no idea, but he's watching and learning, making friends in dark corners. In fact, he says he's recruited two of Nassif's sidekicks as deep-cover agents, paying them out of his own pocket. O'Sullivan is building a dossier. A dossier, ultimately, on police chief Selebi.

In April 2005, O'Sullivan buys a cheap pay-as-you-go cell phone, easy to ditch once it's served its purpose. He uses it to call CNSG, posing as a security consultant whose clients are interested in the firm's services. They say, come in, we'll show you around. The tour starts in a skyscraper that houses Johannesburg Consolidated Investments, or

JCI, one of the city's oldest and richest gold mining houses, now controlled by a young stock market wizard named Brett Kebble. Kebble is Nassif's most important client, and O'Sullivan is impressed by the work CNSG has done for him. "It was a sophisticated setup," he says. "Skilled managers, modern control room, closed-circuit surveillance of almost everyone in the building."

On the other hand, O'Sullivan doubts that this aspect of Nassif's business is generating enough to subsidize the boss's flashy lifestyle. The Mayfair homeboy has moved up in the world. He owns two properties in the northern suburbs, a posh weekend retreat at Hartbeespoort Dam, shares in various IT companies, and wristwatches worth around R3 million. Nassif is also a fan of rare and expensive cars. He's been seen driving a Lamborghini, a Mercedes-Benz SC65, and a Porsche GT2. He seems to own an entire fleet of Hummers. Where's all the money coming from?

Some potential answers emerge in the next phase of the tour, which features a visit to CNSG's headquarters on Loveday Street. "It was like a warehouse," says O'Sullivan, "a big semi-industrial indoor car park with a suite of offices inside." As they move around the site, his guide is boasting about the firm's police connections. They have several legendary (some would say notorious) Murder and Robbery Squad veterans on the payroll. Several serving cops are moonlighting for them, too. "They took me into a control room from where they ran dirty tricks and undercover ops," says O'Sullivan. "All these people tapping away at computers. They told me, 'From here we can do wiretaps, get phone records and police records.' The message was, 'Between us and this brick wall, you can get anything you want here.'"

As he leaves, the guide hands O'Sullivan a glossy brochure hyping CNSG's capabilities. In it, there's a color photograph of a young woman named Ntombi Matshoba. A caption identifies her as a director of CNSG. The name means nothing to the Irishman, so the guide gives him a nudge: "Keep it to yourself, but she's Jackie Selebi's mistress."

At this point in the telling, O'Sullivan's eyes widen comically and he exclaims, "Hello?" It turns out Matshoba was Selebi's secretary in the early 1990s, when the ANC tasked him to supervise the return of exiles from military bases elsewhere in Africa. They fell in love and had a child together. Selebi still lives with his wife, Ann, but he and Ntombi are often seen together in public. What on earth is the police chief's girlfriend doing in a firm that, by Sullivan's reckoning, is involved in protection rackets, money laundering, industrial espionage, and assassination?

Meanwhile, another line of investigation has thrown up the name of Glenn Agliotti, a charming glad-hander who usually introduces himself as an investor and commodities trader. The Italian–South African has no record, but O'Sullivan's police connections tell him that Agliotti's nickname was the "Landlord," who runs counterfeit goods, drugs, and black market cigarettes through Johannesburg Airport.

O'Sullivan pays little attention until the late winter of 2005, when a police reservist friend of his responds to a "robbery in progress" call at an exclusive address in Sandton. While he's interviewing the victim, a muscular neighbor comes over and introduces himself as Glenn Agliotti. When he hears what's happened, Agliotti whips out a cell phone, dials a number, and hands the receiver to the cop, who finds himself speaking to police chief Selebi. The commissioner says, "Glenn is a friend of mine, take good care of him," or words to that effect. The astonished reservist hands the phone back to Agliotti, who seems very pleased with himself. He says, "Ja, Jackie's my mate. We had breakfast just this morning." Then he hands the cop a business card that identifies himself as an employee of Brett Kebble's company JCI. It's another "Hello" moment.

So now O'Sullivan's got Nassif, Agliotti, and the police chief and his mistress locked in a mysterious orbit around Brett Kebble. What makes this particularly intriguing is that Kebble has become very big news in recent weeks. On August 30, 2005, the flamboyant young wheeler-dealer lost control of the mining house JCI in a shareholders' revolt triggered by deepening doubts about his integrity. Forensic accountants are beavering in JCI's books, where they will shortly uncover billions missing. In months to come, some will claim that Kebble wanted to die rather than face the music and was begging underworld connections to help him stage an "assisted suicide." Others maintain he'd lost the confidence of his criminal associates, who feared he was about to cut a deal with prosecutors and sacrifice them all to save his own neck. Whatever the truth, Kebble dies on the night of September 27, 2005, cut down by seven bullets on a lonely road on his way to a dinner engagement.

Newspapers initially portray the murder as a botched hijacking, but Paul O'Sullivan says he heard an entirely different story from his underworld connections. They say the shooting was orchestrated by Agliotti in conjunction with John Stratton, Kebble's partner, and Clinton Nassif, whose bouncers are said to have pulled the trigger. They say Agliotti was lurking nearby when the hit went down and called police chief Selebi on his cell phone to report its successful conclusion.

O'Sullivan can't remotely prove any of this. In fact, the story is so big and strange he barely believes it himself. "I swallowed hard," he says. "I mean, put yourself in my shoes. Who do I tell?" According to news reports, Nassif's operatives were all over the Kebble murder scene, tampering with evidence and chatting happily with police investigators, one of whom had a brother who worked for Nassif's security firm. Under the circumstances, O'Sullivan fears that disclosing his informers' scuttlebutt to police might result in bullets in the head for all concerned. So he started a process he likens to "planting a trail of aniseed balls and letting the hounds smell them out."

In early October 2005, eight days after the murder, the Irishman drafts what he calls "an overview of personalities around Kebble, mentioning Nassif, Agliotti, Selebi, Selebi's girlfriend, and many others." He hands the memo to the Scorpions, hoping it will be enough to get the bloodhounds baying. But there is no response. Nothing at all. By Christmas, O'Sullivan has come to the dismaying conclusion that Jackie Selebi is truly untouchable. He is wrong.

Enter the Scorpions

The Directorate of Special Operations, aka the Scorpions, is an elite crime-fighting unit established to combat the perception that post-apartheid South Africa has become a relaxed and congenial operating base for some of the world's nastiest crime syndicates. Trained largely by the FBI, the Scorpions are a great success, credited with solving more than 80 percent of cases they investigate. The unit has a knack for making sure that TV cameras are on hand when it raids the homes of prominent suspects, which leads to heated charges of trial by media. But this is part of the plan. The Scorpions are intended to be seen as Hollywood-style supercops who drive fast cars, carry special weapons, and strike unexpectedly. They're supposed to be invincible, incorruptible, deadly.

On the day of Kebble's death they are also in grave political trouble, largely as a result of their pursuit of corruption charges against Jacob Zuma, whose recent dismissal from the deputy presidency has caused a major split in the ruling African National Congress. The Scorpions say they're just doing their job, but Zuma supporters believe President Thabo Mbeki is using them to eliminate Zuma as a rival.

This argument seems to have some merit, but meanwhile, the growing populist clamor to disband the Scorpions is providing cover for a host of other agendas. ANC parliamentarians are still smarting over the unit's "Travelgate" investigation, which revealed that at least thirty-eight government MPs had fraudulently padded their expense accounts. In Cape Town, ANC militants are angry about the Scorpions' involvement in the jailing of their hero MP Tony Yengeni, convicted of lying under oath about favors from a German arms manufacturer. A Durban-based cabal is furious about the Scorpions' probe into the finances of former Transport Minister Mac Maharaj, and several ANC figures are anxious about the unit's investigation of Brett Kebble, who pumped millions of other people's money into flimsy "joint ventures" with influential political figures.

Against this backdrop, the last thing the Scorpions need is another high-profile investigation of a senior ANC leader, which might explain why O'Sullivan's memo about Selebi has gone unanswered. Behind the scenes, however, the plot is thickening.

The Kebble murder investigation is initially a joint police–Scorpions effort, with the rival forces sharing information and apparently pursuing clues with equal zeal. By January 2006, however, Johannesburg chief prosecutor Charin de Beer has come to suspect something is wrong somewhere. A top secret letter to President Mbeki expresses it thus: "In essence, the complaint was that the National Commissioner of the SAPS, Mr. J. S. Selebi, was perceived to be protecting a target of the investigation." The letter goes on to state that "analysis of phone call data" shows "suspicious" calls between Selebi and certain suspects "on the night of and after the murder," and that Selebi has warned these suspects to watch their backs. Only at this point—on March 28, 2006—is an investigation formally authorized.

Within days, O'Sullivan is summoned to a coffee shop to meet a fast-talking, chain-smoking Scorpions investigator named Robyn Plitt. She tells him the Scorpions are looking into Selebi's organized crime connections, and that she'd like to compare notes with him. O'Sullivan's heart leaps: at last, a real investigation. "Think of my situation," he says. "You're out there doing your thing in the playground and all the other children are spitting and throwing stones at you and nobody's backing you up. Then all of a sudden you've got five hundred guys behind you. I thought, we're on the move at last, so I dropped everything else and ramped up the speed of my investigation. I worked seven days a week, flat out, to bring all the pieces together."

O'Sullivan says he was operating in accordance with the domino theory of organized crime investigation: you start at the very bottom, catch a small fry, force him to roll over on his boss, and so on up the rungs. In this case, the bottom is easy to plumb: O'Sullivan knows an East Rand bar owner whose joint was trashed by CNSG boss Nassif's bouncers when he declined to pay protection. The bar owner provided police with the bouncers' names and closed-circuit TV footage of their rampage, but no arrests were made. O'Sullivan visits the injured party and says, "Want justice? I can help you." The bar owner agrees to cooperate.

A second aniseed ball involves a brand-new Mercedes E55, apparently totalled in an accident in 2004. The car belonged to Nassif, who insisted that insurer Lloyds pay him out for his loss. According to O'Sullivan, insurance investigators suspected that there was something fishy about the claim but couldn't prove anything, so Nassif walked off with a check for R500,000. Two years later, O'Sullivan asks the insurance assessors to reopen their file for him. They refuse. He speaks to their lawyer, who says, "I have a wife and kids," and hangs up.

"I realized I had to start again from scratch," says O'Sullivan, "so I went to the scene of the accident looking for tow truck operators. I went back night after night until I found a guy who helped load Nassif's vehicle onto a flatbed. He told me the name of the flatbed driver, and that he lived somewhere in Alexandra township. I drove around Alex for days, knocking on doors. Do you know what it's like, looking for an address in Alex? I made six or seven visits and in the end I found this guy, and he confirmed what we'd suspected: when Nassif's car was loaded onto that flatbed it had a flat tire with a damaged rim, nothing else."

O'Sullivan says he booked the driver off work, gave him a stipend, and sent him to Cape Town, "where he could not be got at." Then he arranged for the Scorpions to be tipped off about his breakthrough. It subsequently emerged that Nassif took the barely damaged Mercedes to a panel beater and had it dropped repeatedly off a forklift. After this, the car was indeed a write-off and Nassif was able to file a fraudulent insurance claim that he would come to bitterly regret.

A third aniseed ball involves a trucker who has been doing odd jobs for Glenn Agliotti for years, moving consignments of drugs, untaxed cigarettes, and counterfeit goods around town. When the Scorpions' Robyn Plitt mentions this guy's name, it rings bells in O'Sullivan's brain. "I realized I'd met him about ten years earlier, so I set out to find him." The Irishman traces the trucker, wins his trust, and documents every delivery he's ever made for Agliotti. The cherry on the cake is a giant consignment of hashish and compressed marijuana, shipped to South Africa from Iran by an international drug syndicate a year earlier. Part of the consignment is still sitting in the source's warehouse.

On April 27, 2006, O'Sullivan hands the trucker and his electrifying information to the Scorpions. Ten weeks later, Johannesburg wakes up to news of a R200 million hashish bust in the city's eastern suburbs. After that, the dominoes tumble. Confronted with video footage of themselves trashing an East Rand pool hall and other evidence, bouncers Mikey Schultz and Nigel McGurk start cooperating. Nassif collapses when investigators tell him he's going to prison for the fraudulent insurance claim. As for Agliotti, the giant hashish bust results in charges likely to earn him fifteen years in jail unless he cooperates. By the end of 2006, everyone is talking, and the investigation has moved into realms darker than anything O'Sullivan has dreamed of.

According to court documents, the conspiracy dates back to December 2002, when financier Brett Kebble learned that the Scorpions were investigating him. Incensed that anyone should treat him thus, Kebble "initiated a project to get Bulelani Ngcuka and Penuell Maduna out of office." Safety and Security Minister Maduna was the man who'd ultimately authorized the Kebble investigation, and chief prosecutor Bulelani Ngcuka controlled the Scorpions, who'd carried it out.

These targets placed Kebble in alignment with a powerful ANC faction that was also gunning for Scorpions boss Ngcuka, largely on account of his pursuit of corruption charges against Jacob Zuma. According to insiders, Kebble felt that the best way to solve his own legal problems was to support Zuma's counterattack. His motives were "purely selfish," says Kebble biographer Barry Sergeant. "If he could show that Zuma was the victim of a malicious, politically based smear campaign, Kebble reasoned that he might also be able to discredit the charges he faced as part of a power play within the ANC." Kebble thus became an outspoken Zuma supporter, haranguing journalists about the Scorpions' "sinister machinations" and financing ANC rebels who shared that view.

Glenn Agliotti came into the picture as a result of his friendship with Jackie Selebi. They'd known each other since the early 1990s, when Selebi was just another penniless returned exile, struggling to survive on an ANC stipend of R3,000 a month. Agliotti settled some medical bills on Selebi's behalf, and Selebi never forgot his kindness. When Selebi became police commissioner, Agliotti let it be known around town that he and "the chief" were close. It was this connection that brought Brett Kebble and his partner John Stratton to Agliotti's door.

"They wanted to know how much it would take to secure a relationship with Jackie, to have him in their camp," says Agliotti's confession. "I made up my own figure—a million dollars." Agliotti also suggested that Kebble retain the services of his friend Clinton Nassif, and organized the first of several dinners where police chief Selebi and Kebble met face-to-face.

In early 2004, Kebble deposited R10.7 million into a slush fund, and cash started flowing to the various conspirators. The lion's share allegedly went to Nassif, who was running a dirty tricks operation that reportedly included the attempted assassination of an investment analyst who'd come dangerously close to uncovering Kebble's grand swindle. Agliotti helped himself, too, and "more than R1.2 million" is said to have gone to Selebi, who allegedly made frequent visits to Agliotti's Midrand office to collect his cut.

Among the scores of affidavits filed in court by the Scorpions was one by Agliotti's sometime girlfriend Dianne Muller, who said she was frequently instructed to count and package large amounts of cash allegedly destined for Selebi. In at least one instance, she witnessed the actual handover. Muller said she packed R110,000 in cash in a bag and carried it into the boardroom where Agliotti and Selebi were waiting. Agliotti allegedly took the cash and slid it across the table to the commissioner, saying, "Here you go, china."

In return, Selebi lobbied for the Scorpions to be disbanded or placed under his command. In fairness, the police chief was antagonistic toward the Scorpions long before these payments commenced, and needed no inducement to act as he did. But if Agliotti is to be believed, Selebi eventually became a de facto member of his and Kebble's criminal enterprise. The drug dealer used Kebble's hot money to finance Selebi's campaign for the presidency of Interpol. The world's top policeman reciprocated by giving Agliotti access to secret documents, including a British Customs "activity report" indicating that he and his drug-dealing associates were under surveillance in the UK. In June 2006, Selebi passed on a document showing that Paul O'Sullivan had a mole inside Nassif's organization. As the Irishman says, "This was tantamount to putting out a hit on me, my source, and my family."

With evidence like this, the Scorpions had no further need of O'Sullivan's help. Indeed, court records show that Scorpions investigators were ordered to distance themselves from him in June 2006, on the grounds that his parallel investigation was threatening to muddy the waters. This didn't suit the powerful men who'd come to see the Irishman as a weapon whose timely detonation might blow the Scorpions to pieces.

"Destroy Lucifer"

To understand the next move in this game, it's essential to grasp an underlying paradox of South African politics. Our constitution guarantees a full range of Western-style freedoms, but the upper reaches of government are populated by Marxist ex-revolutionaries who are a bit suspicious of such things. All comrades pay lip service to the need for a free press and independent judiciary, but some comrades seem to expect these institutions to function according to Soviet rules: all freedoms are permissible save those that question the wisdom or integrity of senior party members, with any deviation treated as evidence of a counterrevolutionary plot. By 2006, this had become the first line of defense for politicians accused of corruption.

As Jackie Selebi's problems deepened, intelligence operatives in police headquarters claimed to discern "a multitude of insidious activities" on the part of those seeking to put the police chief behind bars. Countering this threat called for a counterintelligence campaign involving "telephone interceptions, remote data mining, source cultivation, and agent penetration." The ultimate aim of "Operation Destroy Lucifer," as this campaign came to be called, was to prove that the Scorpions had fallen under the control of "enemy formations."

O'Sullivan's first inkling of all this comes on November 6, when he comes home to find an angry message on his telephone answering machine. The caller is deputy police commissioner Andre Pruis, and he's upset about a newspaper story linking him to a putative "police mafia." Pruis maintains the story is rubbish and wants to know who planted it. O'Sullivan rigs up a recording device, then returns the call. After fifteen minutes of inconclusive sparring, Pruis lands a blow that leaves the Irishman momentarily speechless.

"What's your background, Paul?" says the policeman. "I'm an engineer," says the Irishman. Pruis chuckles. "Oh, yes? And your intelligence background?"

Someone has clearly burrowed into British military computers and unearthed something interesting: O'Sullivan *does* have an intelligence background. It's right there in his CV—a cryptic reference to "foreign intelligence work" during his stint with the British military in the 1970s. O'Sullivan says he can't discuss this aspect of his life, other than to say he went to places he can't name, where he did things he can't talk about. But there's little doubt that he's had intelligence training. You see it in the way he drives, the cleansing rites he follows to make sure he's not followed, his easy familiarity with espionage gadgetry: all classic British spycraft, straight out of a John le Carré novel. Pruis says, "I'm not a moron, Paul. I'm not a child. You run sources. You act as a handler. What is that? It's an intelligence role."

O'Sullivan says, "So I worked in intelligence. So what?" He maintains this has nothing to do with his crusade against police corruption, but Pruis doesn't buy it. The Afrikaner says he knows a spy when he sees one, and as far as he's concerned, the Irishman is exactly that. "Paul," he growls, "I'm after you."

A few days later, police start circulating a "top secret" report stating that O'Sullivan is "believed to be an active agent" of MI5, the British intelligence agency. The Irishman is said to have "embedded" himself in the Scorpions and established "direct and covert links" to hostile journalists who've been publishing "concocted allegations" about police commissioner Selebi. The report speaks of "conclusive evidence" of clandestine spy activity. "O'Sullivan has been handling human resources, debriefing these resources, conducting electronic, physical, and aerial surveillance operations, and engaging in covert communications," it says. Conclusion: the Irishman is "on an agenda to undermine the South African government."

On its face, this sounds persuasive, but the underlying logic is defective. Granted, there was a time when O'Sullivan's behavior resembled a professional spy's, but since the Scorpions took over the investigation, he has confined himself largely to psychological warfare in the public domain. A deep-cover secret agent doesn't file lawsuits, shoot his mouth off on talk radio, or share his gleanings with investigative reporters. He definitely does not call a press conference where he stands up in a firestorm of camera flashes and calls on Selebi to resign. These are, beyond doubt, the acts of a man with a score to settle.

But South Africa is not the most logical country. When it first emerged that the Scorpions were investigating him, Selebi made a joke of it, turning out his pockets at a press conference to show they weren't stuffed with organized crime cash. Now his prospects are less certain. In this context, the spy charges against O'Sullivan are a masterful countermove, especially when the "top secret" police report is decoded for its racial content. All but one of the five investigative reporters imputed to be his pawns are white. The same applies to all the Scorpions investigators supposedly "linked" to his alleged spy network. These pale-faced sleuths are, in turn, said to be "linked" to American, British, and German spies stationed at various embassies.

In short, Selebi's team is playing the race card, insinuating that the ANC is once again under attack by evil whites. The spy allegations make their way into the press, into private security briefings by Selebi's deputy Andre Pruis, and, ultimately, onto the desk of the state president. Toward the end of November, Thabo Mbeki alludes to O'Sullivan's intelligence background in an address to clergymen, "supposedly to indicate that this man was undermining our national commissioner at the behest of a foreign government," as the *Sunday Times* put it.

Did Mbeki really believe this? Is that why he blew up when he learned, nearly a year later, that chief prosecutor Vusi Pikoli had obtained a warrant for Selebi's arrest and was about to execute it? Pikoli was fired on the spot. Mbeki initially offered a misleading explanation for his action and, when the truth leaked out, seemed to deny the Selebi warrant's very existence—a development that prompted the police chief to boast, "I will never be arrested."

The following morning, senior staff at police headquarters received an anonymous e-mail cautioning against premature celebration. "Hello Sewer Rats," it said. "As I have it, the warrant does exist, and you will get your collars grabbed very soon. You pricks will rue the day you decided to use tax payer's resources in messing with me to protect your criminal friends."

The missive was signed "The Scarlet Pimpernel," but O'Sullivan admits it was his handiwork. By then, he'd spent nearly five years chasing Selebi, and the effort had pushed him to the brink of ruin. "At the outset I was probably worth ten million rand," he says. "Now it was one." He says his phone bills alone were running at R30,000 a month. He'd spent a fortune on legal fees and payments to his underworld informers. His wife and two daughters were living in England, where they could not be "got at" by his enemies. O'Sullivan himself carried a gun at all times and checked under his car for bombs every morning. "I was living on the edge," he says. "I had to push it through to get back to where I was in the beginning."

But how? The game had moved into realms where he had no influence or access. All that was left was the dubious pleasure of baiting his opponents. On one occasion, he slipped a note under the door of Selebi's hotel room, warning that he was under surveillance. On another, he turned up outside an Interpol conference in Morocco, brandishing a placard accusing Selebi of criminality. Police director Selby Bokaba recognized the "Sewer Rats" message as yet another provocation from the Irishman, and sent a mocking reply. O'Sullivan responded in kind, and the exchange degenerated into acrimony, with O'Sullivan fulminating about criminality in high places while Bokaba longed for December 16, opening day of the ANC's upcoming national conference, where supporters of presidential hopeful Jacob Zuma were expected to push for the Scorpions' disbanding. "Your handlers will be history," writes Bokaba. "You will never set foot in South Africa again, not even under a disguise. Your time is running out. GET LOST!"

Bokaba's reading was accurate in at least one respect: six weeks later, at Polokwane, the ANC was taken over by Zuma loyalists whose ambiguous platform contained but one solid plank: the Scorpions had to go. A resolution to this effect was passed on the spot, but the Scorpions staggered on into 2008, mortally wounded but still capable of delivering a last dying sting.

On the fourth day of the new year, key witness Glenn Agliotti was summoned to a luxury hotel where a group of extremely senior ANC officials was waiting to see him. Among the heavyweights present were police crime intelligence head Mulangi Mphego and National Intelligence Agency boss Manala Manzini, who described himself as "the most powerful man in the country." Apparently eager to ingratiate himself, Agliotti signed an affidavit saying he'd lied about Selebi at the behest of the Scorpions, who were said to be engaged in a "political game" aimed at causing the demise of Jacob Zuma and Jackie Selebi "for the benefit of outside forces, namely the CIA and FBI."

On January 9, 2008, this bizarre claim formed the centerpiece of an urgent high court application seeking to quash Selebi's arrest warrant. South African law forbids the disclosure of evidence prior to trial, but there was little left to lose at this point, so the Scorpions retaliated with the legal equivalent of a nuclear weapon—a sprawling, 335-page filing that laid out the history of the Selebi investigation in painstaking detail, along with the report of an independent panel that had weighed the evidence and found it credible. Agliotti's about-turn had raised doubts about his credibility, but there were many other witnesses, and their testimony was collectively damning. As for Selebi, his reputation was instantly destroyed: the Scorpions' documents showed that he became aware of Agliotti's criminal bent as early as 2002 and yet continued to see him almost weekly, to accept gifts of clothes and cash, and to share state secrets with him and his paymaster the swindler Brett Kebble. The judge ruled Selebi's argument that he was framed meritless and ordered him to stand trial.

And so the drama proceeded at last to its denouement: on February 1, 2008, South Africa's—indeed the world's—top policeman appeared in court on corruption charges. A few months later, the triumphant Zuma faction removed Thabo Mbeki from the state presidency, a development that stripped Selebi of any hope of further political protection. The law took its course and Jackie Selebi was eventually sentenced to fifteen years' imprisonment.

As the disgraced commissioner made his sad and lonely exit from the courtroom, a balding middle-aged man rose to his feet and shouted, "Shame on you, Selebi! Shame on you!" It was Paul O'Sullivan, and he looked, as one reporter remarked, "like the cat who'd got the cream."

—first published in *Maverick*, March 2008; revised 2010

Postscript: A week after this story first hit the streets, *Maverick* deputy editor Phillip de Wet and I were summoned to police headquarters to account for ourselves. We feared the worst, but Deputy Commissioner Andre Pruis was the epitome of Boer hospitality, ordering coffee and seating us on easy chairs in an alcove adjoining his office. The lecture that followed was tinged with sympathy, both for Paul O'Sullivan, described as a harmless fantasist, and for us, on the grounds that we'd been suckered into publishing absurd untruths about Pruis's boss Jackie Selebi.

The Scorpions took a similar tack, claiming that O'Sullivan had exaggerated his role in the commissioner's downfall. "The critical breakthrough in this case," said the anonymous agent deputized to deliver the message, "was the turning of Clinton Nassif. O'Sullivan had nothing to do with it. Someone else gave us Nassif's head on a plate." Confronted by this charge, the Irishman didn't even blink. "What the Scorpions don't know," he said, "is that I was controlling their source from behind the scenes." It was impossible to know who was telling the truth, so we invited all injured parties to write letters to the editor and left it at that.

In truth, I had my own doubts about O'Sullivan. Fifteen minutes into our first meeting, I looked him in the eye and said, "You're not really Irish." I could have sworn his accent was British Midlands, rounded off by a few years in Rhodesia, perhaps as a mercenary. When the police exposed his secret history of cloak and daggery, another theory occurred to me: here was a British soldier who'd carried out some extraordinarily dangerous mission for the queen (infiltrating the IRA, say), and then been given a new identity and enough money to start a new life in Africa. Such speculations solved most of the riddles attached to the man, but they were entirely my own invention.

O'Sullivan's problem, from a writer's point of view, was that he had no psychological interior, or at least none that he was willing to share. While trying to turn his raw material into something at least vaguely readable, I kept asking questions about pivotal points in his sprawling narrative, like, "What were you thinking at that moment," or, "What did your wife say when you got home?" It was like trying to draw blood from a stone. He revealed absolutely nothing. In fact, he seemed irritated even to be asked such nonsense. All the relevant facts were to be found in the thousand-page dossier handed over at our first meeting. My job was to write the facts, not probe his private life and personal feelings.

This made it difficult to deliver the end he seemed to desire—a yarn in which he featured as the superhero, single-handedly overcoming impossible odds in a long and lonely battle for justice. His response to skeptical questions could be chilling. "I hope you're not on the other side," he said one night. "If you are, I'll fucking kill you." Our dealings became strained. In the end, I turned down an offer to make a film about his escapades and tried to forget about him.

But a character so vivid does not easily fade. As the Selebi case wound its way through court, I often returned to transcripts of my interviews with O'Sullivan, trying to assess the extent to which the hard evidence could be reconciled to his version, the one in which he starred as the master puppeteer, cultivating agents who recruited other agents whose anonymous tip-offs caused the Scorpions to kick down doors behind which they found secrets to which the Irishman had been privy from the outset. There is no doubt that he engineered the hashish bust that set the dominoes tumbling in the early stages of the Selebi investigation. The Scorpions' interest in Glenn Agliotti's friendship with Selebi was likewise prompted by information from an unnamed outsider, almost certainly O'Sullivan. Beyond that, it was all a mystery. Like all journalists, I fudged my conclusions with admiring generalizations about the "important" role O'Sullivan had surely played.

I last saw the Irishman in Soweto, on the eve of his departure for God knows where. He'd been in Johannesburg to see lawyers about his ongoing attempts to claim millions from the Airports Company for wrongful dismissal. Some said he was going to Australia to hunt down a suspect in the Brett Kebble murder case. Others said he was returning to England, where he claimed to be based, although I had doubts about that, too; he'd claim to be calling from London, but background noise suggested he was actually in Cape Town. All I can say with certainty is that he was there that night, sitting under the stars with a beer in his hand, surrounded by black men who admired him hugely.

These were figures from O'Sullivan's previous life, the one where he was a solid businessman with a powerful sense of civic duty. Tebogo Motswai told me he'd known O'Sullivan since the mid-1990s, when the latter was managing a shabby shopping mall in Johannesburg's northern suburbs. The Irishman spruced the place up, drove out the bad elements, and offered him a prime restaurant site in the rejuvenated complex. When Motswai opened a second joint in Soweto, O'Sullivan organized a shuttle to bring nervous white customers to his doorstep.

By 2008, Motswai's restaurant/bar, the Rock, had evolved into one of Soweto's top nightspots, popular with tourists seeking an authentic township experience and black businessmen in search of soul food. The burly man seated beside me turned out to be Zukile Nomvete, an aeronautical engineer and former executive director of South African Airways. Bra Zuki, as he was known at the Rock, said he'd met O'Sullivan in some tourism body where a senior employee had fingers in the till. The Irishman solved the problem, and Nomvete joined the ranks of those who saw him as an honorable and credible figure.

After a drink or two, Bra Zuki asked O'Sullivan to tell a few Irish jokes. Jackie Selebi's nemesis hitched up his pants, slipped into character, and treated us to a carnival of ribaldry that sounded authentically Irish, even if the accent wasn't exact. An hour later, the Soweto brothers were gasping for breath and begging for mercy, and I was thinking, This must be it: the performance that convinced hard men to entrust a stranger with secrets that blew great, gaping holes in the

271

South African firmament, allowing us to see into the heart of an African power machine.

What we saw there was dismaying. Police corruption is an everyday phenomenon. Political machinations surrounding the Selebi case were something much darker. When he found himself in a corner, Selebi threw police resources into the battle against the Scorpions, whose corruption probes threatened a range of powerful political figures. Hopelessly outgunned, the Scorpions were hounded into oblivion in January 2009. In their place came the Hawks, a police unit with a similar mission but considerably less appetite for controversy. Shortly after coming into being, the Hawks abandoned an inquiry into the present whereabouts of the billion-odd rand in bribes generated by South Africa's notorious arms deal. An investigation into swindler Brett Kebble's "joint ventures" with powerful politicians seems likewise to have withered on the vine. As for the Scorpions' case against presidential candidate Jacob Zuma, it was dropped amid huge controversy on the eve of South Africa's 2009 general election.

I was at the tumultous press conference where this decision was announced. As the world's media exited the building, opposition leader Helen Zille was waiting outside, shuddering with indignation. "This is a travesty," she declared. "All evidence presented here today indicates that [prosecutors] have buckled to political pressure." General Bantu Holomisa, leader of a rival opposition party, concurred. "This is the culmination of a campaign by dodgy characters in the ANC to reduce this country to a banana republic," he said, noting that "vast numbers" of senior ANC leaders had until recently been the targets of corruption investigations. For them, Zuma's exoneration seemed to set a delightful precedent: if you had enough political clout, your legal problems could be made to vanish. "Our justice system is crumbling," said Holomisa.

The weeks that followed were . . . interesting. The ANC had recently split, spawning an offshoot known as Congress of the People. Zille's Democratic Alliance was showing well in the polls, and General Holomisa's United Democratic Front was a force in his home province. Collectively, these three parties presented the first credible threat to the ANC's dominance, and Zuma's exoneration had placed a potent weapon in their hands. They spent the last two weeks of their 2009 election campaigns telling anyone who'd listen that electing Zuma would mark the beginning of South Africa's end. Their warnings fell on deaf ears, and the ANC romped home with a crushing majority.

It was time to pray.

MESSIAH OF
THE POTATO FIELDS

Oh, ye of little faith, ponder the parable of Michael Rosen, a holidaymaker who was traveling across Zululand on Friday, April 8, heading toward a game farm on the upper Tugela River. Rosen thought he'd reach his destination in time for dinner, but he's a creature of the secular world and had no idea of the tribulations awaiting. Some twenty kilometers short of Greytown, he ran into the rearguard of a giant traffic jam. Assuming there had been an accident, he turned on his radio, but there was no mention of any such thing, so he got out and asked the men in the van behind him what was up.

"They were Boers," he says. "Big tough guys in khaki shorts who said they'd driven all the way from the Kalahari to hear a preacher called Uncle Angus." Same applied to the men in the buses, the leather-clad bikers revving past on the verge, and even the light planes passing overhead. Like most residents of the secular world, Rosen had never heard of this Angus person. Like most residents of the secular world, he was heading toward a revelation.

Angus Buchan is a white African of Scots extraction, born in Zimbabwe and raised in Zambia, where he farmed as a young man. When Zambia's economy collapsed in the 1970s, he sold out for a pittance and bought some wasteland near Greytown. He built a crude mud house in the Zulu style and set forth to hew a living from the soil, but it was tough: no water, just one tractor, and too little capital to clear the fields of alien vegetation. He says his neighbors thought he was "some sort of Gypsy" who'd soon give up and drift away.

For a while, it was touch and go. Buchan started taking tranquilizers, drinking heavily, and taking out his frustrations on his laborers. Shamed by his actions, he turned to the Lord on February 18, 1979, and lo, miracles ensued. His potato crops flourished. Boreholes struck water. Rain quenched a bush fire that threatened to ruin him, and a Zulu employee struck by lightning was raised from the apparent dead by prayer. These and other wonders were recounted in *Faith Like Potatoes*, his 1998 autobiography, made into a movie seven years later by Frans Cronje, brother of the ill-fated cricket captain Hansie Cronje.

By then, Uncle Angus had become a minor star on the evangelical circuit, with tours pending in several countries, but the Lord was not entirely pleased with him. Indeed, the Lord spoke to him at a bush retreat, instructing him to scrap other plans and become a light unto the lost men of his native land. Toward this end, in 2004, he staged the first Mighty Man Conference on his farm. It drew 170 people. The next year, some 600 turned up, and the year after, 1060. In 2007, the crowd swelled to 7,500.

Angus was "petrified" by his success but the Holy Spirit warned that even greater things were coming, so he went to Johannesburg and hired "the largest tent in the world" for the next year's event. A tent that took three weeks to erect and seated 30,000. People thought he was nuts. Not even Billy Graham could pull that many to a potato field in the middle of nowhere. But as the event neared, it became clear that Buchan's prayers were yielding abundant results. With three days to go, his webmaster informed him that registrations were coming in at the rate of one per second. Shortly after, the server crashed, and it became clear that a huge army was converging on Greytown. "We panicked," says Buchan, but it was too late to do anything but pray.

This then was the crisis into which Michael Rosen drove on that fateful Friday evening. He sat in bumper-to-bumper traffic for three hours, hugely irked that his pleasure should be disrupted by something as anachronistic as a revival meeting. And when he reached the turnoff to Shalom Ministries, he did not go in. If he had, he would have seen something amazing: a tent the size of a cathedral and, beneath it, on stage, an unlikely figure in baggy jeans and farm boots, yelling himself hoarse about the coming transformation.

"God is looking for Mighty Men," thundered Angus Buchan. "God is looking for valiant soldiers! The tide is turning in South Africa because the Holy Spirit is here! It's here!" Buchan is sixty, but when the spirit moves him, he skips around the stage like a child, his excitement barely containable. "There's enough men at this conference to change the destiny of this country! Do you understand that? *Do you?*" In response came an uncanny rumble: the sound of sixty thousand mostly white males saying, "Amen."

Sixty thousand men. By several reckonings, it was the largest gathering of white males since the 1938 Voortrekker centenary celebrations. Every third farmer in the country was there. One in twenty adult white males. English-speaking South Africans tend to be embarrassed by this sort of thing, but Afrikaans papers splashed Angus across their front pages, causing a furious debate over a thousand Web sites. Some thought Angus was the real thing. Others dismissed him as a money-grubbing charlatan. Progressives were horrified by his Old Testament views on almost everything, and right-wingers wondered if he might be The One whose coming was prophesied nearly a century ago by Siener van Rensburg, a wild-eyed Boer holy man. The One who would defeat the forces of darkness and restore the Afrikaners' freedom.

As for cynics like Mr. Rosen, they yawned. It was wildly inconceivable that a country as advanced and complex as South Africa could be swayed by a mere evangelist. But Angus was not done yet. One of his followers, a Middelburg farmer named Paul du Toit, heard a voice in his dreams instructing him to stage an Uncle Angus rally at Loftus Versveld, the nation's largest rugby stadium. Everyone laughed at him, too, but du Toit did as he was told, and lo: by early July, advance bookings had accounted for every seat in Loftus Versfeld's towering stands, along with 14,000 on the sacred field itself. This suggested—God help us—that Angus was a bigger draw than rugby.

This was an event of seismic dimensions. I set forth to investigate it.

In which the narrator assesses his relationship with God (such as it is)

We're on the stoop of a farmhouse overlooking a row of vineyards and a line of blue gums that mark the banks of the Orange River. This place has no name, as far as I know, but it's seventy clicks downstream from a village called Grootdrink, bounded on one side by the Kalahari desert and, on the other, by the arid wastes of Bushmanland. I'm drinking tea with F. J. Nesar, a bearded young Afrikaner with broad shoulders, callused hands, and a face as open as this landscape. F.J. is desperate to sell his farm and I'm a potential buyer, but he's one of those religious Afrikaners who can't quite bring themselves to dissemble. Fertilizer prices have risen 150 percent in the past year, he says. Diesel is up 70 percent. This has shaved margins to almost nothing, he says, and now the raisin price is collapsing because of foreign competition, and because South Africans are becoming too poor to buy.

F.J. is a man in anguish. He has three children under ten, and wants to save them from the apocalypse that is surely coming to South Africa. He has a visa for New Zealand, but can't leave until he sells his land, and who in their right mind would buy a farm at this time? You will bleed here, he says. I suspect that's true, but I can think of worse things. The climate of paranoia in Johannesburg, for instance. Crime. Corruption. Pogroms against foreigners. A government that seems to

277

be foundering on most fronts, and a state president who seems to support the murderous Robert Mugabe. And atop all this, a surge in food prices that threatens to sink tens of millions below the breadline, with consequences that can't fail to be grim.

This jeremiad pushes F.J. even closer to despair and he starts talking about God. Faith is the only answer, he says. I tell him I have none, and then I tell him about Tolstoy, who wrote that there are four kinds of human beings. Those too dumb to ask themselves, "What is the meaning of life?" Those who ask the question, find it disturbing, and numb themselves with drink and debauchery. Those who ask the question, and find an answer in God. And finally, those who find no answer at all, and ought by rights do the rational thing and kill themselves. I find myself in the latter category these days but lack the courage to act consequentially.

In short, I'm just another white man rolling down a road that seems to disappear in darkness around the next bend. When I heard about the miracle of the potato field, I thought Angus was talking directly to me, and I wasn't put off by the antediluvian tenor of some of his views. On the contrary: it was amusing to see someone giving the progressives a go on issues like family values (Angus believes they're critical), abortion (Angus thinks it's murder), and the position of women (Angus says husbands should be "king, prophet, and priest" in their homes). He also thinks corporal punishment is good for unruly children and that homosexuality is an aberration that can be cured by love and prayer. Yes, these are terminally unfashionable positions, but so what? South Africa is a nation of conservatives presided over by a tiny elite that seems to imagine it's in Sweden. If you despise what Angus stands for, you despise most South Africans.

That said, you probably despise me, too, but the hour is late and I'd rather not waste time arguing about social rights and gender issues. For me, the astonishing thing about Angus Buchan was that he seemed to have found seeds of optimism on the hard and stony ground of our present realities. "There's enough men at this conference to change the destiny of this country! Do you understand that? *Do you?*" I didn't. But I liked the sound of it.

A crash course in the theology of born-agains

Joy! magazine is created in Cape Town by evangelical Christians for evangelical Christians, and the news it carries is sometimes strange to the layman. There are world-famous Christian rock bands the secular world has never heard of. Famous Christian movies and novels likewise. It turns out that South Africa is awash with Bible colleges whose names ring no bells and miracles that pass unnoticed by the mainstream media. (On November 22, 1998, for instance, Bill Wiese of Cape Town spent twenty-three minutes in hell, and has now written a best seller about his experiences there.) *Joy!* has no discernible political stance, but the magazine seems to enjoy the support of the tiny African Christian Democratic Party, which runs an ad in every edition. "It is time for change," reads one such. *"When there is moral rot within a nation, its government topples easily.* —Proverbs 28:2."

Angus Buchan's face often graces the cover of *Joy!*, and its pages bring news of his services and offerings. He has published nine books over the years, and filmed more than three hundred episodes of *Grassroots*, a show carried by five cable or satellite TV channels. The entire body of work is available by mail order, but time enabled me to absorb only a tiny fraction of it—one book and a boxed set of six DVDs chronicling the most recent Mighty Man conclave. These open with an eerie trancelike soundtrack and visuals of clouds boiling over the cathedral tent in time-lapse slow motion. "Faith is the ability to believe things you cannot see," intones the disembodied voice of Angus, "and the reward of that faith is to see the things you believe in."

The music ends, sunlight floods the screen, and Angus appears, in a jaunty Stetson, sitting astride a horse. He tells the camera of the extraordinary venture he has embarked on, and then we cut to footage of pickups and buses streaming into the Mighty Man campsite. Most of the attendees are sunburned farmers but there are also many surprises: shaven-headed bikers, youths with body piercings, long-haired Christian heavy metallurgists, executives with soft hands, and a fair smattering of persons of color. These men are shown hugging each other and choking back tears as they contemplate the situation unfolding around them.

In due course, the sun sets and Angus appears onstage, wearing his trademark farmer's work clothes and carrying a battered red Bible, which he refers to as "my agricultural manual." He raises both hands to acknowledge thunderous applause, opens the book, and starts preaching. Most of his parables involve the land, and are populated by tractors and harvesters, dry boreholes, and strong men rendered desperate by adversity. No, not farm murders or land claims. Drought is the eternal theme of African prophets. Sun beats down, crops whither, humans face ruin and starvation. Then a man of God arises to purify the community and salvation comes in the form of rain.

Buchan has a vast repertoire of such stories, all of them riveting. At Mighty Man 2008, he came up with a cracker involving a visit to the Eastern Cape, then in the throes of a crippling drought. Angus flew down there in a sponsored light plane and, when he beheld the suffering of his fellow farmers, made a rash promise: "Boys," he said, "before I leave here, it's going to rain." Not, it will rain, God willing. His promise was categorical: if you repent your sins, rain will come before next Monday.

Word spread, and at every stop, more people turned out to hear the good news. Angus picks up the story: "Guys said, 'Where's the rain?' And I said, 'It's coming.' But it didn't. Thursday, no rain. Friday, no rain. Saturday, not a cloud in the sky. Come Sunday night, I was lonely and scared. I died, boys. I died. I was sitting in a tin-roof sheep-shearing shed in a place called Kroomie. In the cow dung, like Job. I said, Lord, I have sullied everything, because I got a heart for these men. They going bankrupt, Lord, their sheep and cattle are dying. That's why I shouted my mouth off, Lord. Not because I want to be a hero. Because I want them to prosper. But there was no sign of rain. I wanted to run. The way farmers were looking at me, I could see they were thinking, ja, big mouth, liar. I could hear cars coming for the last service. I said, Lord, you never let me down before, and I got to preach in ten minutes. What am I going to say?"

Angus's voice sinks to a whisper and sixty thousand men lean forward in their chairs as he describes slinking out onto the stage, dreading what's to come. And then, just as he starts preaching, rain starts

drumming on the tin roof. At this point in the telling Angus goes mes-
sianic, eyes bulging and neck tendons straining. "Do you hear that?"
he shouts. "DO YOU HEAR THAT? That's the king! That's my Lord!
He's the rainmaker and He's coming!" The roar that follows is so loud
the earth seems to tremble.

My neck hairs are standing on end by now, and Angus is only just
hitting his stride. "We're in a war here," he thunders. "This is not a
Sunday school picnic! This is the real thing! We will leave here as an
army . . . sixty thousand men! Sixty battalions signed up for Jesus!"
And later, "We are not taking no for an answer! We are claiming this
country!" In context, these statements pertain to the war against Satan,
but I could almost swear I heard something else there—a veiled call to
militancy directed mostly at people like myself and aimed at inciting
us to rise against the Romans of our time and place.

Was this Farmer Buchan's underlying message? There was only
one way to find out. I packed my bags and set forth to kneel at the
prophet's feet.

Among the faithful

Buchan's Shalom Ministries stands on a rise five miles south of Greytown, the surrounding land falling away in all directions in a tapestry of
green fields and pine plantations. There is a towering cross that lights
up at night and, at its feet, a small chapel and a white building that
seems to have done previous service as a dairy or stables. As I enter,
the receptionist is talking to a distraught woman in Britain who says
her niece is threatening suicide. Chantal slips the details into a folder
bulging with prayer requests, three or four of which arrive daily.

On her desk, there is a glossy magazine with a cover featuring two
blow-dried grotesques of the sort that typically populate American tel-
evangelism but, otherwise, there's no sign of Elmer Gantryism. The
women who work here look like hippies with their long straight hair,
mostly unmade-up faces, and sensible jeans and sweaters. The cars
outside are humble, and there's a plaque on the wall in which Uncle

Angus disavows all interest in money. "We are committed to preaching the word of God to a dying world," it says. "God has promised He will provide for our needs. We are therefore against fund-raising of any description."

There are those who say this is too good to be true, but if Angus Buchan owns a gold-plated Cadillac, he keeps it well hidden. His wife Jill is a serene, otherworldly creature whose style runs to simple cotton frocks and sandals. Her nails are unvarnished and if she ever had a soap-opera hairdo it grew out years ago. They still live in the mud house Angus built when he first came here, still cook on the cast-iron woodstove that dominates their lounge. The roof is bare corrugated iron—no ceiling and no insulation. In winter, the cold in that house must be unbearable, which is possibly why Angus showed it to me. The prophet is at pains to present himself as a simple rural everyman, clad in working clothes and forever pausing to scrape dung off his boots. "I'm just a farmer," he says. "I didn't even finish school, man. I'm nothing special."

In the flesh, Buchan has a bluff hello-howzit manner that is initially slightly disconcerting. He slaps you on the back, calls you *boet*, or brother, and spices his talk with clumsy jokes and Zulu phrases. His smile is impish, his enthusiasm contagious. "I've got one hour," he says as we sit down to talk. "One hour. That's it." Then he launches into a spirited description of all he's up to. Newspaper interviews. Calls from Christian radio stations. Preparations for the forthcoming Loftus Versfeld rally and the national stadium tour that follows. "Is this really happening or am I dreaming?" he says. "It's awesome, man. Awesome."

Agreed, I say, but what does it mean, and why is it happening now? Angus turns serious. "I'm telling you my heart now, Rian. I believe it is God. If revival doesn't come, this nation is doomed."

But how will revival save us?

"Good question," says Angus. "We talking reality here. We not talking froth and bubbles. I'm not into that, hey. I'm a farmer. Feet on the ground." He pauses to gather his thoughts. I sit back, anticipating visions of righteous Christians flogging Pharisees and so on, but all that comes forth is a slightly lame anecdote about a coal mine where workers and managers pray together, and an even lamer one about a man who broke off an adulterous affair after hearing Angus preach. "That," says the prophet, "is the fruit of revival."

It's not quite what I had in mind, so I inquire about his politics. "No," says Angus, "that's one thing I will not be drawn into. I'm not a politician. Can't even spell the word." How about race? "Apartheid was not God's will," he says. "Definitely not. I want to make that straight and clear. There's white racialism in this country, and as much racism in reverse, maybe more. But God has set me free from that. A man is a man. Treat him with respect. My biggest desire is that this thing should be multiracial."

Oddly, this longing for interracial love and understanding lies at the root of the only act of dishonesty I can lay at the door of Angus Buchan's organization. Last year, *Joy!* magazine published a photograph purporting to show a multiracial crowd hanging on Buchan's lips. On closer inspection, the image had been doctored, with several Indian and African figures inserted into the sea of white faces. Some might be dismayed, but it was a forlorn and hopeful little sin, so let's let it pass.

By now, I'm thinking a spot of confession might hasten our progress to the heart of the matter, so I start telling Buchan about my own despair. He nods sympathetically. "Lots of people are in despair," he says.

I observe that in my case hopelessness seems to breed a spiritual infection that manifests itself in poisonous racial tirades. Angus chuckles sympathetically. "Well said, Rian!" he cries. "That's exactly right, my *boet*! If you hang around negative guys long enough . . . ja, the blooming country's in a mess, there's no manners on the road, there's hijacking, the blooming economic situation, the government's gone to the dogs, this and that, let's drink because tomorrow we die. And the guys just pull each other down. We got to draw the line somewhere, *boet*. We can't let this carry on."

But how do we stop it? With marches and strikes? With guns?

"No," says Angus, "there's no victory in that. I want to tell you the good news—there's Christians in every political party in this country, and there's lots of strong African Christians in government." He says the head of the South African air force attended Mighty Man 2008 in mufti, and that this black man was so moved by the experience that he's decided to bring his friends to the upcoming Loftus Versfeld affair. "This is fantastic," says Angus. "Hatred is not the answer. Retaliation is not the answer. We got to find a common denominator."

And that is?

"His name is Jesus," says Angus. "I'm telling you now, his name is Jesus."

That's it? All this talk of war, soldiery, and determining the destiny of the nation ends right here? *Eish.* I came looking for John Knox, the Calvinist whose political sermons made Queen Mary tremble, or Martin Luther, who shook the Holy Roman Empire to its rotten foundations in 1517. I am bitterly disappointed but I guess it's unfair to judge Buchan against history's great revolutionary holy rollers. "I believe," says Angus, "that when a man's heart turns to God, he's going to feed the poor and treat his subjects with respect. He's not going to be racist. He's not going to steal. He's going to be just, compassionate, and merciful. That's what I believe."

On balance, Buchan is right; a nonracial government of law-abiding and God-fearing Christians would be a considerable improvement on our present one. Let us therefore pray that his revival brings our politicians to their knees, promising to walk the straight and narrow and never sin again.

My friend Rosen was appalled to hear that I thought Buchan was a good man and should be supported. "He's a televangelist!" shrieked Rosen. "They're all the same! At some time he'll start collecting. First it will be power, then money. They prey on desperate people who clutch at any straw in the hope that somehow tomorrow things will be better. It's a symptom of confusion and dire despair." I sighed and said, "You're right, Mike. Dead right."

—unpublished, 2008

Postscript: I wrote this piece for Branko Brkic, the immigrant who dreamed of creating a *New Yorker* in Africa. By the time it was done,

Maverick magazine had gone under, but I pressed on regardless. I wasn't following Angus for money. I was looking for salvation.

A few weeks later, I persuaded photographer Greg Marinovich to accompany me to Angus's revival rally at Loftus Versfeld, Pretoria's famed rugby stadium. As we pulled up outside, we saw a cryptic Afrikaans graffito on a concrete embankment. *"Die Rebellie,"* it said. The rebellion. I thought, Is this how it starts? Here, in the Boer heartland, on ground hallowed by generations of heroic rugby bloodshed? Greg said he could think of better ways to spend a Saturday, but I was like, "Shaddup, Greg. Rain is going to fall on our parched and cynical souls. We will see the light and be saved." Marinovich rolled his eyes. He thought I was joking. I wasn't.

Quite a spectacle awaited in the stadium—a hundred thousand Christians flooding the bleachers, Christian rock bands on stage, and a helicopter in the heavens above, filming the proceedings for a satellite channel called God TV that goes out globally to a billion homes. Uncle Angus was oddly subdued that afternoon. His theme was the story of Abraham and Sarah, who laughed when Jehovah declared that she would give birth to a son, even though she was already one hundred years old. Moral of the story was that the faithless stand to be humbled by God's power. I strained my ears, but if there was a coded message I couldn't hear it.

"Humble yourself today, sir," cried Angus. "There's a spirit of pride in South Africa that's got to stop! The younger guys are open, but the older guys . . . chaps, I want to tell you, put the past behind you. Jesus resists pride, but he gives grace to the humble." I was like, Huh? Angus seemed to be telling me to bow down to the forces of history and accept my helplessness. At times, he sounded just like Archbishop Tutu. "Today I am believing in reconciliation for this nation. Reconciliation between father and son, between black and white," and so on.

The multitudes were waving their hands in the air, weeping, shouting hallelujah. I was outside, smoking. The spell had worn off. This is pure conjecture but I suspect the moguls of God TV had a hand in this. I think they told Angus that his global audience didn't give a hoot about South Africa's agony. I think they said, "Keep it general, Angus. It'd be nice if you could mention Mandela, but otherwise . . . just say something about reconciliation, okay? And how about some references to the African wild?" As if on cue, the prophet started talking about an eagle soaring over mountaintops in some lonely African wilderness. I ground out my cigarette and walked away.

PART SEVEN
MUTATIONS

DID YOU HEAR THE ONE
ABOUT APARTHEID?

Once upon a time there was a liberation movement whose plans for utopian socialism were derailed by the collapse of Communism. Forced to lay down arms and buy into the dreaded Washington Consensus, these revolutionaries never quite abandoned their egalitarian faith. Their dream (aside from enriching themselves) was a society where everyone would be perfectly equal, and their instrument was a constitution that granted formidable new rights to children, women, gays, and others previously disadvantaged. The rich were required to give corporate equity to the previously poor. The dull-witted were assisted by a lowering of standards in school-leaving examinations, the lazy shielded by workplace laws that made it almost impossible to fire anyone. School curricula emphasized the joys of multiculturalism, and almost everyone observed an unwritten law stating that criticism of black people was unfair on the grounds that any failings they might exhibit were attributable to poverty, oppression, and bad education, otherwise known as "the legacy of apartheid."

We speak of course of South Africa, which evolved in the course of the 1990s into the most politically correct society on the planet.

After losing power, white conservatives withdrew into psychic exile, leaving the chattering classes to do as they pleased. Newspapers were soon filled with great billows of soft-left pabulum. Radio talk shows sounded like sociology conferences, peppered with terms like "gendered," "community-based," and the unspeakable "othering." In time, your narrator came to feel as if he were suffocating in a fog of high-minded pieties, a condition that often reduced him to cursing and throwing things at his TV set.

In the course of one such episode, I switched channels and came upon a demented comedy sketch in which a gunman was tutoring a class of tiny black schoolchildren in the finer points of armed robbery. "You need an inside source to tell you where the money is," yelled the gunman, "and when you get inside you have to take charge immediately. And if you get caught"—I just love this bit—"if you get caught, you blame it on the legacy of apartheid. Okay! So what have you learned today?" The children chorus, "Blame it on the legacy of apartheid!"

If you're not South African, you'll never understand how dumbfounding this was, so let's proceed without explanation to the trendy Johannesburg suburb of Greenside, where Takunda Bimha maintains his office. A twenty-nine-year-old lawyer who wears designer jeans and Italian smoking jackets, Takunda forsook the law for TV production a few years back and now he's a capo in Johannesburg's comedy underworld, manager of a stable of comedy stars who first came together on the *Pure Monate Show*, the TV series that provided satirical armed robbery lessons, among other delights. The title meant "absolutely delicious scrumptious show" in a local African language, but fans called it PMS for short.

As Takunda tells it, the PMS gang were middle-class boys with good educations who wanted to do a satirical comedy show in the style of *Saturday Night Live*. Since most of them were young, gifted, and black, state-owned SABC TV gave them a deal in 2003. God knows what the broadcaster was anticipating, but what it got was sacrilege.

"Memories of apartheid were fading," says Takunda, "and the guys were like, 'Let's move on, you know.' They felt the culture had become boring, and that it was time we started laughing at ourselves." Toward this end, they staged a conversation between dildos of various races, mocked politicians, told ethnic jokes, skewered black soccer bosses for gangsterism, lampooned African dictators, and, in one memorable sketch, portrayed South Africa as a country where politics were so boring that most people stayed in bed on election day, thereby allowing the white rulers of yore to stage a comeback. This was presented as a trailer for a horror movie—"*Apartheid II*, coming to a cinema near you."

If the PMS boys were white, they would have been fired, but black authorities seemed dazed by the fact that those responsible for this mockery of all that was sacred were bright young men from their own side of the racial divide. "They thought we'd care," says David Kibuuka, twenty-seven, a leading light in the PMS collective. "But actually, we don't."

Kibuuka is a droll young sophisticate who drives a convertible, writes clever pop songs, and affects to be vaguely bored by almost everything, including my questions. He says he has no regrets about the trouble PMS caused, and no serious grievances about the show's ultimate demise. (It was axed in 2005.) "The SABC is a public broadcaster," he yawns. "Citizens were complaining, so they had to listen." The PMS gang just packed their bags and moved on to greater things, beginning with a pseudodocumentary about young comedians and their girlfriends traveling into the backwoods to perform stand-up at a rock festival.

Bunny Chow (2006) did well on the local circuit, but foreigners found it a bit bewildering. There was an *Easy Rider*–esque scene where a small-town redneck threatens to murder the funnymen because they're trying to seduce his wife, but otherwise this was a South Africa that was totally unfamiliar to outsiders. The whites were likable slackers, the blacks cocky and urbane. Characters of various races were constantly hopping in and out of each other's beds, and apartheid cropped up only in jokes.

In short, the film was a fairly accurate depiction of the lifestyle and attitudes of, say, university students who were in grade school when apartheid ended and find their parents' politics passé. This in itself was a sin in certain eyes. "I thought politicians would be smart enough to treat comedians and satirists like court jesters," says Kagiso Lediga (age thirty), another PMS veteran. "You let them do their thing, and then you stand back and say, of course I believe in freedom of speech, look what I'm willing to put up with." But South Africa isn't like that. "They expect you to take sides," says Lediga. "That's one of our problems. They feel the black youth is apathetic and we should be inciting them to take up arms or whatever."

The source of one such critique was Christine Qunta, a black power activist and writer who sits on the state broadcaster's governing body and is said to be close to President Thabo Mbeki. After the Cape Town premiere of *Bunny Chow*, she fired off a text message to a relative who leaked it to the comedians. "Christine was, like, very upset," says Lediga. "Apolitical, cynical . . . black men fornicating with white women . . . completely unacceptable!" His heart sank when he read Ms. Qunta's verdict. There was clearly no chance of the *Pure Monate Show* getting a second chance on state TV.

But hey, no worries. The PMS boys were making money on South Africa's live comedy circuit. In fact, some were making a great deal of money, wearing sharp suits, and driving pimped-out cars with TV sets in the backseat. It was time, as Takunda puts it, to start plotting world domination. Their chosen vehicle was *The Dictator*, a movie script about the rise and fall of Edson Nyirembe, president for life of a fictitious African country named Jambola. Part Idi Amin and part Robert Mugabe, Nyirembe is a sinister buffoon with certain, shall we say, painfully lifelike characteristics. Lediga was sent to New York and Cannes to pitch the project to potential investors. "It was quite funny," he says. "White liberals are happy to finance harmless African art movies but they get anxious about ideas that might draw the attention of the Thought Police."

If *The Dictator* cuts a bit close to the bone, one struggles to imagine the Thought Police's reaction to the PMS boys' other movie project—a comedy about apartheid, loosely inspired by *Life of Brian*, Monty Python's heretical parody of the story of Jesus. Christ, I say, this is going to get you in truly serious trouble. What was funny about apartheid? Lediga shrugs. "It was absurd," he says, "and that's always funny. It was also painful, so there has to be a lot of comedy in there some-where." "Ja," says his sidekick Kibuuka, "like white racists with black lovers and morons trying to free Mandela."

Morons? Ouch. These guys are lucky they're working in Africa's most tolerant country. Elsewhere, they'd be in dungeons. According to British historian Martin Meredith, almost every country on the conti-nent has "insult laws" to protect the dignity of its leaders, and if those don't work, there are other forms of joke suppression: African culture commands youngsters to respect their elders, and Africa's embarrass-ments provide a powerful incentive for self-censorship.

What do you do if you're young, gifted, and African, when the *Economist* describes your home as "The Hopeless Continent"? Con-test this assessment and you sound like an earnest white liberal in kaf-tan and sandals, which is anathema to a cool dude like David Kibuuka. "The way the foreigners see Africa is sort of the way it is," he says. "Wars, people dying of diseases that were cured long ago, and so on." But acknowledging such truths is dangerous, too—some brothers are always going to accuse you of being a self-loathing sellout, and that's enough to keep many quiet. Not the PMS boys, though. Their atti-tude, says Lediga, is "Get lost if you can't take a joke. Our job is to talk about things that are wrong, and we'll keep doing it unless you kill us."

Am I making these guys sound like raving neocons? If so, that's en-tirely unfair. In person, they're thoughtful young men who lament the poverty in which most black South Africans still languish and acknowl-edge how lucky they are to have escaped it. They are also staunch anti-imperialists, always delighted to find an American in the audience so they can crack jokes about moronic presidents and so on. Local whites get frequent lashings, too.

The other night, a friend and I walked into a Soweto club where a black stand-up comedian was holding forth to two hundred dark-skinned fans. The man behind the microphone greeted our arrival with a howl of malevolent glee. "Look!" he shouted. "White men!" Two hundred heads swiveled in our direction. The joint fell dead si-lent. We felt like missionaries bound for the cooking pot and, verily, we were in for a roasting. "These whites all have penis dimension anxiety," declared comedian Jackson Mathebula. "They stand next to a black man at the urinal and their eyes cut sideways and you can see they're thinking, Christ, this just isn't fair. And you know what?" he cried, pointing at me. *"That's exactly how blacks feel when we go into a bank!"* The joint erupted. People slapped us on the back and offered us drinks. By the time they arrived, Mathebula had moved on to more interesting targets.

Over the past year or two, the ruling African National Congress has been torn asunder by a vicious power struggle, allowing the mesmerized nation a rare glimpse of our leaders with their pants around their ankles. State President Mbeki stands accused of misusing organs of state security to block the rise of his archrival, Jacob Zuma. Zuma is something of a joke in his own right, a much-married Zulu polygamist who has yet to clear two hurdles in his race for the presidency—corruption charges and wisecracks arising from an unprotected sexual encounter with an HIV-positive woman who subsequently accused him of rape. Zuma's followers see him as the victim of an Mbeki-inspired dirty tricks campaign. Mbeki loyalists see Zuma as a rural oaf incapable of keeping his dick in his pants and his hands out of the public purse.

It was against this backdrop that dignitaries gathered at Johannesburg's Emperor's Palace casino for the Black Management Forum's 2008 gala dinner. Jacob Zuma was the keynote speaker, and entertainment was provided by Trevor Noah, age twenty-four, the newest star in Takunda Bimha's stable. Trusting that Zuma was big enough to take a joke, Noah launched into a monologue that went something like this: in apartheid's dying years, he said, hundreds of thousands of terrified white South Africans moved to Australia rather than live under a black government. Those who remained were charmed by Mandela, but when the old man stepped down in favor of Thabo Mbeki, in 1999, whites thought, uh-oh, and there was a renewed exodus to the antipodes. Blacks were amused by these outbreaks of paranoia, Noah concluded, but now that a Zuma presidency is in the cards, they aren't laughing anymore. Now it's blacks who are asking, "How much is that ticket to Australia again?"

The audience tittered nervously. Noah had challenged several African taboos here, and some Western ones besides. All eyes swiveled in Zuma's direction, and lo: "He was laughing like crazy," says Noah. "Killing himself." And that in turn brought the house down.

This was a pretty optimistic moment, if you ask me—a banquet hall of glamorous black-tied Africans laughing at a joke that would have been considered racist a decade back. Is this not a sign that they're transcending victimhood and coming into their own? "Yes," said Kagiso Lediga. "Learning to laugh at yourself is a great sign of human evolution." As he notes, the Jews and the Irish went through a similar process generations ago. Black Americans made the critical breakthrough in the seventies. Indians followed suit about ten years later, and look at them now—rising giants of international trade and authors of every third work on the West's best-selling book charts. Take this as a joke if you like, but I think the PMS boys might foreshadow a similar renaissance in Africa.

—Wall Street Journal, 2008

Reprinted by permission of *The Wall Street Journal* Europe, Copyright © 2012 Dow Jones & Company, Inc. All Rights Reserved Worldwide

THOSE FABULOUS ALCOCK BOYS

We're en route to an advertising shoot and I want to know if GG is carrying a gun. Anywhere else in the world this would be a wretched pun, but here in Soweto it seems a legitimate and fairly pressing question. I know GG owns a Colt, and that he usually stuffs it down the back of his pants. Personally, I would be reassured to know that at least one of us is armed, but I don't want to display my cowardice by saying, "Trust you're carrying your gat, GG."

In the bad old days, I would have been chain-smoking at this point, dreading what lay ahead. Soweto was bandit country, home to two million angry black people corralled in a grim and depressing labor barracks by the mad scientists of apartheid. Anything could happen here, but today, under the bright autumn sun, it looks oddly cheerful. Liquor billboards line the highway. The landscape is scarred with building sites where developers are erecting a billion rands' worth of shopping malls. Old Potch Road is clogged with gleaming new cars, all presumably piloted by members of the Black Diamond tribe, a dark-skinned bourgeoisie whose numbers have grown tenfold since Mandela came to power in 1994. The Unilever Institute, which coined the term, says Black Diamond spending power is about £12 billion a year and growing at the dumbfounding rate of 50 percent per annum.

Unilever reaches for terms like "economic tsunami" to describe the consequences. Judging by what I see out the window, Unilever is on to something.

GG is a white male, aged thirty-nine, with muscled forearms, bulging biceps, and a square jaw topped off by a crew cut. On the deceptive surface, he looks rather like a Boer cop from the apartheid era. This is not exactly a style associated with Soweto, but GG loves this place. He is jabbering like a cokehead about its glories. That there is the Back Room, a dance club owned by one of his buddies. The dam over yonder is where GG stages the annual "Soweto Beach Party," of which more later. This is the route followed by the Tour de Soweto, a GG-organized bicycle race that drew international attention two months ago. And this is Pimville.

In the struggle years, my heart would sink into my boots as I turned in to Pimville. It was less dangerous than other zones of Soweto, but you were still liable to encounter feral comrades who threw stones if they saw white skin in a passing car. Back then, Pimville was a sea of identical matchbox houses, all dusty and unpainted, marching over the horizon in all directions. Now it's a suburb.

When apartheid ended, residents were given deeds to their houses, and with ownership came pride—trees, lawns, rose gardens, cars in every second driveway, every third house undergoing renovation. Here and there, the old apartheid matchboxes have been torn down entirely and replaced with double-story monstrosities that resemble nothing so much as the houses Afrikaners built when apartheid first lifted them out of poor white squalor. "Ja," chuckles GG, "there's no difference between the Boers and the Bantu. Wait till you see Mrs. Phetlo's house."

Mrs. Catherine Phetlo is in many respects your classic Black Diamond. Her husband made money in the transport business. She is a supermarket supervisor. In her living room, leather-upholstered sofas face a giant TV set. Her display cabinets are crammed with china, crystal glasses, and pink porcelain ducks my middle-class mother would consider "nice." The walls are lined with photographs of children in mortarboards, and a brass plaque offers a Victorian platitude—"Bless this house, oh Lord we pray, make it safe by night and day."

The lady of the house is a matronly person who exemplifies the Black Diamond virtues. She is optimistic and resourceful, keeps an immaculate house, prides herself on her five children's achievements, and keeps up with the Joneses. That is why Mrs. Phetlo has been selected to appear in a TV advertorial sponsored by Sunlight washing powder, a brand eager to win the Black Diamonds' favor.

She woke up this morning to find a film crew in her driveway. They're lugging gear, setting up for the shoot. Mrs. Phetlo has gotten herself up for the occasion in a silky beige pants suit with gold accessories. Her neighbors, equally resplendent, have turned out in force to support her. One is adjusting her hem, another helping with makeup. A third is making tea. "This is why I will never move to the white suburbs," says Mrs. Phetlo. "Things are not right there. There is no neighboring." Her neighbors sigh in regretful assent. White suburbs are cold. Black people who move there get homesick and sad. One last touch of the powder puff and Mrs. Phetlo is ready. GG nods to a young man with a clipboard, who cries, "Action."

The shooting of Mrs. Phetlo gets under way and GG and I step outside to smoke and catch up. "By the way," I ask, "have you got that Colt on you?" He laughs and says, "Nah, I hardly ever carry a gun anymore. Soweto is safe these days."

What a strange day this is turning out to be—Soweto booming, Black Diamonds turning up their noses at the white suburbs, GG telling me that the once mean streets are now quite tame. Would you mind if I resurrect that painful old saw about Africa's knack of always producing something new? Well, here it is. I should have seen it coming. Let's dig up its roots and examine its nature.

It's the winter of 1986 and I'm sitting on a mountaintop overlooking the Tugela River, discussing the art of war with an ancient Zulu named Mankomaan Mabaso. Mabaso prefers to live here, a three-hour walk from the nearest road, because his business is illegal. He has an anvil, a hand-cranked drill, a file, and a pile of scrap metal that he fashions into homemade rifles. Technically, his guns are about two centuries behind the times, but they are much in demand in this wild valley where maidens still go bare-breasted and women crawl on all fours in the presence of kings. Mabaso himself is a grand old savage. He has an old .303 hunting rifle secreted somewhere and is said to be deadly with it, capable of hitting an enemy from a thousand yards away. This makes him a man of distinction in the Thembu clan of the Zulu nation.

All Zulus enjoy a warlike reputation, but the Thembu and their neighbors the Mchunu were arguably more warlike any other. Their territory was known as Msinga, and it was notorious for opaque feuds that sometimes boiled over into full-scale fratricidal warfare, with armies of warriors armed with spears, homemade rifles, and the occasional machine gun hunting one another in the canyons and broken hills that lined the slow brown river. There were jets in Msinga's skies and buses crawling along its dusty roads but in many respects it was a place of the Iron Age. Women wore traditional regalia—purple cloaks, leather skirts, and great coagulations of beads and bangles around wrists and ankles. Their husbands sported huge colored discs in their earlobes. Everyone was poor and hungry. And everyone save the Alcocks was black.

Neil Alcock was a rural development worker who came to Msinga with dreams of turning a poverty-stricken apartheid dumping ground into a land of green and plenty. It turned out to be a greater challenge than he'd anticipated. Drought and war ruined his agricultural projects. His waterwheel was washed away in a flood. His white neighbors, outraged by his interference in their medieval labor practices, were constantly threatening to kill him. In the end, though, the bullet came from a different direction—he was caught in the crossfire while attempting to broker a truce between warring Thembu and Mchunu factions and was murdered for his trouble.

I'd come to Msinga to talk to his widow, Creina, a strange and bewitching creature who spoke mostly in riddles. She conceded that she and her dead husband had largely failed in what they came to do in Msinga, and yet there were tiny increments of progress. She said she'd recently seen a Zulu child building play-play soil-retaining walls on an eroding footpath. Saving the topsoil was an idea Neil had brought here, and it had taken root in the child's consciousness. It wasn't a big thing, but it was something.

Another thing Neil left behind was two teenaged sons, one of whom once asked his father what his future would be. "I can't afford to send you to university," said Neil, "but I will prepare you for life in Africa." Colonial Africa was full of whites who grew up playing with pickanins in farmyards, but there were only two who grew up in a mud hut, with no running water, no electricity, no TV, no lights, no windows even—just rafts of logs lowered against holes in the walls to keep out the winter cold. For the Alcock boys, hunting small game with their Zulu peers wasn't sport. They did it because they were hungry, like everyone else.

One cringes at the term "white Zulu," which has been much debased by urban fakers whose Zuluness consists largely of dreadlocks and tribal bangles. The Alcock boys were strangers to such self-indulgence. Their Zulu peers regarded them as Zulus, and when it came to the boyhood ritual of stick fighting, they were expected to stand and fight, never flinching in the face of blood and pain. They learned the Zulu warrior code—hammer anyone who messes with you—and the allied art of shooting straight. And they learned the Zulu language.

The Alcocks had the only phone for miles around. When Zulu migrant workers in distant cities needed to communicate with relatives, they would call to leave messages with the Alcocks. Sometimes they found themselves speaking to creatures whose Zulu was so immaculate that they refused to believe the person on the far end of the line was white. In South Africa, a handful of white farmers and policemen speak Zulu, but their accents betray their race. With the Alcock boys, you couldn't tell. Such a thing was unheard-of, and Mabaso found it unsettling. "Those boys are dangerous," he said.

He was laughing as he spoke. Indeed, one of the Alcock boys was sitting beside me, translating. Mabaso loved the Alcock boys, but still, the language thing was troubling. A Zulu could penetrate the white world more or less at will, provided he was willing to adopt an alias (John or Peter), learn a bit of English, and take a job as a houseboy. But whites couldn't enter the Zulu world, because they were too arrogant to learn the language. This gave Zulus a strategic advantage in certain situations. You could stand a yard away from a white man and openly plot picking his pocket, so long as you spoke only Zulu. You could crack jokes about him, admire his wife's breasts, plan his overthrow, and he'd be totally clueless.

Ceding this advantage to anyone, even to boys he liked, did not appeal to Mabaso. But what could he do? The boys were there. They were growing big and tall, with unruly mops of blond hair. They were squabbling with their mother, chasing girls, and developing attitude. Soon they would finish school and go out into the world, armed with the only legacy their dead father could bestow on them: the skills to live in Africa.

One wonders if Neil Alcock understood the riches he was bequeathing. He began life as a commercial farmer but got increasingly involved in liberal politics as apartheid blighted the lives of his Zulu neighbors. In the 1960s, he became a sort of secular missionary, obsessed with the idea that hunger would be wiped out if African peasants could be taught to use their land effectively. Toward this end, he and Creina moved to Msinga, where they planned to live among Africans, like Africans, until such time as Africa's pain became their own. Only in this way, said Neil, could you earn the peasants' trust and begin to make progress.

The boys born into this insanely idealistic social experiment are now in their thirties. The younger was named Rauri, but Zulus called him Khonya. The other was Marc, known to friends as GG. This is his story.

The Palace bar is located on the ground floor of a high-rise in Randburg, a suburban business district just north of Johannesburg proper. Once upon a time, Randburg was strictly whites-only, but as apartheid crumbled the area was infiltrated by blacks who liked the low rents and made the Palace their watering hole. Initially, owner Lance Smith was thrilled to have the extra business but as time passed his white clientele vanished entirely and Lance grew paranoid in his isolation. As he mounted the stairs to open his doors, he'd find dozens of black customers waiting to get their hands on a cold beer. Lance was sure it was just a matter of time before these guys clocked his vulnerability and killed him in an armed robbery, so he was ecstatic when a madman offered to take the business off his hands.

GG spent his first several years out of school doing upliftment work in rural areas but didn't like it much—too many limp-wristed pieties from the NGO types, no adventure, and above all no money. Having grown up in a mud hut, GG did not find poverty glamorous. Most of his Zulu brethren shared this view and trekked to Johannesburg as soon as they were old enough, dreaming of smart clothes, fast cars, and big money. In 1990 or thereabouts, GG gave up the struggle and joined them.

He worked on a construction site before linking up with businessmen who wanted to install manned phone booths in black areas. Elsewhere in the world, this would have been easy, but in those anarchic times, doing business in Johannesburg's townships was almost impossible. White-owned companies routinely had their vans stoned or burned, their employees robbed or shot. As a rule, white civilians never set foot in the townships. There were areas where even policemen were scared to venture, but the white boy from Msinga had seen worse. He cruised the city's hellholes in jeans and a T-shirt, setting up phone shops at the rate of two or three a day and installing tough Msinga homeboys to run them. The grateful businessmen gave him 5 percent of the takings, and GG moved on to bigger things.

For a man accustomed to hellholes, Randburg held no terror at all. GG bought Lance out, repainted the place, put paper in the toilets, and reopened it as the Palace of Kwaito. Again, his Msinga homeboys were a critical part of the operation. The Zulu nation has produced its share of poets, cowards, and gentle intellectuals, but they do not feature in the great legend of Zulu militarism. In Jo'burg, a certain kind of Zulu—especially a rural Zulu, and *especially* a rural Zulu from Msinga—is held to be very dangerous. You do not cross these guys. You do not even look at them askance. You view them as Romans viewed Asterix and Obelix, because they are presumed to be capable of berserkery when their blood is up.

There are a thousand yarns in this regard, but for the moment one will suffice. GG's manager at the Palace of Kwaito was Fana Dlada, a twenty-two-year-old who'd grown up in a mud hut a few hundred yards from GG's own. Fana was definitely that certain kind of Zulu. One afternoon, he looked up from his newspaper to find four armed robbers leveling weapons at him. He dropped the paper and charged, bellowing frightening Zulu war cries. The robbers ran, one in such a state of terror that he broke an ankle leaping down a staircase. According to GG, Fana was sorely disappointed at this outcome. "He hadn't had a scrap for ages, because locals were too scared to take him on," says GG. "He thought the four-to-one odds would stiffen the robbers' resolve, but no such luck."

While Fana and his crew kept antisocial elements at bay, GG was holding down a day job with a company that owned a fleet of gaily-colored trucks whose appearance in rural villages would cause all normal activities to cease. Thousands would gather in the town square, whereupon staff would drop the sides of the truck, revealing a stage. The show that followed featured pop music, comedy sketches, morality playlets, beauty pageants, and, every now and then, a word from the sponsors, who ranged from soap manufacturers to AIDS awareness campaigns.

GG started as a lowly organizer, but his unique African skills soon elevated him to a directorship in a company that was turning over around R65 million a year. As such, he took it personally when gunmen started hijacking company trucks. "We went through a patch where we had twenty-three trucks hijacked in three months," he says. "We were being targeted by an organized crime syndicate that was threatening to murder our drivers if they refused to cooperate. We knew exactly who was doing this. Not the big guys—they had whites and Indians moving the vehicles out of the country—but the operators we knew. So we went to the police and said, 'What can we do?' They said, 'Get a court interdict.' The criminals would have laughed at us. So we tried the politicians, but they had succumbed to white liberal weakness and said, 'Be vigilant, not vigilante.' We thought, Okay, let them dream, this is our Africa.

"So I talked to these guys I grew up with—Fezela, which means *scorpion*, and Dumisani, which means *thunder*. They were famous for not taking shit. They organized four or five others and we went to the East Rand at three am. When we arrived at the first house, the guy wouldn't open his door until he saw there was a white guy in the group. He thought I was a cop, so he said, 'Wait, wait, I will open, I want to talk to the sergeant.'

"He opens and says, 'Sergeant, where is your search warrant?' I shove the barrel of my shotgun up his nose, and he realizes he's in trouble. Scorpion says, get out of the way, you don't want brains on your clothes. Then he cocks his pistol and shoves it into this guy's ear. The guy thinks he's going to die. He starts peeing. Please, please please. We said, Okay, take us to your boss and we'll let you live.

"It was like a Western, all these heavily armed guys walking down the road with our captive in front. We arrived at a nice house, surrounded it. They wouldn't open the door, so we shot out the lock. The owner comes out in his underpants, saying, 'I don't even know this guy.' We knew he was lying, but it was getting light and we were worried about the cops coming, so I gave them all a business card and said, 'If you ever see this logo on a truck you hijack, we will come back and there will be a war like you have never seen before. You will all die.'"

Later that week, Thunder and Scorpion visited several houses in Soweto, where they distributed more business cards and similar messages. The hijackings stopped immediately.

Meanwhile, in Msinga, Khonya Alcock was building himself a mud hut a few hundred yards downstream from his widowed mother's. Khonya is the younger and some say gentler of the brothers, although I would dispute that assessment. Let's just say Khonya is the more cerebral of the two, and seems to have inherited his parents' indifference to worldly comforts. Like his mother, he reads avidly and writes letters full of vivid descriptions and wise insights. Like his father, he's interested in the land and the Zulu peasants who live on it.

The lot of those peasants changed radically after 1994, when Nelson Mandela's government announced that land taken from blacks under discriminatory laws would be returned to its original owners.

Zulus responded by laying claim to vast swathes of territory along their border with white South Africa. Their own land was barren and eroded, ruined by overgrazing. The white farms were verdant, and Zulu cattlemen couldn't wait to drive their scrawny herds over the apartheid boundary. But first, there were disputes to settle. Some white farmers threatened to shoot anyone who tried to take their land away. Some Zulus claimed land to which they weren't entitled. In some instances, rival clans laid claim to the same farm and threatened violence if the prize was denied them.

The authorities were at a loss. How to control the process and quell the looming anarchy? They needed someone who could explain the Zulu position to white farmers, and vice versa. Someone willing to venture into remote areas where the locals were armed and sometimes dangerous. In short, they needed Khonya Alcock.

If this was a sentimental Hollywood movie, it would now evolve into a story of the good brother versus the bad, Khonya striving for racial justice in the heartland while the violence-prone GG pursues a variant of capitalist gang warfare in the distant and sinful city. Well, yes. The Alcock boys are indeed prone to rivalry. GG admires Mitsubishi off-road vehicles. Khonya feels the Toyota is more rugged. GG favors the Colt, whereas Khonya swears by the Glock. GG feels one owes criminals the courtesy of a warning shot, whereas Khonya jokes about "two warning shots through the heart."

On the page, this sounds rabidly racist, but in context it's something else entirely. The Alcock boys are almost always surrounded by blacks who seem to delight in their company. They laugh, spar, crack jokes about you in a language you can't understand, then turn to you and say something outrageous, like, "Hey, Rian, we're just talking about the solution for crime. Two warning shots through the heart, hey. What do you say?" Everyone falls silent and watches your reaction. They find it particularly amusing if you turn red and start sputtering liberal pieties about constitutional rights and due process.

This is about the only subject the Alcock boys agree on—the inanity of white liberals who think all Africans are humble Christians or kindly practitioners of *ubuntu* but flee the country as soon as anyone points a gun at them. Such liberals admire the results of Khonya's land reform work, but tend to be disconcerted by his methods. He drives into a dispute with his guns and his dogs, dazzles the opposing parties with his language skills, and charms them into a deal. If that fails . . . On one occasion, rival claimants started threatening to kill each other rather than compromise. Khonya slapped his Glock on the table and said, "I'm the only armed man in this room." By sunset, he had a signed settlement.

One imagines nostrils twitching in Hampstead as liberals digest this, but that's Hampstead for you. South Africa is a frontier state where the rules are still being written and the state is struggling to impose its progressive values on an unruly populace. What would you do if you lived here? Weep? Bow down to the hard men? Emigrate? The Alcock boys are made of sterner stuff. As far as I know, they've never actually shot anyone, but they exist in a world I can liken only to Hollywood westerns. The town has been taken over by evil men. Widows and orphans are suffering but the good citizens are too timid to resist until a lone rider shows up to save them.

In the outside world, such men would be regarded as deranged fantasists, but here they seem saner than most. "They have their own moral universe that they almost chopped out of the rock they grew up in," says Christine Hodges, a film editor who has known the boys for years. "It's very hard-core but there is no black and white about it, excuse the pun. They never muddy things with doubts about moral worthiness and relative merit because they've already decided that. They just do it."

Do what, exactly? Over the past decade, Khonya has reclaimed an area half the size of Wales for landless people. His brother figures his labors have altered the lives of 200,000 Zulus, but Khonya is reluctant to claim credit. He just shrugs and says, "Ah, change the subject." GG owns a company called Minanawe (you and me) that does advertising and promotions in black communities, employing up to five hundred people at peak periods. Both boys are married with children, and both concede the other's achievements, within limits.

"As far as I'm concerned," says GG, "the one with the most toys wins." He lives in a ranch house in a suburb favored by the black nouveau riche because Soweto is just ten minutes down the freeway. He owns a Mitsubishi pickup, a VW Touareg, a 1200cc BMW motorcycle, a motor boat, sundry mountain bikes, several kayaks, and a paraglider. Khonya lives in a modest Pietermaritzburg flat and might, in crassly materialistic terms, be judged a failure, but a far more profound assessment lurks hereabouts. Let's seek it.

Can we talk about market research for a moment? One hears yawns, but South Africa is a country where research commissioned by soap powder firms often reveals truths that elude the daily papers. In the 1980s, for instance, journalism gave the impression that black South Africa was a seething hotbed of Marxist insurrection, foursquare behind the Soviet-aligned ANC. Market research told another story entirely, finding massive levels of admiration among urban blacks for all things American, including capitalism. The sole exception was a tiny segment of university-educated black women who thought Margaret Thatcher's UK was the finest country on the planet.

Today, South African newspapers are full of stories about crime, unemployment, and the decay of our electricity supply network, which is increasingly prone to plunge us into days-long blackouts. On bad days, you get the impression of a doomed nation, septic with despair. But market research reveals blinding optimism in places like Soweto. Upwards of 80 percent of the black middle class feel life is great and getting better. They have money in their pockets and access to well-paid white collar jobs. Some own cars and take seaside holidays.

Johannesburg's advertising companies are, naturally, keen to talk to these people, but it is not easy. Advertising was traditionally a white industry, staffed by cosmopoles who took their cues from New York and London. When the new dawn broke over South Africa, these cosmopoles turned their gaze on the black market, assuming that cool was a nonracial thing and that blacks were prey to exactly the same status cravings as whites. The result was an epidemic of TV ads featuring slender African models with long straight hair and English accents, consorting with Armani-clad beaux in "international" settings.

Blacks were not impressed. Indeed, the aforementioned Unilever research project found that two-thirds of Black Diamonds disliked the way they were portrayed in advertising. They did not want to see trendies mimicking whites. They wanted real Africans. "People like us," with African accents and African attitudes.

GG was delighted by the resulting consternation, because he'd been telling advertising agencies this for years. In fact, his career is built on rubbing white noses in white ignorance. "There was a time when the agencies hated us," he says, "because we were always telling them their campaigns were absurd. They'd say, 'Ah, rubbish,' and commission research that would always confirm the answers we'd already given."

We're driving around Soweto in bright sunshine, talking about market research and the light it sheds on the African female derriere. This is no small thing, pardon the pun. South African folk wisdom maintains that black men love big butts, but you never see a big behind in advertising. "Whiteys don't want to show large African women because they think it's a racist stereotype," says GG. "I've been telling them for ages that large African women are very happy with themselves. They don't need whitey's approval."

This was precisely the sort of sentiment that advertising agencies found offensive, but research commissioned by Levi Strauss showed GG was right: African prejudice in favor of the ample derriere is real and widely held. African women are not ashamed of their large butts. On the contrary, they want skin-tight jeans that show them off to best advantage. Levi's obliged by introducing a brand called Eva, cut to suit African requirements, and laughed all the way to the bank.

Levi Strauss is not one of GG's clients, but this is the sort of thing he does for a living—telling first world companies who their African customers are and how to talk to them. A soup company hired him to find out why blacks wouldn't buy their minestrone. Answer: a strong cultural aversion to the mushrooms pictured on the package. Captain Morgan rum wants to sell its product to blacks but doesn't know how. GG says, Well, your advertising is based on palm trees and Caribbean beaches, and black South Africans don't get it. But this can, of course, be changed.

Then he and his men dump four hundred tons of white sand on the banks of a power station dam, moor eight oceangoing yachts offshore, and invite Soweto's elite to a "Soweto Beach Party," which subsequently turns into an annual event. Last year, they had the nation's hottest pop stars on stage, 12,000 fans inside the fence, and another 15,000 clamoring to get in. Traffic was gridlocked for five miles in all directions. Captain Morgan was ecstatic.

We pull up outside a joint called Masakeng, a Sotho term for cattle kraal. In the bad old days, this would have been a shebeen, an illicit drinking spot, but now it's an upmarket entertainment venue frequented by Soweto's upper class. We are here to meet Billy Chaka, a dashing, dark-eyed playboy who quit a job in academia to become GG's partner. Billy drives an Audi 180 turbo, dates celebrities, and seems to know everyone. "I work, he networks," jokes GG. Billy recently lured Doctor Khumalo, the greatest striker in South African football history, to spearhead a soap powder promotion. Last year, every impresario in town was battling to book Kelly, a sexy pop tart who surged to megastardom when the tabloids revealed she was performing onstage without panties. Billy convinced her to headline the beach party.

Billy and GG have actually come to confer with Masakeng owner Sonwelo Mautloa about their next wild party, but today's newspapers feature a story that has aggravated them hugely. Foreigners are saying South Africa is too disorganized to stage the 2010 Soccer World Cup. Indeed, Australia is reportedly plotting to take our World Cup away on grounds that football fans will never set foot in a country so dangerous. "Preposterous," says Billy. "Racist," says GG. "Completely uninformed crap."

"Look," says GG, "nobody's denying that there's crime, but we've repeatedly shown that we can run world class events and make sure there's no shit." Minanawe's last beach party drew 27,000 punters, most of whom were drunk. Video footage of the event shows thousands of half-naked bodies writhing in firelight while fireworks detonate in the sky and a dark human tide batters the perimeter fence, begging to be let in. And yet, thanks to "strong local boys" doing the security, the event passed off with less aggro than an English folk festival; two fans cut themselves on broken glass, and some guy bit his girlfriend's face when he found her dancing with a rival.

Last March, GG and Billy pulled off a similar feat with the inaugural "Tour de Soweto." You must understand that cycling is a lily-white sport in South Africa, and that most whites view Soweto with terminal dread. At the outset, GG and Billy thought they'd be lucky to lure a few dozen white cyclists, but they formed an alliance with Soweto's taxi associations, who agreed to provide marshals. Soweto's taximen are hard; nobody messes with them. When word of the arrangement got out, GG started getting tentative inquiries from nervous white cyclists. Will I be safe? Can women participate? Will police line the route? And so on. GG cajoled them into taking a chance, and on the day two thousand showed up and had a wonderful time. The sun was bright, the roads great, crowds friendly and cheerful. A few punctures and traffic jams aside, there wasn't a single problem.

Perhaps the bosses of international soccer should talk to GG about the appropriate African response to crime. Toward sunset, he and I ran into Archie Sepoyo, chairman of the Soweto Cycling Association. Archie said some of his chums had recently fallen victim to muggers as they rode across a stretch of open land. This prompted GG to tell a story about the day someone tried to rob him of his mountain bike on a lonely footpath north of Jo'burg.

Interestingly, GG never carries a gun in Soweto, but he finds it advisable to pack a gat on the mostly white and supposedly safe side of town. The Colt was thus stuffed down the back of his pants when a stranger stepped into his path and pulled a gun on him. "He shot at me from point-blank range," he says. "I was so shocked I fell off and this guy takes off with my bike." GG draws the Colt, fires a shot into the air. The robber abandons the bike and runs, but it is too late: he's reawakened the Zulu berserker in GG's corporate breast. GG screams, "Someone is going to die today," and gives chase.

When the robber realizes he's being followed, he stops and shoots. GG shoots back. The race resumes but GG's losing because he's wearing clumsy cycling shoes. Then two off-road motorbikes appear. The riders want nothing to do with this madness, but GG says, "Just get me close," so they give him a ride. Now they're gaining on the robber, who keeps turning to fire at them. The bikers are terrified, but GG urges them on.

"When I'm maybe fifty meters away," says GG, "I jump off and aim. I'm waiting for him to turn and fire at me. As he starts turning, he sees I've got him covered. He drops the gun and says, 'Sorry.' I say, lie down. I go over, take his gun. It's still got one bullet in. I give it back to him and say, in Zulu, 'Pick up the gun.' He says, 'No, you're going to kill me.' I say, '*Pick up the fucking gun!*' The two whitey bikers get between us at this point, shouting, 'Hey, no ways, 'bro, stand back, you can't just shoot this guy!' I wasn't really going to. I just wanted to scare him, but things are getting out of hand so I lower the Colt and say something very stupid. I say, 'Don't worry, I'm a white liberal.'"

Archie and I burst out laughing. GG looks slightly shamefaced and says, "I have no idea what I meant." But I do. The idea of the white liberal has become ridiculous. That's why we're all laughing. Readers in Hampstead might be appalled, but South Africa is becoming, at last, part of Africa.

And so we come to the end of this story and consider its moral. Some years ago, in Tanzania, I met an old Afrikaans lady who, in 1950 or there-abouts, committed the unforgivable sin of getting herself knocked up by a black lover. The trekboer community under Mount Kilimanjaro expelled her, and Tannie Katrien Odendaal spent the rest of her life as a peasant farmer, living in a mud hut with her African family and, when the occasion presented itself, making soap out of hippopotamus fat. Tannie Katrien was a mutant. The Model C schoolgirls who con-gregate at my local shopping center are mutants, too. They are black, but their English is upper middle class and, as far as I can tell, their in-terests are as vacuously suburban as mine were at that age. The Alcock boys are, of course, mutating in the opposite direction.

It is hard to say where all this mutation is leading, although the trend seems generally promising. A century hence, historians might look back and identify the Alcock boys as primitive incarnations of a new African life-form. On the other hand, there might not be a posterity at all, so let's just say Neil Alcock's experiment has produced hybrids whose world is infinitely more interesting and optimistic than the gloomy one I inhabit. For them, just visiting the supermarket can turn into an extraordinary experience.

Picture this: you're in a supermarket in some Johannesburg suburb where all the tills are manned (pardon) by African ladies who are chatting to each other in Zulu, serenely confident that none of their white customers will understand a word they're saying. One of these customers is a strapping young man with crew-cut hair, pushing a trolley of groceries. When he reaches the head of the queue, the lady behind the till says, in Zulu, "Look at the hair on this one's arms. It's a baboon, I tell you." Her colleagues titter. The white man says nothing. He's writing a check. He rips it out, hands it over. Then he says, "Ever see a baboon write a check?"

The till lady freezes. She says, "Oh, God. Sorry, boss." The white man laughs and says, "*Senge suki kwe mfene ngaya kubasi?*—so I've gone from baboon to boss in a couple of seconds?" This is seriously weird; the skin is white but the voice is African. The till lady shrieks, claps a hand over her mouth, and runs to hide behind a pillar.

By now, the rest of the till ladies are convulsed with merriment and the entire supermarket is paralyzed. A supervisor appears, apologizing profusely. GG says, "I don't mind. I think it's funny." The guilty till lady is coaxed back to her post and finishes the transaction amid gales of laughter and ribald Zulu banter. GG gathers his groceries and waves good-bye. As he leaves, they give him a standing ovation.

—*Observer,* June 2007

POSTSCRIPT

When this collection was first suggested, I said, Sure, but only on condition that I get to write a postscript in which I settle old scores, gloat over my enemies' humiliations, and exhume all the stories I couldn't get published because nobody wanted to know. Having laid waste to all around me, I intended to stand on their corpses and render a magisterial final verdict on the South African situation. But writing is a process of discovery, and I have discovered that I have nothing worth saying. I've been sitting here for weeks, typing furiously, but it's all rubbish. The same old what-ifs chase the same if-onlys around the same old obstacle course, usually working their way toward conclusions so dismaying that I want to shoot myself.

So I just hit delete and liquidated all of it. What a relief. I sounded like an old Africa hand with skin cancer on his bald spots, holding up the bar in Salisbury or Nairobi and complaining about the way the natives are buggering things up. They *are* buggering it up, for the most part, but I can't stand myself when I slip into that mode of virtuous outrage. I am not entitled, and what's the point anyway? We all know where we come from, and where we're going. Empires are always rising and falling. The one I was born into—the empire of white males—was a mighty thing until a few decades back, but now it's in decline everywhere and the end is likely to be messy. Nothing I say will affect the outcome, so I think I'll just shut up and cede the last word to a photograph that speaks far more eloquently than any of us.

It was taken just the other day in Cape Town and shows a blonde girl, seminaked, draped over the bonnet of a sports car in a cavernous nightclub. Above her looms a jovial black man wearing designer shades and a white tuxedo jacket with pink trimming. This is Kenny Kunene, who has recently become famous for all the wrong reasons. He is eating sushi off the model's pale flesh while a gallery of leering drunkards applauds in the background.

Four years ago, Kenny was a penniless ex-convict. Today he reportedly owns two Porsches, a BMW, and a Lamborghini. The source of his money remains a mystery, but there is a lot of it, and Kenny spends it lavishly, among other things, on parties where he sips Dom Perignon while eating sushi off the bodies of seminaked girls in a firestorm of camera flashes. These orgies are publicity stunts for Kenny's chain of ZAR nightclubs, expensive joints that cater to rich black businessmen and their political friends. Some find the ZAR clubs obscene, given that most South Africans struggle to find enough to eat. Others, like Kenny's best friend, Julius Malema, think Kenny is "a role model for the new generation."

Julius is the president of the ANC Youth League, famous for his radical anticapitalist utterances and his admiration for Robert Mugabe, the dictator who reduced neighboring Zimbabwe to penury. Julius claims to speak for the poor, but his own style is the epitome of capitalist piggery—Breitling watches, Italian suits and shoes, giant SUVs, and gleaming suburban mansions, also acquired by mysterious means. Julius loves a party, so he's here tonight, sweat pouring off his shaven pate as he swills Kenny's champagne. Mr. Malema can be quite dangerous in party mode. A year or two back, he punched one of his neighbors for daring to suggest that he turn the music down. Tonight he's picking a fight with opposition politician Helen Zille, whose Democratic Alliance controls Cape Town and the region surrounding. Zille's administration is clean, efficient, transparent—and loathed by Malema, who bitterly resents the fact that there remains a corner of the country where a "racist little girl" can tell him what to do. "Helen Zille will not close ZAR at two am, like these other nightclubs in Cape Town," he declares. "The ANC owns ZAR—and we will party till dawn!"

Ah, what a rich canvas. It's all here—the ostentatious display of wealth by a greedy elite, buffoonish utterances from a politician re-nowned for crass racial demagoguery, and the insinuation that this bac-chanalia is taking place under the auspices of the ruling party and is therefore above the law. All that's missing is the reaction, which was equally interesting. Older, wiser ANC leaders issued a coldly furi-ous press release, denouncing the eating of sushi off naked women as "antirevolutionary." The mighty ANC Women's League was equally scandalized. The press emitted a great roar of derision. Kunene was so viciously ridiculed that he begged forgiveness, and even Malema was forced to issue a grudging clarification of his behavior. It was a nothing event in the overall scheme of things, but it shows something worth remembering: the battle for South Africa is not over yet.

But it is certainly moving into interesting new terrain, with Ju-lius Malema now rising like a meteor, dismissing all whites as "crimi-nals," and demanding the nationalization of almost everything. In a way, Julius is the first post-apartheid politician, a thirty-year-old who despises the historic compromise of the Mandela era and yearns for revolutionary transformation. His stated model for this crusade is Rob-ert Mugabe's Zimbabwe, where a similar Africanist ideology has led to economic catastrophe, but no matter—populist radicalism evokes a powerful response in a country where 60 percent of young black people have no jobs or money, and young Julius is laying waste to the ANC's old guard as he battles his way toward power. We knew in our bones that something like this was inevitable, and right now, the end seems imminent. But the end has seemed imminent ever since I opened my eyes, and somehow it hasn't arrived yet. Maybe it never will. Maybe we'll just mutate out of our present incarnations and become some-thing else entirely.

I've always loved the passage in the opening pages of *Heart of Darkness* where Marlowe eyes the mud flats lining the Thames estuary and says, "This, too, was once a place of darkness." Conrad was, of course, looking through the eyes of Caesar and Plautius, who arrived to find the banks of the Thames thronged with half-naked Celts in blue war paint. The Romans subjugated these savages with ease and introduced them to the benefits of empire: level roads, comfortable villas, advanced systems of social organization, and so on. In due course, the Roman Empire succumbed to the laws of entropy and the Romans sailed away again.

The results, as Churchill noted, were catastrophic: Roman roads were overgrown, Roman villas crumbled, Britain was without central heating or indoor plumbing for centuries. And when the Britons pulled themselves out of the slump known as the Dark Ages, a hallucinatory sight awaited the visitor to Oxford or Cambridge: descendants of the blue-painted savages of yore wearing togas and declaiming the classics in Latin, the tongue of their ancient oppressor. And not just that: venerating the Romans as a higher form of life, poring over their texts for clues as to their greatness, and lamenting their downfall. The Britons went on to formulate a culture that combined naked self-interst with early Roman ideals of public service and self-sacrifice, and lo: they wound up with an empire of their own while the descendants of Caesar and Plautius became a jokey nation of waiters and ardent swains.

I suspect the gods of irony are planning similar reversals for South Africa. Johannesburg as we know it will vanish, and something new will arise in its place. Many centuries hence, visitors to this New Jerusalem will encounter something presently inconceivable—Africans wearing safari suits and struggling to decipher the crumbling texts of a race that once lived here, planting cornfields that stretched farther than the eye could see, splitting atoms, and making the trains run on time. That race will be gone, of course, but the new order will preserve and venerate its ruins, in much the way that Europeans preserve Roman roads and aqueducts. Outside universities, Afrikaans will be a ghost that rattles its chains in the depths of some new African tongue, and white and black skins will have given way to something closer to golden. The issues that divide us now will seem absurd in retrospect. The good that white men did will be acknowledged, the evil forgotten. The wounds of history will be healed. Would that I could live to see it.

> *"I ache to move beyond this time."*
> —Jefferson Airplane, 1967